THE EPISTLE TO THE COLOSSIANS & PHILEMON

THE EPISTLE TO THE COLOSSIANS & PHILEMON

by

H. C. G. Moule

WIPF & STOCK · Eugene, Oregon

Wipf and Stock Publishers
199 W 8th Ave, Suite 3
Eugene, OR 97401

The Epistle to the Colossians and Philemon
By Moule, Handley C.G.
ISBN 13: 978-1-4982-0828-4
Publication date 1/1/2015
Previously published by Cambridge University Press, 1893

Reprint of the 1977 Kregel edition.

CONTENTS

INTRODUCTION TO COLOSSIANS
Chapter 1. Colossae and Its Neighboring Churches 11
Chapter 2. Date and Occasion of the Epistle 22
Chapter 3. Alien Teaching at Colossae 30
Chapter 4. Authenticity of the Epistle 37
Chapter 5. The Ephesian Epistle and the Epistle from Laodicea 41
Chapter 6. Parallels Between the Colossian and Ephesian Epistles 47
Chapter 7. Argument of the Epistle 53

COMMENTARY
Colossians 1 63
Colossians 2 94
Colossians 3 117
Colossians 4 134

INTRODUCTION TO PHILEMON
Chapter 1. Authenticity of the Epistle 147
Chapter 2. Testimonies to the Epistle 148
Chapter 3. The Chief Persons of the Epistles 152
Chapter 4. Slavery and the Attitude of Christianity Towards It 154
Chapter 5. Argument of the Epistle 164

COMMENTARY
Philemon, Verses 1-25 167

APPENDICES 179
INDEX 193

JESUS CHRIST is the true God of men, that is to say, of beings miserable and sinful. He is the Centre of everything and the Object of everything; and he who does not know Him knows nothing of the order of the world, and nothing of himself. For not only do we not know God otherwise than by Jesus Christ; we do not know ourselves otherwise than by Jesus Christ...In Him is all our virtue and all our felicity; apart from Him there is nothing but vice, misery, errors, clouds, despair, and we see only obscurity and confusion in the nature of God and in our own.
PASCAL, Pensées sur la Religion.

ALLIED to Thee our vital Head
We act, and grow, and thrive;
From Thee divided each is dead
When most he seems alive.
DODDRIDGE, Hymns founded on
Texts in the Holy Scriptures.

INTRODUCTION

Chapter 1

COLOSSÆ AND ITS NEIGHBOUR CHURCHES

THREE Churches, or, as we may call them in the language of modern evangelization, three mission-stations, are named in the Epistle to the Colossians, and evidently as standing in close connexion; Colossæ, Laodicea, Hierapolis. These towns lay in the great peninsula now called Asia Minor, in a district where Lydia and Phrygia touched and as it were overlapped each other, and which was included by the Romans in a department of proconsular Asia called the Cibyratic Union (*conventus Cibyraticus*)[1]. The sites are found about 100 miles east of that of Ephesus, near the 38th parallel of north latitude and midway between the 29th and 30th parallels of east (Greenwich) longitude, in a minor valley of the system of the river Mæander, now called the Menderè. The Lycus ("Wolf"), now the Tchoruk Su, rising in the south-east, flows westward through this valley into the larger valley of the Mæander, and passes, not long before the waters meet, Colossæ and Laodicea on its left, and Hierapolis, opposite Laodicea, on its right. A space of less than twelve miles divides Colossæ from the two other sites, which are about six miles distant from each other; thus the three places are easily accessible in one day's walk. Colossæ stood close to the stream; in fact the waters ran through the town. Laodicea and Hierapolis stood

[1] The district lies, according to the Turkish division of the peninsula, in the province of Anadoli, in the *sanjak* or department of Kermian.

further back, each on a hill side, Hierapolis on the steep lower buttresses of a true mountain range. In the northern horizon, above this lower rampart, are seen the long ridges of Messôgis, now called Ak Dagh, "White Mountain"; in the south towers the snowy pyramid of Baba Dagh, "Father of Mountains," also called Chonas Dagh, the Cadmus of ancient geography[1].

The whole region is volcanic, and earthquakes have been frequent throughout its history. Laodicea was ruinously shaken at least four times between B.C. 125 and A.D. 235; the third shock falling, probably[2], in A.D. 65, a few years later than the writing of the Colossian Epistle, and striking all three towns. As late as 1720, 12,000 people perished in a great convulsion of the region. Less than thirty miles north of the valley of the Lycus is a vast district, anciently called *Catacecaumenê, Burnt-up Land;* it still presents a scene of blackened desolation, as after a recent eruption of volcanos.

The rocks of at least part of the Lycus valley are calcareous, of the formation called travertine. In such a bed, flowing water rapidly lays a stony deposit, almost snowy white; and accordingly the country is sprinkled with glacier-like streams and cataracts of limestone. These are especially remarkable at the site of Hierapolis; the Rev. S. C. Malan's sketch in *The New Testament Illustrated* (ii. 254), shews the steps of the mountain-side almost covered with solid white cascades.

The pastures of the valley are rich, especially on the side of Colossæ and Laodicea, and the breed of sheep was excellent; their wool, according to one account, was naturally dyed a glossy black by the minerals in the waters. The artificial dyes of Colossæ and Laodicea were famous, as were those of their provincial neighbour Thyatira, Lydia's city[3].

---

[1] See for an engraved general view of the Lycus valley, Churton and Jones's *New Testament Illustrated* (1865), vol. ii. p. 246. The accuracy of the sketch is warranted by the name of the artist, the Rev. S. C. Malan. On the topography of the valley see the recent work (1893) of Prof. Ramsay, *The Church in the Roman Empire*, pp. 468 etc. A large local map is inserted opposite p. 472.
[2] Lightfoot, *Colossians*, p. 38, *note*.
[3] Acts xvi. 14.

Introduction / 13

Of the three towns of the region of the Lycus the most important was LAODICEA. Its name dates from about B.C. 250, when Antiochus Theos designated it from his queen, Laodicè; but it had existed long before under other names, Diospolis and Rhoas. Not long before the Christian Era it had risen, somewhat rapidly, to wealth and importance, and was made the *metropolis*, or district-capital, of the Cibyratic Union, a civil *diœcêsis* ("diocese") of twenty-five towns. In its court-house Cicero, when Governor of Cilicia (B.C. 52—50)[1], held more than one assize. Its tutelar God was Zeus, who is sometimes called, on Laodicean coins, *Aseis*, "a title which perhaps reproduces a Syrian epithet of this deity, 'the mighty'"[2].

Laodicea is now a wilderness of ruins. The traveller finds on the hills traces of a stadium, a gymnasium, theatres, the wrecks of temples, the relics of a street with side-colonnades, a gateway in a broken wall, and some of the arches and stone pipes of an aqueduct. "Nothing can exceed the...melancholy appearance of the site; no picturesque features...relieve the dull uniformity of its undulating and barren hills; and, with few exceptions, its grey and widely scattered ruins possess no architectural merit"[3]. The Turks call the site of Laodicea, Eski Hissar.

The Christian history of Laodicea, after St Paul's time, presents some interesting landmarks. The Apocalyptic Epistle[4] indicates a superficial prosperity, spiritual and perhaps also material, as the condition of the "Angel" and probably of the

---

[1] Soon after that date the Cibyratic Union was transferred to the province of Asia.

[2] Lightfoot, p. 8. The word is perhaps akin to the Aramaic *Aziza*, and the Arabic *Aziz*. See also Ramsay, *The Church in the Roman Empire*, p. 142.

[3] Hamilton, *Asia Minor*, i. 515.

[4] Rev. iii. 14—22. Against a tendency to *Angel-worship* in the Asian Churches the whole book would utter a mighty protest, shewing as it does, in all its prophetic visions, "Angels made subject *unto Him*." (And see Rev. xix. 10, xxii. 9.) At the same time the book testifies throughout to the objective reality of the angelic host and its order.—This is not the place to discuss the date (under Nero or under Domitian) of the Revelation. Notwithstanding the main current of recent opinion we prefer the later date. Cp. David Brown, D.D., *Structure of the Apocalypse* (1891), pp. 7—25.

14 / Introduction

Church. But beneath it lurked the fatal malady of spiritual self-complacency, and a consequent "lukewarmness" in witness and work for the Lord. Nothing in the Epistle throws light on the special dangers which in St Paul's time beset the Churches of the Lycus; unless indeed we trace a connexion of thought between the solemn assertions of Col. i. 15—18 and the glorified Lord's self-designation, in His message to Laodicea—"*The Beginning of the creation* of God."

About A.D. 155 Sagaris, bishop of Laodicea, died a martyr, in the same persecution which saw the burning of Polycarp at Smyrna. Just at that time the "Paschal Controversy" arose within the Church, and made Laodicea its centre. This was a conflict between the Asiatic observance of Easter, which regarded the day of the month irrespective of the day of the week, and the Palestinian and Western observance, which required the day of the week to be followed, as we do now. Melito[1], then bishop of Sardis, wrote a book, now lost, *On the Pascha*, to defend the Asiatic usage.

Bishops of Laodicea and of Hierapolis took part in most of the great Councils of the fourth and fifth centuries, with a curious vacillation between orthodoxy and its opponents. In the fourth century (probably A.D. 363) a small council[2] was held at Laodicea, at which, for the first time on record, the question was formally discussed and pronounced upon, what Sacred Books should be recognized as inspired, and as such read in the Christian Churches. A list, purporting to be that then made, is extant. It contains the entire Old Testament, with Baruch and the Letter of Jeremiah, and the New Testament as we have it, except the Revelation. But Bp Westcott[3] has given strong reason to think that the list is a later addition to the (undoubtedly genuine) decree, which forbids the reading of "things uncanonical" (ἀκανόνιστα).

The same council dealt with other matters, and among them with some which throw a light on local beliefs and practices,

---

[1] See Smith's *Dict. of Christian Biography*, iii. 897.
[2] "It was in fact only a small gathering of clergy [59 at most] from parts of Lydia and Phrygia." Westcott, *Canon of N. T.*, part iii. ch. ii.
[3] *Canon*, as just cited.

Introduction / 15

and indicate a continuity in these with some phenomena of the days of St Paul. Canon 29 forbids a "Judaizing" observance of the (seventh-day) Sabbath, as distinguished from the Lord's Day. (Cp. Col. ii. 14, 16, 17). Canon 35 forbids Christians "to abandon the Church of God, and invoke (lit., 'name') Angels, and hold assemblies" for secret angelolatry[1]. (Cp. Col. ii. 18.)

"No place in the world," writes M. Svoboda[2], "is so remarkable for its natural phenomena as HIERAPOLIS....From a great distance may be seen, overlooking the valley of the Lycus, a white mass, of considerable extent, resembling snow, and called by the natives Pambouk Kalesi (the 'Castle of Cotton'[3]). This is the site of ancient Hierapolis, which was in the time of the Roman Empire so renowned for its marvellous mineral hot springs, unique in Asia, and possibly in the world. From many parts of Asia, and also of Europe, people repaired thither to bathe. By the great influx of visitors the city increased in wealth and importance, and became filled with fine temples and elegant baths. The wonderful effects of the water of the *Plutonium*, exhaling vapour which killed instantly any animal that approached the opening, as this was generally believed to be the effect of a Divine power, earned for this city the name of Hierapolis, 'the Holy City.' An immense quantity of hot water bubbles out from the ground in the middle of the city, and thence takes different directions, forming solid dams across the watercourses by its calcareous deposits, until it reaches the falls. These are about 400 feet in height, and form an amphitheatre of more than 1000 yards in extent, where...thousands of basins are formed by the calcareous deposit...from...the size of only a few inches to masses of about 20 feet in diameter and height, superimposed one upon another, and supported by stalactites, presenting the appearance of natural columns." The

---

[1] Lightfoot, p. 68. See also Ramsay, *The Church &c.*, ch. xix.
[2] *The Seven Churches of Asia* (1869), p. 28. The letterpress of the book is explanatory of the photographs taken by the writer.
[3] See also Lightfoot, p. 9, note. Other forms of the name are Pambouk Kalè, Tambouk Kalesi, or Kalè. Hamilton (*Asia Minor*, i. 517) says meanwhile that "in the lowlands between the river and Hierapolis are many cotton-fields."

16 / Introduction

great spring fills a basin whose width varies from 30 to 60 feet, and the depth from 15 to 20 feet. M. Svoboda found by experiment that its exhalations are still almost instantly fatal to birds. The city lay on a platform just below the stony waterfalls, and the site is covered with ruins. "The theatre is one of the best preserved in Asia Minor; the seats are complete; the ornaments and figures...all heaped as they were overthrown by the earthquake." Above the falls lie the vast ruins of the Baths (*thermæ*); "they are composed of many large halls, covered by arched roofs, built with stones of immense size, beautifully joined together without cement." Among the other ruins stands a building whose shape indicates a church, of the third or fourth century[1].

The Christian history of Hierapolis is marked by some important names. It is probable[2] that after the fall of Jerusalem St John migrated to Ephesus, and with him some other leaders of the Palestinian Church; the Apostles Andrew and Philip, and "Aristion and John the Presbyter, among other personal disciples of the Lord, are especially mentioned. [See Euseb., *History*, III. 39.] Among the chief settlements of this Christian Dispersion was Hierapolis....Here at all events was settled Philip of Bethsaida...and here, after his decease, lived his two virgin daughters[3], who survived to a very advanced age, and thus handed down to the second century the traditions of the earliest days." From them, from Aristion, and from John the Presbyter, Papias, the native bishop of Hierapolis (his name is Phrygian), about A.D. 130, gathered materials for his work, at present lost, entitled *Expositions of the Dominical Oracles*,

[1] M. Renan (*Saint Paul*, p. 359) paints in brilliant colours the view seen from the theatre of Hierapolis: "On the right side of the Lycus the heat is extreme, the soil being one vast plain paved with limestone; but on the heights of Hierapolis the purity of the air, the splendid light, the view of Cadmus, floating (*nageant*) like an Olympus in dazzling ether, the scorched summits of Phrygia vanishing rose-coloured in the blue of the sky, the opening of the Mæander valley, the side-long profiles of Messogis, the white summits of Tmolus far away, fairly dazzle the beholder."
[2] Lightfoot, p. 44.
[3] Not to be confused with the four daughters of Philip *the Evangelist* (Acts xxi. 8).

Introduction / 17

i.e., probably, of the Gospels[1]. Within the last half-century the name of Papias has been associated with a memorable controversy over the origins of Christianity. The notices of his work in Eusebius shew no reference to the writings of St Paul; and it has been maintained (notably by Baur, of Tübingen, and more recently by Renan[2]) that the school of St John entirely repudiated St Paul, and succeeded in effecting a total break of continuity between his teaching and their own, and that Papias accordingly will have nothing to say to the Pauline Epistles. Lightfoot (*Colossians*, pp. 51 etc.) amply shews the weakness of the evidence for this astonishing paradox. Papias' main object, apparently, was to gather up *personal reminiscences* of our Lord's works and words; and for these of course he would not go to *Pauline* sources. And Polycarp, Papias' friend, and Irenæus, who quotes Papias with respect, were as loyal to the authority of St Paul as any Christian teachers of any age. And Eusebius himself, who entirely accepted the same authority, and who freely criticizes Papias on other grounds, gives no hint that Papias thought amiss in this matter. And again, Eusebius may well have found in Papias' work abundant *Paulinisms*, and yet made no note of them, for his object is not to give an abridgment of the "Expositions," but to note special points of interest and curiosity in them[3].

Papias was succeeded in his pastorate, probably, by Abercius, or Avircius, and he by Claudius Apollinaris (St Apollinaris), about A.D. 180; an active and important writer, author of an *Apology*, or Defence of Christianity, of discussions of paganism and Judaism, of a book on the Paschal controversy, and

---

[1] See Smith's *Dict. Chr. Biography*, s.v. *Papias*, for an account of what is known of Papias and his work, and of the questions which gather round him and it. Papias (Euseb., *Hist.*, iii. 39) mentions by name St Matthew's and St Mark's Gospels, and there is the highest internal probability that he had also before him, as canonical, St Luke's and St John's.

[2] "The second and third chapters of the Apocalypse are a cry of hatred (*cri de haine*) against Paul and his friends." Renan, *Saint Paul*, p. 367. The proof offered for this statement is a chain of ingenious special pleading.

[3] See, besides Lightfoot, the notes to Euseb. *Hist.* iii. 39 in the *Select Library of Nicene &c. Fathers* (New York and Oxford, 1892).

of others on that raised by Montanus, with his claim to a special inspiration, and his revolt against a too formal ecclesiasticism. Apollinaris gathered at Hierapolis a council, which excommunicated Montanus and his associate Maximilla. Of the works of Apollinaris only fragments now survive; one octavo page could well contain them all.

Lightfoot remarks that the controversies of the second century themselves bear impressive witness to the "solidarity" of the Church. The most distant Churches, and teachers, are seen "bound together by the ties of a common organization and the sympathy of a common creed;" and in proportion to our acquaintance with this fact will be our suspicion of any theory of vast divergences, afterwards completely silenced and healed, among the leaders of the first age of Christendom.

Besides the Christian celebrities of Hierapolis one illustrious native must be mentioned, Epictetus, the Stoic ethical philosopher (*obiit* about A.D. 120); once the slave of Epaphroditus, freedman and favourite of Nero. Lightfoot calls him "the loftiest of heathen moralists".[1] His *Enchiridion* ("*Manual*") is a small treasury of noble principles and precepts, of which the writer appears to have been a genuine embodiment. The interesting question is raised by Lightfoot, whether he ever met Epaphras, or St Paul himself. The answer is that "history furnishes no hint of such intercourse" (Epictetus must have been very young at the supposed time of it); but that some coincidences of language between Epictetus and St Paul "would thus receive an explanation."

COLOSSÆ alone remains to be noticed of the Churches of the Lycus valley. Apparently it was never a city of the size and wealth of Hierapolis and Laodicea; but its position gave it a strategical importance in the ages of Persian and Greek empire. It lay in the mouth of a pass in the Cadmian range[2],

---

[1] *Colossians*, p. 13. Cp. Lightfoot's *Philippians*, pp. 313, etc.
[2] Ramsay (*The Church &c.*, p. 472) writes thus from personal observation: "Colossæ was situated at the lower western end of a narrow glen some ten miles long....On the south Mount Cadmos rises steep above (the glen)....The river Lycus flows down the glen, rising in a series of vast springs at its upper eastern end." See further, Appendix A.

on the military route from the Euphrates to the west. Here Xerxes' host (B.C. 481) halted on its march to Thermopylæ and Platæa; and Herodotus (vii. 30) takes occasion to call it "a large city of Phrygia, in which" (the phrase is remarkable) "the Lycus disappears in a subterranean gulph, and, reappearing about five stadia further down, so flows into the Mæander."[1] Eighty years later the younger Cyrus, with his 10,000 Greek mercenaries, halted a week at "the populous, prosperous, large city of Colossæ" (Xenophon, *Anabasis*, i. 2, § 6), on his march into the heart of Persia to attack his brother Artaxerxes Mnemon. In later days it sunk in size and consideration. The geographer Strabo, about the Christian era, describes it as a small town (*polisma*). The astronomer and geographer Ptolemy, about A.D. 140, does not even mention it among the places of the region. Its ruins are meagre compared with those of its sister cities. Hamilton (ii. p. 509) found "a field full of large blocks of stone and foundations of buildings, with fragments of columns and broken pottery...The road was lined with marble blocks...among which were fragments of columns, architraves, and cornices. A little further, near the roadside, was the hollow *cavea* of a theatre, built on the side of a low sloping hill, and of which several seats were still *in situ*; some traces of the wall of the right wing were also visible: a grassy sward covered nearly the whole space." Near this a small bridge spanned the rapid Tchoruk Su (the Lycus), itself the union of three streams which met just above; one of these, the Ak Su, or White Water, was highly petrifying. Crossing the united stream, which falls into a deep chasm just below the bridge, the traveller found himself in another field of ruins, which proved to be the site of the necropolis of the ancient town. "Many rude grotesque-shaped pedestals, resembling elongated truncated pyramids," were to be seen; they appeared to be sepulchral monuments of an Oriental type.

The ravine into which the Tchoruk Su rushes from amidst the ruins was examined carefully by Hamilton. He found unmistakable signs of the ceaseless work of petrifaction, and

---

[1] But see Ramsay, below, Appendix A.

thought himself able to identify the place for certain as the tunnel mentioned by Herodotus, but long since laid open by earthquake. "It is most apparent that...the two cliffs have here been joined." Near this ravine a church was erected in honour of St Michael, in memory of a preservation from flood.

Colossæ was at length deserted for Chonæ, three miles away. Chonæ is mentioned by the Byzantine historians of the twelfth century as a rich and populous city[1]; it is now a large straggling village, Chonos. The name is connected with the Greek word *chônê*, a funnel.

The name Colossæ is perhaps connected with *colossos*, a gigantic statue; in possible allusion to the fantastic shapes of the stony deposits. But "in a Phrygian city over which so many Eastern nations swept in succession, who shall say to what language the name belonged?"[2]

The form of the name, at, before, and long after St Paul's time, was certainly *Colossæ*; it appears unaltered on coins of nearly two centuries later. But the form *Colassæ* ultimately came in also[3]. The manuscripts of the Epistle shew considerable evidence for the use of this form in the Title, but not in the text. Lightfoot has "written confidently ['*in Colossæ*'] in the text, and with more hesitation ['*To the Colassians*'] in the superscription."

It remains only to ask, what was the history of the Colossian mission-station, and its neighbours, up to the date of our Epistle? The materials for the answer lie entirely in the Epistle (with that to Philemon), and in the Acts. From the Epistle we gather that on the one hand the Colossian Church looked to St Paul as its father (certainly he addresses the converts in a father's tone); and on the other, that he had not visited Colossæ personally. This latter assertion indeed has been disputed, as we have explained in the note to ch. ii. 1. M. Renan (*Saint Paul*, p. 331), holds that the Apostle, on his third missionary journey (Acts xviii.), passed from Galatia and Phrygia to Ephesus by Apamea Cibôtus, and thence down the valley of the Lycus, touching the

---

[1] Findlay, *Byzantine Empire*, ii. 235, 294.
[2] Lightfoot, p. 17, *note*.   [3] Lightfoot, p. 16, *note*.

Introduction / 21

three towns which lay in it, but so slightly as to make no personal acquaintance there. Bp Lightfoot[1] labours to prove that the region intended by St Luke (Acts xvi. 6, xviii. 23) under the term "the Phrygian and Galatian *country*" was not (as M. Renan thinks) the Roman province of Galatia, but the districts properly and naturally so described, and therefore (as a map will shew) districts which would *not* put the traveller, moving from them to Ephesus, in the line of the Lycus[2].

Combining the notices in the Acts (xix., xx.) with those in Colossians and Philemon, we gather that St Paul was practically stationary (xx. 18) at Ephesus for three years (probably A.D. 55—A.D. 57) after his arrival there from the interior ("*the upper coasts*," xix. 1) on his third journey; and that during that time not only was Ephesus powerfully affected but "all they which dwelt in (proconsular) Asia heard the word".[3] The great city was naturally the centre of a large intercourse, and visitors from the remotest districts, coming there for business, or worship, or pleasure, would be brought across the Missionary's path, and, finding Christ for themselves, would return to their homes to report their discovery[4]. Some of them, coming under the Apostle's developed teaching, would be sent back by him with a definite commission to evangelize and to form Churches.

Such an ordained native evangelist we may believe Epaphras to have been. And Nymphas, Philemon, Apphia, Archippus, who all evidently were personally known to St Paul, must have made his acquaintance on visits to Ephesus from their valley; perhaps guided to him by Epaphras, if Epaphras was "the first-fruits of the Lycus unto Christ."

In our Epistle St Paul would thus be addressing a commu-

[1] *Colossians*, p. 24, *note*.
[2] But see further, Appendix A, for Ramsay's recent conclusions.
[3] See *Ephesians* in this Series, pp. 12, 13.
[4] So it is still. Not many years ago a mountain district in the Chinese province of Cheh-kiang was evangelized by a native of one of its villages. He had visited the provincial capital, Hang-chow (the Quinsay of Marco Polo), and, seeing an unwonted combination of hieroglyphics, making the name JESUS, over the door of a Christian preaching-room, was led by literary curiosity to "the foreign teacher," and so to the feet of Christ.

nity which he had not seen, but many representative individuals of which he had seen; persons who were his dear friends in Christ of some five or six years' standing.

Chapter 2

DATE AND OCCASION OF THE EPISTLE

IT is assumed in this Commentary that the Epistle was written from Rome, at some time during the imprisonment recorded at the close of the Acts. In Acts xxiii., xxiv., another imprisonment, also of about two years' duration, is mentioned, at Cæsarea Stratonis, on the Syrian coast; and many historical critics assign the Epistles to Ephesus, Colossæ, and Philemon to that time and place. Among recent continental writers Weiss (*Einleitung in das N. T.*, pp. 249, 250) decides for this alternative, certainly as regards the Epistles to Colossæ and Philemon. It is to be remembered that "the evidence is curiously scanty; few would imagine how rash it would be to express a confident opinion without close examination".[1]

In seeking a decision, the first question is, what is the relation of time between *Colossians* (to speak now of it only) and *Philippians*, which is generally allowed to be dated from Rome. Lightfoot[2] argues for the priority of *Philippians*, and to us his argument seems convincing. The doctrinal affinity between Phil. iii. and *Romans* is remarkable, while *Colossians* presents no such traces. The type of error combated in *Colossians* is, in some important respects, of a different order, and such, in our opinion, as to suggest a somewhat later development. In the Acts, St Paul appears beset by Jewish opposition of an altogether Pharisaic type, which was to be

---

[1] We quote these words from MS. notes of lectures by the late Dr Hort (Lady Margaret's Professor of Divinity at Cambridge,) kindly put into our hands by the Rev. G. A. Schneider, M.A., Vice-Principal of Ridley Hall. To these notes we are much indebted in this whole context.

[2] *Philippians*, *Introd.*, ch. ii. A statement of the case is given in *Philippians* in this Series, ch. ii.

Introduction / 23

met with the watchwords "grace," "justification," "righteousness of faith." It seems likely then that the type of teaching which invaded Colossæ, in which Judaism appears tinged with the mystic elements afterwards developed in Gnosticism[1], came later than this in the experiences of his work. If so, *Philippians* marks his last great protest against the older type, *Colossians* his first against the newer.

The late Dr Hort, however, remarks that "Lightfoot's view has found few friends," and recommends that *Philippians* should not be employed as a certain factor in the argument.

Weiss' contention is, (*a*) that in *Philippians* (ii. 24) St Paul hopes to visit Macedonia, in *Philemon* (practically one with *Colossians*) Phrygia; (*b*) that at Cæsarea he must have had considerable hopes (Acts xxiv. 26) that Felix would summarily release him, while at Rome he had to await the regular course of his trial; and that therefore it was not likely that *from Rome* he would write asking for "a lodging" at Colossæ; (*c*) that Colossæ was too far from Rome to make such an announcement of speedy arrival likely. Other critics have urged also that Onesimus was more likely to have fled to Cæsarea than over sea to Rome; but Weiss (p. 250 *note*) rightly says that we know nothing of the details of Onesimus' flight, and dismisses this reason. And it seems likely, from what we know of St Paul's comparative freedom at Rome, compared with the rule made at Cæsarea (Acts xxiv. 23; partly no doubt to protect him from assassination) that only "*his own*" should come to him, that a fugitive slave would more easily approach him at Rome than at Cæsarea. Weiss argues indeed that the centurion on guard would not know who Paul's "own" were; but surely the rule was not made for nothing, and in any case it would be enough to make admission difficult for a deplorable-looking slave.

As regards Weiss' main arguments[2], it may be replied to (*a*), that St Paul might well pass through Macedonia to Phrygia, and so carry out both purposes in one journey; supposing him

---

[1] See below, ch. iii.
[2] See too the able statement of and answer to Meyer's plea for Cæsarea by Alford; *Greek Test.*, iii. 20—23.

to start from Rome. As regards (*b*) it seems fair to remark that *he does* express a hope (Phil. ii. 24), while his case was pending at Rome, that he should "come *shortly*" to Philippi. And the language of Philem. 22 must not be pressed as though it were a formal announcement of arrival at an early date; he is hoping for a release before very long, in answer to prayer, and, perhaps not without a touch of loving pleasantry, bids Philemon make haste to receive him, as if he was coming to see that his request about Onesimus had been carried out.

In favour of the earlier date of *Colossians* it has been urged that Colossæ was visited by a tremendous earthquake in A.D. 60 (according to the account of Tacitus, *Annals*, xiv. 27), and that it would be strange if a letter written after that date should make no allusion to it. But Eusebius (*Chronicon*, Olymp. 210) dates the convulsion quite four years later; and Lightfoot[1] gives reasons for thinking that Eusebius had better information.

On the whole, we think the evidence goes for the Roman origin of our Epistle, and of *Philemon* and *Ephesians*. The strongest arguments of detail to the contrary are certainly not conclusive; and there remains the general probability that the two years at Rome, on whose spiritual activity St Luke lays such stress, were more likely than the scarcely-noticed two years at Cæsarea to be the time of production of these truly wonderful Epistles[2].

With these considerations before us, we now sketch the circumstances under which probably they were written[3].

St Paul arrived in Rome, from Melita, in the spring of A.D. 61, probably early in March. There he spent "two full years" (Acts xxviii. 30), at the close of which, as we have good reason to believe, he was released.

In the long delay before his trial[4] he was of course in

[1] *Colossians*, pp. 38—40.
[2] See Appendix B, for some remarks on the relation of time between *Colossians &c.* and 1 *Peter*.
[3] The following paragraphs, as far as the end of par. 2, p. 28, are transferred nearly verbatim from our *Ephesians*, pp. 16—20.
[4] Due probably to procrastination in the prosecution and to the caprice of the Emperor. See Lewin, *Life &c. of St Paul*, vol. II. p. 236, for a parallel case.

custody; but this was comparatively lenient. He occupied lodgings of his own (Acts xxviii. 16, 23, 30), probably a storey or flat in one of the lofty houses common in Rome. It is impossible to determine for certain where this lodging was, but it is likely that it was either in or near the great Camp of the Prætorians, or Imperial Guard, outside the Colline Gate, just N.E. of the City[1]. In this abode the Apostle was attached day and night by a light coupling-chain to a Prætorian sentinel, but was as free, apparently, to invite and maintain general intercourse as if he had been merely confined by illness.

The company actually found in his rooms at different times was very various. His first visitors (indeed they must have been the providers of his lodging) would be the Roman Christians, including all, or many, of the saints named in a passage (Rom. xvi.) written only a very few years before. Then came the representatives of the Jewish community (Acts xxviii. 17, 23), but apparently never to return, as such, after the long day of discussion to which they were first invited. Then from time to time would come Christian brethren, envoys from distant Churches, or personal friends; Epaphroditus from Philippi, Aristarchus from Thessalonica, Tychicus from Ephesus, Epaphras from Colossæ, John Mark, Demas, Jesus Justus. Luke, "the beloved physician," was present perhaps always, and Timotheus, the Apostle's spiritual son, very frequently. One other memorable name occurs, Onesimus, the fugitive Colossian slave, whose story we have to study more fully below. His case is at once a striking evidence of the liberty of access to the Apostle granted to anyone and everyone, and a beautiful illustration both of the character of St Paul and the transfiguring power and righteous principles of the Gospel.

No doubt the visitors to this obscure but holy lodging were far more miscellaneous than even this list suggests. Through the successive Prætorian sentinels some knowledge of the character and message of the prisoner would be always

---

[1] See Lightfoot, *Philippians*, pp. 9 &c., 99 &c.

passing out. The right interpretation of Phil. i. 13[1] is, beyond reasonable doubt, that the true account of Paul's imprisonment came to be "known in the Prætorian regiments, and generally among people around;" and Phil. iv. 22 indicates that a body of earnest and affectionate converts had arisen among the population of slaves and freedmen attached to the Palace of Nero. And the wording of that passage suggests that such Christians found a welcome meeting-place in the rooms of the Apostle; doubtless for frequent worship, doubtless also for direct instruction, and for the blessed enjoyments of the family affection of the Gospel. Meanwhile (Phil. i. 15, 16) there was a section of the Roman Christian community, probably the disciples infected with the prejudices of the Pharisaic party (see Acts xv. &c.), who, with very few exceptions (see Col. iv. 11 and notes), took sooner or later a position of trying antagonism to St Paul; a trial over which he triumphed in the deep peace of Christ.

It is an interesting possibility, not to say probability, that from time to time the lodging was visited by enquirers of intellectual fame or distinguished rank. Ancient Christian tradition[2] actually makes the renowned Stoic writer, L. Annæus Seneca, tutor and counsellor of Nero, a convert of St Paul's; and one phase of the legend was the fabrication, within the first four centuries, of a correspondence between the two. It is quite certain that Seneca was never a Christian, though his language is full of startling superficial parallels to that of the N.T., and these are most full in his latest writings. But it is at least very likely that he heard, through his many channels of information, of St Paul's existence and presence, and that he was intellectually interested in his teaching; and it is quite possible that he cared to visit him. It is not improbable, surely, that Seneca's brother Gallio (Acts xviii. 12) may have described St Paul, however passingly, in a letter; for Gallio's religious indifference may quite well have consisted with a strong personal impression made on him by St Paul's bearing. Festus himself was little

---

[1] See Lightfoot, *Philippians*, pp. 99 &c.
[2] The first hint appears in Tertullian, cent. 2—3.

interested in the Gospel, or at least took care to seem so, and yet was deeply impressed by the personality of the Apostle. Again, the Prefect of the Imperial Guard, A.D. 61, was Afranius Burrus, Seneca's intimate colleague as counsellor to Nero, and it is at least possible that he had received from Festus a more than commonplace description of the prisoner consigned to him[1].

Bp Lightfoot, in his Essay, "St Paul and Seneca" (*Philippians*, pp. 270, &c.), thinks it possible to trace in some of the Epistles of the Captivity a Christian adaptation of Stoic ideas. The Stoic, for example, made much of the individual's *membership* in the great Body of the Universe, and *citizenship* in its great City. The connexion suggested is interesting, and it falls quite within the methods of Divine inspiration that materials of scriptural imagery should be collected from a secular region. But the language of St Paul about the Mystical Body, in the Ephesian and Colossian Epistles, reads far more like a direct revelation than like an adaptation; and it evidently deals with a truth which is already, in its substance, perfectly familiar to the readers[2].

Other conspicuous personages of Roman society at the time have been reckoned by tradition among the chamber-converts of St Paul, among them the poet Lucan and the Stoic philosopher Epictētus[3]. But there is no historical evidence for these assertions. It is interesting and suggestive, on the other hand, to recall one almost certain case of conversion about this time within the highest Roman aristocracy. Pomponia Græcina, wife of Aulus Plautius, the conqueror of Britain, was accused (A.D. 57, probably), of "foreign superstition," and tried by her

---

[1] We cannot but think that Bp Lightfoot (*Philippians*, p. 301) somewhat underrates the probability that Gallio and Burrus should have given Seneca an interest in St Paul.
[2] It appears in 1 *Corinthians*, written a few years before *Ephesians*. See 1 Cor. xii., and cp. Rom. xii.
[3] See above, p. 18. For the curiously Christian tone of Epictetus' writings here and there, see Bp Lightfoot, *Philippians*, pp. 313 &c. The *Manual* of Epictetus is a book of gold in its own way, but that way is not Christian.

husband as domestic judge. He acquitted her. But the deep and solemn seclusion of her life (a seclusion begun A.D. 44, when her friend the princess Julia was put to death, and continued unbroken till her own death, about A.D. 84), taken in connexion with the charge, as in all likelihood it was, of Christianity, "suggests that, shunning society, she sought consolation in the duties and hopes of the Gospel"[1], leaving for ever the splendour and temptations of the world of Rome. She was not a convert, obviously, of St Paul's; but her case suggests the possibility of other similar cases. And she would assuredly seek intercourse with the Apostle during his Roman residence.

At what time of the Two Years the Epistle to the Colossians was written we cannot hope to determine with precision. It is a prevalent theory that the Ephesian and Colossian Epistles date somewhat early in the period, and the Philippian late. Bp Lightfoot (*Philippians*, pp. 30, &c.), as we have observed above (p. 22), has given some strong reasons for the reversal of the order. The strongest, in our view, is the consideration of style in the respective Epistles. *Philippians*, so far as it is dogmatic, approaches certainly much nearer to the type of *Romans* than *Ephesians* does; and this suggests a comparative nearness in date. The test of style demands caution, in its application, in the case of a writer of such compass and versatility as St Paul; circumstances might suggest similarity of subject to his mind at widely separated times, and the subject rather than the time would rule the style, within certain limits. But in this case we have further to observe that the style of the Ephesian Group (so to call it) is manifestly, in some aspects, a new style, and charged with dogmatic materials in many respects new. And this suggests at least the probability of an interval between the Roman and Ephesian Epistles as long as the chronology will reasonably allow.

We may conjecture that it was at some time in A.D. 62, or even early in A.D. 63, that the Colossian Epistle, with its companions, *Philemon* and *Ephesians*, was written. Tychicus (iv. 7; Eph. vi. 21), an Asiatic, and perhaps Ephesian, Christian,

---

[1] Lightfoot, *Philippians*, p. 21.

had been at Rome at St Paul's side, and was now ready to return eastward as his representative. And with him was going another and more recent convert, Onesimus, fugitive slave of a leading Colossian convert[1], who had somehow found his way from Phrygia to Rome, and to St Paul, and through him to faith in Christ, and was now, at St Paul's instigation, returning to his master. Meantime a visitor had come from Colossæ, Epaphras, himself a Colossian (iv. 12) and the first missionary to Colossæ (i. 7). Perhaps he had acted, like many a modern missionary, as pastor also in the place where he had first preached Christ, and in its neighbourhood (iv. 13); certainly some time had elapsed since the first evangelization, as the tone and contents of *Colossians* and *Philemon* bear witness; and Epaphras appears as both the original evangelist and the anxious watcher afterwards over the flock once gathered out. Circumstances of the mission, apparently, had suggested to him a visit to Rome, to consult his apostolic chief; and he had come, leaving behind him, it would seem, as his successor or assistant in the missionary pastorate one Archippus (iv. 17; Philem. 2), probably the son of Philemon.

Other reasons may have concurred to occasion the visit. Like Epaphroditus of Philippi Epaphras may have brought alms from the mission to the afflicted Apostle; but no allusion to such a gift occurs. However, the main purpose of the visit is clear from the Epistle. At Colossæ, as earlier in Galatia, the infant Church was invaded by alien teaching and influence; the Colossians and their neighbours were in great danger of serious spiritual harm, above all as regarded a full realization of the glory of the Person of the Lord, and of the all-sufficiency of His atoning and mediating work to secure both the pardon and the moral purity of the believer. This Epaphras must report to St Paul, and either carry a message back, or procure its going by other hands. In the following chapter we examine in some detail the question, what was the alien teaching thus reported from Colossæ.

---

[1] See further, *Introduction* to the Ep. to Philemon, ch. ii.

Chapter 3

ALIEN TEACHING AT COLOSSÆ

WHAT does the Epistle indicate as the kind of danger which beset the faith of the Colossians? Combining the passages of explicit warning with others which evidently emphasize a somewhat discredited truth, we get the following result.

The new influences tended in practice, if not in theory, to throw into the background the unique greatness of the Son of God as the Divine King; as the perfect Propitiation, who by the blood of His Cross has won our peace; as the Vital Head of the Church; as the Bearer of the Plenitude of Deity; as the living Likeness of the invisible God, and also as the Origin of all created being, including the angelic orders (i.13—20) whose Head as well as Cause He is (ii. 10). They were tempted to forget that He is the ultimate "Secret of God" (ii. 2), in whom the Christian possesses *all* that God has to reveal for his salvation; in whom he has access to all the wealth of the Divine wisdom; in whom he is "filled full," being united to the incarnate Abode of all the Plenitude of God (ii. 2—10). They were tempted to forget that union with Jesus Christ by faith, of which union their baptism was the Divine pledge and seal, was everything for their spiritual life and health; that "in" Him, He being what He was, and having done what He had done, they were "circumcised" into the true Israel of faith and holiness, were disburthened of the awful debt of guilt, were "buried" to sin, and "risen again" to acceptance, and moral purity and power, possessing a life "hidden with Him in God" (which life in fact was He), and looking forward to His Return as the occasion and cause of the outburst of this life into glory (ii. 11—14; iii. 1—4). They were tempted on the other hand to adopt substitutes for this Divine Secret, Christ, in the pursuit of spiritual peace and purity. Teachers, or a teacher, were among them who spoke speciously of a "philosophy," and claimed to hold a "tradition" (the mere product, as a fact, of human thought), independent of the Message of Christ and tending away from Him (ii. 8); not, apparently, by way of direct denial but as teaching a need of supplements to Him and His work, and of other intermediations between the disciple and God. This preacher, or school, advocated a strict ascetic rule of food (ii. 16, 21), a diligent observance of the Jewish yearly, monthly, and weekly holy days, and also recourse to angelic beings as subsidiary mediators with God (ii. 8); mediators apparently, not with *Christ* (or there would be little point in the stress laid by St Paul on His creative and regal relation to angels, and on His conquest (ii. 15) over rebels from among them in His crucifixion), but with God absolutely. Angels were presented as another and as it were rival path of communication with the Supreme, and so far they broke the Christian's hold upon his Head (ii. 19) as his direct and all-sufficient Union with God. Traces may perhaps be found in the same teaching of a tendency to an esoteric and exclusive theory; a doctrine of secrets and initiation. The reference to Christ as the true Depositary of "hidden treasures" (ii. 8) may point this way. However, the openness and universality of the Gospel are powerfully emphasized in the Epistle.

Such on the whole were the principles and influences of which Epaphras had to speak as he sate with the Apostle in the Roman lodging. What may we infer as to their source and historical connexion?

In the first place, it is reasonably plain that the influence on the whole was *one*. Some critics have assumed *two* independent but concurrent invasions of Colossian faith, one speculative, the other ritualistic[1]. But let the reader take the Epistle as a whole, and he will surely feel that such a division is arbitrary; the insistences on truth and warnings against error are too freely interwoven for the theory. Allusions to "philosophy" glide imperceptibly into allusions to circumcision, sabbaths, and ascetic rules, and again into allusions to fancied insights into the unseen world.

Again, the danger comes rather from within than from without

[1] Lightfoot, pp. 74, 75.

the pale of Christianity. It is not indicated that any direct assault on the claims of Christ was in question; the risk was rather that principles and practices (see ii. 6) really inconsistent with His claims should be adopted unthinkingly, to the *ultimate* wreck of faith.

Again, the movement was Judaic (however much it was *Christiano*-Judaic). This is plain from the allusions to the Jewish feasts, and to rules of abstinence. True, the Old Testament has no express restrictive rules about drinks (ii. 16), except for the Nazirite; but Rabbinical Judaism, which would certainly influence the Judaizer of St Paul's day, had such rules. (And see Heb. ix. 10 for a similar allusion to "meats *and drinks*," as matters about which the Law was held actually to speak.) It is implied in ii. 17 that the new teachers taught the permanence of the ritual Law. And the marked allusion to angel-worship (ii. 18) points to a practice widely-spread in later Judaism. Again, we may compare the Epistle to the Hebrews (i. 4—14), as indicating such a risk in Palestine as well as at Colossæ.

Meantime elements appear in this Colossian movement which are not altogether of the ordinary Judaic type. The new doctrine presented itself as not only a "tradition" (cp. Matt. xv. 2), but as a "philosophy." Too much must not be made of this word, as if it necessarily suggested a system of independent speculation on problems of existence, and the like; for in some quarters of the Jewish religious world, about the apostolic time, there was a tendency to disarm Gentile prejudice by representing Jewish doctrine and practice as a sort of "philosophy," practical rather than speculative[1]. Still, the presence of this tone in the movement at Colossæ indicates a somewhat different school from that which had invaded Galatia; in the

---

[1] In the Jewish tract, *The Fourth Book of the Maccabees*, the writer represents the refusal of the Maccabees to eat unhallowed food as a use of "reasoning" (λογισμός), and appeals to the reader, in the opening of the book, to "give heed to philosophy." We owe this reference to memoranda of the late Dr Hort's Lectures (see above, p. 22, *note*). Dr Hort inclines on the whole to see less than Bp Lightfoot sees of a "Gnostic" element in the Colossian movement, and to account for its phenomena rather on the theory that it was Judaism of a more ordinary type, but using a somewhat Grecized phraseology.

Galatian Epistle we find no trace of such aspects, or at least of such a phraseology, of error. So the Judaists of Colossæ may very possibly have tinged their thought and teaching with some of those attempts to combine Hebrew or Christian revelation with independent speculation, or reverie, which later, in a more developed form, came to be known as Gnosticism.

The Gnostic, as he is seen in his maturity, is occupied with two great problems; the mystery of Creation and the mystery of Evil. He attempted to account for finite Existence by a self-limitation of the Infinite, such that a chain of Emanations (called "*Angels*" by Cerinthus, the first historical Gnostic, St John's younger contemporary) bridged the gulph between the world and the Supreme. And he practically identified evil with matter, and taught that the true purification lay in the spirit's emancipation from material trammels. As to practical results, this theory led some to an extreme asceticism, others to an unrestrained licence; the one insisting on the need of so to speak attenuating the body to the utmost, the other on that of an absolute indifference to its motions. If such theories, which doubtless were far and wide "in the air" about the date of our Epistle, had at all affected the new teacher, or teachers, at Colossæ, it must have been (ii. 21) in the ascetic direction. As regards the problem of creation, we may perhaps see in Col. i. an indication that this also was in their minds. We seem to see that they failed to grasp the glorious suggestions of a solution given in the revelation of the Incarnate Son, One with God and One with man, Head of Creation and Head of the Church, Cause of finite being and Cause of the sinner's salvation; but sought an ineffectual answer in a theory of angelic agency between the Supreme and the world and man.

Bp Lightfoot, with great learning and labour, and admirably clear exposition, has discussed in this connexion the question whether the new teaching at Colossæ was influenced, directly or indirectly, or at least was akin to, the belief and teaching of *the Essenes*[1].

[1] Incidentally to this discussion he has written the fullest and most learned dissertation in existence on the Essenes. *Colossians*, pp. 114—179.

The Essenes, otherwise Essæans[1], are described by Josephus[2] as the third Jewish sect or school with the Pharisees and Sadducees. He gives an elaborate and curious picture of their life, characteristics, and doctrines, which is supplemented for us by other Jewish notices[3], and by a passage in the *Natural History* of the elder Pliny (v. 17), who gives a brief epigrammatic account of them, as "a people of all most wonderful," living near Engadda (Engedi) on the west side of the Dead Sea, without money and without marriage, but continually replenished in numbers by accessions from the outer world[4]. Here apparently was their headquarters, and there is little certain trace of their diffusion beyond Palestine and Syria; but Josephus says, vaguely, that they were to be found everywhere. They were "rather an order than a school;" observing a rigid rule of life; divided into grades; making a prolonged scrutiny of every applicant for membership; absolute communists, and (as a rule) celibates; bound together by sworn fidelity and secrecy, while also industrious and kindly. Their characteristics as religionists were curiously anomalous; on the one hand they were sabbatarians far more strict than the Pharisees, and observed extremely rigid laws of ceremonial purity, on the other hand they repudiated animal sacrifices. Meanwhile they held that the body was the mere prison of the soul, and they apparently looked for no bodily resurrection. And they were certainly in some degree sun-worshippers, however this was reconciled with Hebrew monotheism. They reverenced Moses next to God, but they had sacred books of their own (apparently) over and above the Old Testament Scriptures; which Scriptures possibly they received only in part. They appear to have cut themselves off from national interests, aiming only at the highest good of the individual. They disappear

[1] The names are of uncertain derivation; of the many suggested Lightfoot inclines to that from the Hebrew *châshâ*, "*to be silent*," with a reference to mystic meditation.
[2] The main passage is *Wars of the Jews*, ii. 8. § 2—13.
[3] Especially Philo, *Quod omnis bonus liber*, §§ 12, 13.
[4] He says that the race is thus "eternal through thousands of centuries." This has been taken to mean (by Lightfoot among others) that Pliny understood them to be of immense antiquity. Does it not rather mean, more generally, that their proselyte system enables them *to defy time?*

Introduction / 35

after the ruin of Jerusalem; the Romans fell on their community with persecuting fierceness, and probably extirpated it[1].

It has been suggested that Essenism was the result of a graft of Greek mystical philosophy (Pythagorean) on Pharisaism. But the concurrence would be a most unlikely one, both geographically and religiously. Lightfoot advocates[2] the view that the influence on Judaism which produced Essenism was that of Parsism, the religion of the Zend Avesta, with its condemnation of matter, its sun-worship, its reverence for super-human intermediate world-rulers, and its intense striving after purity. History and geography alike make such contact and influence, some time before our Era, not unlikely[3].

In applying these facts to the question of the troubles at Colossæ Bp Lightfoot infers that the Essenes exercised an influence, however indirect, on the Judaistic teachers who disturbed the Church. Dr Hort (as referred to above, p. 32, *note*) contends on the other hand that there is no clear evidence of Essene influence at Colossæ, and that it was confined, so far as we know, to Palestine. But Lightfoot thinks it at least likely that the same ideas which produced Essenism animated the alien teachers at Colossæ. And while Essenism as an organization may never have left Palestine, individual Essenes may well have travelled, and may have carried about a medley of Christianity and quasi-Judaism with them.

Obviously, the case is not one for absolute decisions. We venture to think that Bp Lightfoot has drawn somewhat too large conclusions from his vast and masterly collection of data; the references to an *esoteric* system in the Epistle are not, as it

---

[1] In a book ascribed to Philo (cent. i.), *On the Contemplative Life*, is a curious description of the *Therapeutæ*, or Devotees, of Egypt, which is in many respects like that of the Essenes by Josephus and Philo. See an account of it in Eusebius, *History*, ii. 17; with notes in the Series of *Nicene and Post-Nicene Fathers*. But it is at least possible that the book is later than Philo, and really describes a Christian monastic community.

[2] Lightfoot, pp. 148 etc. Lightfoot holds that the suggestion of *Buddhist* influences is certainly to be rejected.

[3] On Essenism and Christianity, see further Appendix E.

appears to us, quite so full as he takes them to be. On the other hand Dr Hort, whose every word on such a question calls for attention and deference as justly as Bp Lightfoot's, seems to us somewhat to overstate the case in holding, apparently, that in essence the teaching was simply Judaism with a special dialect. For firstly, this does not quite account for the indications given in Col. i. of a special need to emphasize our Lord's *Headship over Creation;* and secondly, it seems to neglect the fact that the movement took, in part, the direction of an intense asceticism *with a view to subdue the flesh* (ii. 20—23). This is not Pharisaism, but something much more like Essenism, whether or no the two had a traceable connexion. "The teaching", says Dr R. Sinker, " is probably not Essene, but it is Essenic."

In any case Lightfoot seems to be fully justified in seeing in the troubles at Colossæ, on one side of them, an embryo of the type of speculative thought which so much disturbed the Church of the second century, and is known as Gnosticism. Particularly he regards Cerinthus (see above, p. 33) as a link in history between such a movement as that at Colossæ and the developed Gnosticism[1]. Cerinthus taught in proconsular Asia, within St John's lifetime. The accounts of his doctrine preserved to us indicate a thinker who combined a spurious Christianity, involving utterly inadequate views of our Lord's Person, with some Judaistic principles and practices, and with a theory of creation which included the agency of world-making "Angels"[2].

This review of the actual and possible characteristics of the disturbing movement in the missions of the Lycus will serve in some measure to aid the reader's appreciation of the earnestness with which St Paul, after hearing Epaphras' report, sets himself to emphasize the glory of the Son of God, the mighty fulness of His redeeming work, and the immediate relation between Him as Head and each believer as member. Along this road of circumstance the Inspirer led the apostolic Prophet,

[1] *Colossians*, pp. 107 etc.
[2] See, besides Lightfoot as constantly quoted here, Mansel's *Gnostic Heresies*, especially Lectures i.—iv., and viii.

to give to the Colossians an Epistle which, written to meet a local and peculiar need, now unfolds to the whole Church the radiant mystery of the Person and Work of Christ.

Chapter 4

AUTHENTICITY OF THE EPISTLE

THE external evidence for the Pauline authorship of the Epistle as we have it is abundant. In the second century Irenæus (about A.D. 115—A.D. 190), the Asiatic bishop of Lyons, quotes the Epistle expressly (*Adv. Hæreses*, iii. 14. 1): "Again, in the Epistle written to the Colossians, he says, '*Luke, the beloved physician, salutes you.*'" Clement of Alexandria (perhaps A.D. 150—A.D. 220) quotes the Epistle (*Stromata*, i. p. 325), in favour of using every sort of "wisdom" in the work of the Gospel: "In the Epistle to the Colossians he writes, '*Admonishing every man, and teaching in all wisdom, that we may present every man perfect in Christ.*'" Tertullian, of Carthage (about contemporary with Clement of Alexandria), quotes the Epistle (*De Præscriptione*, c. 7): "Hence these endless fables and genealogies, and fruitless questions, and words creeping like a cancer, from which the Apostle would restrain us (*refrenans*), expressly assuring us that we must be on our guard against philosophy, writing to the Colossians, '*See that no one be beguiling you* (*circumveniens vos*) *through philosophy and empty seduction, according to the tradition of men, beyond the providence of the Holy Spirit.*'"[1] And in his book *De Resurrectione Carnis, c. xxiii.*, (a chapter which is a mass of mainly Pauline extracts), he quotes Col. i. 21, ii. 12, 13, 20, iii. 1—3; with the introduction, "The Apostle thus teaches, writing to the Colossians." Origen, of Alexandria (about A.D. 185—A.D. 254), quotes the Epistle (*Contra Celsum*, v. 8): "In Paul..., in the (Epistle) to the Colossians,

---

[1] In this last clause is he quoting loosely from memory, or merely commenting or supplementing?

we read as follows, '*Let no man beguile you of your reward*'" (and so throughout Col. ii. 18, 19). Possible allusions to the Epistle are traceable in other primitive writers. Ignatius (*ob.* about A.D. 110) uses passingly (*To the Ephesians*, c. iii.) the precise Greek of Col. i. 23, "*settled in the faith*." Clement of Rome (cent. i.) perhaps adopts the phrase "*love, which is the bond of perfectness*" when he writes to the Corinthians (1 *Epistle*, c. xlix.), "Who can describe the bond of the love of God?" Less doubtfully Theophilus, of Antioch (A.D. 176—A.D. 186), in his apologetic work called *Ad Autolycum*, uses the words of Col. i. 15: "He begat this Word to be His Utterance (προφορικόν), *Firstborn of all creation*." The same phrase, probably from the same Colossian source, is used by Justin Martyr, of Palestine (about A.D. 110—A.D. 170), in his *Dialogue with Trypho* (p. 311, B): "In the name of this Son of God and Firstborn of all creation... every demon, adjured, is conquered." And apparent allusions to it occur in two other places of the same book (pp. 310, B, 326, D). The heretic Marcion (contemporary with Justin), "the earliest of destructive critics," admitted Colossians into his *Apostolicon*, or Canon of the Epistles[1].

Not till quite recent times was it suggested that internal evidence was unfavourable to the authenticity of the Epistle. Mayerhoff (1838) and Baur (1845) maintained that it betrays a late date (somewhere in the second century) by variations of style and diction from the supposed normal style of St Paul, by its manifest likeness to the *Ephesians* (which in the opinion of these critics is certainly not Pauline[2]), and by its alleged explicit references to the doctrines either of Cerinthus (Mayerhoff), or of the Ebionites (Baur); the Ebionites regarding "Jesus" as a merely human being temporarily possessed by "Christ," and largely Judaizing their conception of Christianity.

To the first objection it is surely fair to reply by an appeal to the reader to "taste" the style of the Epistle. Can anything be more alive with thought and feeling, and more absolutely unlike an elaborate literary fabrication, produced (on the hypo-

[1] Westcott, *Canon of N.T.*, Pt. i. ch. iv. § 9.
[2] See *Ephesians* in this Series, pp. 22—4.

Introduction / 39

thesis) in an age of declining literary power? Meyer[1] quotes words to this purpose from Erasmus, who is giving his opinion on the style of the alleged *Epistle to Laodicea*[2]: "It is not everyone who can personate Paul's heart (*Paulinum pectus effingere*); Paul thunders, and lightens, and utters fiery flames (*meras flammas*)." It is surely uncritical in a high degree, in examining a work externally well-attested as Pauline, to find a difficulty in the absence from it of some classes of words (e.g. "*righteousness*," "*salvation*," and certain connective particles) elsewhere familiar, and in the presence in it of new words like "*plenitude*" (*plerôma*), or even invented words like "*will-worship*" and "*will-humility*." Such a mind as St Paul's is seen to be in the unquestioned Epistles, e.g. *Romans* and *Corinthians*, was abundantly rich enough, putting Divine inspiration quite aside, freely to vary both its vocabulary and its diction with time and circumstances[3].

To the objections connected with the Ephesian Epistle we must reply in part by the arguments which support the authenticity of this latter[4]. But the literary criticism of *Colossians* may fairly be pursued in great measure independently; the more so as a comparison of the two Epistles favours the hypothesis that *Colossians* was written before *Ephesians*, at whatever interval[5].

The suspicions of Mayerhoff and Baur, due to alleged signs in the Epistle of the writer's acquaintance with a *developed*

[1] *Kommentar über das N.T.*, vii.—x., p. 179.
[2] See below, ch. v.
[3] See Salmon, *Introd. to N.T.*, pp. 469, 470, for some characteristic remarks on "the doctrine that a man, writing a new composition, must not, on pain of losing his identity, employ any word that he has not used in a former one." Salmon quotes from Prof. Mahaffy the observation that the style of Xenophon, "whose life corresponded to St Paul's in its roving habits," shews "a remarkable variation in vocabulary;... so that, on the ground of variation in diction, each single book might be, and indeed has been, rejected as non-Xenophontic."
[4] See *Ephesians*, in this Series, pp. 22—24, for a short summary of them. Here too it is most important that the reader should "taste" the Epistle, putting the controversy as much as possible out of mind, and ask himself if in argument, moral aim, and structure, it reads like an anxious fabrication made at a time when Christian thought was not rising but in some important respects declining.
[5] See below, ch. vi.

Ebionism or Gnosticism, may fairly be met by asking for genuine evidence from the Epistle. It is certain that Gnosticism, and Ebionism, as they appear in history, did not spring suddenly on the Church, but grew from antecedents, some of which lay far in the past, in Judaism or in Oriental mysticism. Thus it was not only possible but highly likely that in the lifetime of St Paul tendencies of thought should appear which called out reasonings and phraseology on his part applicable also as a fact to the Gnostic controversy when developed[1].

Some continental critics (reviewed by Meyer), granting the general authenticity of the Epistle, hold that we have it interpolated with un-Pauline insertions; or that it was mentally formed by St Paul but put into written shape by another hand. Here again the best answer will be the fresh and attentive reading of the Epistle as a whole. It is difficult to say where, in any literature at all similar, we are to look for a close and complex coherence, and for a powerful and sustained individuality of expression, if not in the Epistle to the Colossians[2].

M. Renan (*Saint Paul*, pp. vii—xi) after marshalling, in a spirit of the freest and least reverent criticism, what may be thought the suspicious aspects of the contents of the Epistle, deliberately asserts his conviction of its authenticity: "The Epistle to the Colossians, as we believe, is the work of Paul. It presents many features which negative the hypothesis of fabrication. One of these, surely, is its connexion with the

---

[1] See Meyer, as above, and Mansel, *Gnostic Heresies*, esp. ch. iv. We transcribe the following sentences from memoranda of a Cambridge Lecture on *Colossians* by Bp. (then Prof.) Lightfoot, May 1862: "The language of St Paul, and still more that of St John, often proves that the Gnostics borrowed their language, though no doubt perverting it. Hence it is no argument to infer from the appearance of the same terms in St Paul and some Gnostic writers that Gnosticism was earlier than the Epistle." M. Renan says the same in effect: "Instead of rejecting the authenticity of passages of the N.T. where we find traces of Gnosticism, we must sometimes reason inversely, and seek in these passages the origin" (we should rather say indications of the origin) "of Gnostic ideas of the second century" (*Saint Paul, Introduction*, pp. x. xi). See further, Appendix C.

[2] See Appendix D for some remarks on the phenomena of "the literature of *tendency*."

Note (*billet*) to Philemon. If the Epistle is apocryphal the Note is apocryphal. But few are the pages which shew so pronounced a tone of sincerity. Paul alone, so far as it appears, was capable of that short masterpiece."

Chapter 5

THE EPHESIAN EPISTLE AND THE EPISTLE FROM LAODICEA

IN our edition of *Ephesians* (*Introduction*, ch. iv.) we have reviewed the question whether that Epistle was rather a Circular to a group of Churches than a message only to one. We stated the problem of Eph. i. 1, where the words "*at Ephesus*" are missing from some important MSS., and where collateral evidence shews "that an uncertainty, to say the least, attached very early and very widely to the two words." We noticed the absence from *Ephesians* of any "Ephesian destination on the face of it"; "the salutations are of the most general kind, and the topics of the Epistle are of the highest and least local. The obvious connexion of its contents with the Colossian Epistle, and the name of Tychicus in both Epistles, fix the destination to Roman Asia, but scarcely to a narrower area. The phenomenon is the more noticeable when St Paul's peculiarly intimate and prolonged relations with Ephesus are considered." On the other hand, only two MSS. omit the words (except one other, where a later hand does so); all ancient Versions shew them; and no Church other than Ephesus appears ever to have claimed the Epistle. "As against the suggestion that St Paul, designing the Epistle to be an Asiatic Circular, left out the name of any Church in the very place where in other Epistles a name is found, it may fairly be asked whether it is not far more likely that he would have written, in such a case, '*in Asia*,' or, '*in the Churches of Asia*.'" We summed up the case thus:

"On reviewing the evidence,...the true theory must embrace the phenomena, on the one hand, of a very early variation in the reading of Eph. i. 1, and of the non-local tone of the Epistle; on the other hand, of the universal tradition of its destination to Ephesus, and the immense documentary evidence for it, and the total absence of any serious rival claim. In constructing such a theory it will be useful to remember...that the City stood in the closest possible relation to the Province, both politically and in regard of St Paul's three years' work... Ephesus, more than many another Metropolis, may well have represented its Province to the writer's mind. We believe that the facts are fairly met by the view that St Paul actually addressed the Epistle...'to the saints that are in Ephesus,' but designing it also for the other Asian Churches; and that the transcripts dispersed through the Province frequently omitted this precise original address accordingly, but without introducing any other. It was well understood to be the property of Ephesus, but in trust for the Province."

Archbishop Ussher (cent. 17) first suggested the "Circular Letter" theory[1]. He also suggested that Col. iv. 16 contains an allusion to such a Circular. And the phrase there well suits the theory; it is "the Epistle" (not "*to*," but) "*from* Laodicea." Bp Lightfoot, with his usual thoroughness and fairness, examines this view, and accepts it, and takes "the Epistle from Laodicea" to be in fact our "Epistle to the Ephesians."[2] He states and effectually disposes of the following other theories of "the Epistle from Laodicea": that it was

1. An Epistle written *by* the Laodicean Church, to St Paul, or to Epaphras, or to the Colossians; perhaps complaining of evils in the Colossian Church;

---

[1] *Annales N.T.*, A.M. 4068.
[2] The Bishop's full discussion of the subject of the "circular" is reserved (*Colossians*, p. 347) for his Introduction to the Epistle to the Ephesians; for which now we can no longer hope. The Editor has before him however full MS. notes of the Lectures on *Colossians* delivered by Prof. Lightfoot in 1862 (above, p. 40, *note*). These notes, by the way, quote the Professor as saying, in passing, that the attempt to question the authenticity of the Ephesian Epistle is "quite useless; it is thoroughly Pauline."

Introduction / 43

2. An Epistle written by St Paul *from* Laodicea, and if so either 1 *Timothy*, 1 *Thess.*, 2 *Thess.*, or *Galatians;* conjectures faintly supported by the "Subscriptions" to these Epistles in some MSS. (see e.g. that retained in the A.V. under 1 *Tim.*), but fully negatived by the internal evidence of the Epistles.

He quotes lastly the suggestion that it was

3. An Epistle addressed *to* the Laodiceans; either by St John (1 *Ep.*); or by Epaphras, Luke, or some other friend of St Paul's; or by St Paul himself.

Historical and literary evidence narrows the question to this last point, and it remains to ask, *what* Epistle from St Paul can be that which the Colossians were to procure "from Laodicea"?

As a fact, conjecture has named three of the extant Epistles bearing St Paul's name; *Hebrews, Philemon, Ephesians.* The first suggestion (apart from the question of Pauline authorship) is negatived by the contents of *Hebrews,* which deals with a quite different phase of error and trial from those which would beset Asian Christians of the year 63. The second suggestion is trivial; as Lightfoot well says (p. 347); "The tact and delicacy of the Apostle's pleading for Onesimus would be nullified at one stroke by the demand for publication" of the letter to Philemon. The suggestion of *Ephesians* thus alone remains, with two alternatives from other quarters; one, that "the Epistle from Laodicea" is lost, the other that we still possess it, in a form to be given just below, but as to which we may say beforehand that *that* "Epistle" is a certainly spurious document.

In the theory of a lost Epistle there is nothing *a priori* impossible. The Divine providence which built up the Christian Scriptures was not obliged to employ, for the *permanent and universal* use of the Church, all that even Apostles produced, even under special inspiration. But on the other hand we rightly decline to assume a loss where there is no necessity to do so. And the phenomena of the Ephesian Epistle fairly answer the needs of this case. It is addressed to Asia. It deals with phases of truth and error known to us (from *Colossians*) to be specially prominent there. It is otherwise non-local, and fit for a Circular. It bears traces, as we have seen, of having been addressed not solely to Ephesus. The serious difficulty of the theory lies in the question, whether two letters at once so like and so unlike as *Ephesians* and *Colossians* would be used interchangeably by St Paul's direction. And perhaps the only answer must be that the difficulty is at least far from an impossibility. With all the doctrinal likeness of the two letters, great elements of truth appear in each which are absent from its fellow—the creative Work of the Son in the one, the sanctifying Work of the Spirit in the other[1]; and this may have been enough to justify an arrangement which from other points of view is less intelligible[2].

It may be added that the *metropolitan* position of Laodicea in the Cibyratic Union (above, p. 13) would account for the sending of a Circular thither rather than to any neighbour Church.

It remains only to state briefly the facts about the so-called "Epistle to the Laodiceans."[3]

It is a short composition in letter form, found (so far as we know) only in Latin in the MSS. The earliest known copy

---

[1] See below, p. 50.

[2] Weiss (*Einleitung*, p. 262) thinks that "the Epistle from Laodicea" cannot be our *Ephesians;* at least, that the theory demands artificial hypotheses in support (*künstliche Hilfshypothesen*). He refers to Eph. vi. 12 as indicating that Tychicus was to present the letter personally, and therefore, if it were a Circular, to travel round with it; and thinks that this, if Col. iv. 16 refers to *Ephesians*, would mean that Tychicus *with Onesimus* would go a long round, including Laodicea, *before* reaching Colossæ, where Onesimus was to surrender to his master. He thinks too that it is unlikely that St Paul should greet the Laodiceans in *Colossians* (iv. 15) if he were sending them at the same time a letter (*Ephesians*) by the hand of the same friend. But these reasons seem inconclusive. The hypothesis, if "artificial," is not forced, that Tychicus would only in a general sense *accompany* the "Ephesian" letter; would rather set it going on its round, visiting the Churches personally as he was able. Even otherwise, Laodicea was *on the road from Ephesus to Colossæ*. Tychicus and Onesimus might arrive there together, make a very short stay, and then go on to Colossæ, leaving the "Ephesian" Circular to be brought on after them.

[3] Lightfoot, pp. 347—366.

Introduction / 45

dates from cent. 6. Lightfoot gives good reason however for the belief that it was first written in Greek. The Latin style bears marks of the constraint of translation, and of translation from the Greek. Its (concealed) quotations from St Paul are not drawn from the ancient Latin Versions of his canonical Epistles, as they most probably would have been had the fabricator written in Latin. And there is good evidence that an "Epistle to the Laodiceans" was early known to Greek readers; e.g. Theodoret (cent. 5) writes (in Greek) of a "fabricated Epistle" which "some brought forward." Lightfoot "restores" the Greek from the Latin; the task is not difficult, so truly is the composition, in his words, "a cento of Pauline phrases, strung together without any definite connexion or any clear object;...taken chiefly from the Epistle to the Philippians, but here and there one is borrowed from elsewhere, e.g. from the Epistle to the Galatians."

The "Epistle" reads as follows; we translate from the Latin text as it is printed by Lightfoot.

"TO THE LAODICEANS

"PAUL an Apostle, not of men, nor through man, but through Jesus Christ, to the brethren who are at Laodicea. Grace unto you and peace from God the Father and the Lord Jesus Christ.

"I give thanks to God in (lit. through) every prayer of mine, that ye are abiding (*permanentes*) in Him, and persevering in His works, looking for the promise unto the day of judgment. And let not the vain speech of certain men beguile you, who teach (*insinuantium*) in order that they may turn you away from the Gospel which is preached by me. And now God shall bring it about that those who proceed from me prove serviceable for the furtherance of the truth of the Gospel, and doers of the goodness of the works which belong to the salvation of life eternal.

"And now are manifest my bonds, which I suffer in Christ; wherein I exult and rejoice. And this is to me for perpetual salvation; which also is done by your prayers and by the administration of the Holy Spirit, whether through life or through death. For to me to live is Christ and to die is joy. And His mercy shall do in you this very thing, that you should have the same love and be of one mind.

"Therefore, dearly beloved, as ye hearkened in my presence, so hold fast and do in the fear of God, and you shall have life for evermore; for it is God who worketh in you. And do without disputing whatsoever ye do.

"And for what remaineth, dearly beloved, rejoice in Christ; and beware of them who are defiled with gain. Let all your requests be manifest before God; and be ye stedfast in the mind of Christ. And the things which are whole, and true, and grave, and just, and lovely, do. And the things which ye have heard and received in the heart, hold fast; and ye shall have peace.

"The saints salute you.

"The grace of our Lord Jesus Christ (be) with your spirit.

"And see that (this) be read to the Colossians, and (that which is) of the Colossians to you."

"For more than nine centuries," says Lightfoot, "this forged Epistle hovered about the doors of the sacred Canon." Gregory the Great (cent. 6) appears to receive it as Pauline, though not as canonical. In our own country, Aelfric, abbot of Cerne, in Dorset (cent. 10), ranks it as one of the "fifteen Epistles" of St Paul; and so does John of Salisbury, cent. 12. In MSS. of "all ages from the sixth to the fifteenth century we have examples of its occurrence among the Pauline Epistles." It appears in an Albigensian version, "said to belong to the thirteenth century;" in Bohemian Bibles; in German Bibles before Luther; and in two curious English versions[1] made soon after Wyclif's time, say between 1400 and 1450. But the revival of learning finally disposed of its claims. Erasmus contemptuously dismissed it[2]; "No argument against a Pauline authorship can be stronger than the Epistle itself." A Lutheran scholar, and a Jesuit, both of cent. 16, are quoted as its last defenders; the latter taking it as a proof that the Church might, in her discretion, decline to insert

---

[1] Printed by Lightfoot, p. 364.
[2] See above, p. 39.

even an apostolic letter into the Canon. But "the dawn of the Reformation Epoch had effectually scared away this ghost of a Pauline Epistle, which, we may confidently hope, has been laid for ever."

Chapter 6

PARALLELS AND OTHER RELATIONS BETWEEN THE COLOSSIAN AND EPHESIAN EPISTLES

THE parallelism of the two Epistles can be fully appreciated only through the comparative study of both the details and the whole of each; a study which will also bring out many important differences between the points of view and modes of treatment in the two. In the following table all that is offered is a view of the chief doctrinal parallels, and a few out of the very many instances of parallelism of subject, or expression, not necessarily connected with doctrine.

1. *Christ the Head of the Church:*
   Col. i. 18, ii. 19 = Eph. i. 22, iv. 15, v. 23.

This view of the Lord's position and function is practically confined to these Epistles.

2. *Christ supreme over angelic powers:*
   Col. ii. 10 = Eph. i. 21.

3. *The Church Christ's Body:*
   Col. i. 18, 24 = Eph. i. 23, iv. 12, v. 23, 30, &c.

4. *Articulation and nourishment of the Body:*
   Col. ii. 19 = Eph. iv. 16.

The imagery is peculiar to these Epistles.

5. *Growth of the Body:*
   Col. ii. 19 = Eph. iv. 16.

6. *The Body one:*
   Col. iii. 15 = Eph. ii. 16, iv. 4.

7. *Christians once dead in sin:*
   Col. ii. 13 = Eph. ii. 1, 5.

8. *Once alienated from God and grace:*
   Col. i. 21 = Eph. ii. 12, iv. 18.

The Greek verb is confined to these Epistles.

9. *Once in darkness:*
   Col. i. 13 = Eph. iv. 18, v. 8.
10. *Now risen with Christ:*
    Col. ii. 12, iii. 1 = Eph. ii. 6.
The Greek verb is confined to these Epistles.
11. *Made alive with Christ:*
    Col. ii. 13 = Eph. ii. 5.
The Greek verb is confined to these Epistles.
12. *Reconciled through the Death of Christ:*
    Col. i. 20, 21 = Eph. ii. 13—16.
The Greek verb is confined to these Epistles.
13. *Redeemed, in the sense of pardon of sin, in Christ:*
    Col. i. 14 = Eph. i. 7.
The exact phrase is peculiar to these Epistles.
14. *In the light:*
    Col. i. 12 = Eph. v. 8, 9[1].
15. *Rooted in Christ:*
    Col. ii. 7 = Eph. iii. 17.
The Greek verb is confined to these Epistles.
16. *Built up as a structure:*
    Col. ii. 7 = Eph. ii. 20.
17. *On a foundation:*
    Col. i. 23 = Eph. iii. 17.
18. *Spiritually filled:*
    Col. i. 9, ii. 10 = Eph. i. 23, iii. 19, v. 18.
19. *The Fulness:*
    Col. i. 19, ii. 9 = Eph. i. 23, iii. 19.
20. *The Old Man and the New Man:*
    Col. iii. 9, 10 = Eph. iv. 22—24.
21. *Similar classes of sins reproved:*
    Col. iii. 5—8 = Eph. iv. 25, v. 5.
    Col. iii. 12—14 = Eph. iv. 2, 3.
22. *The wrath of God coming:*
    Col. iii. 6 = Eph. v. 6.
23. *The duties of home enforced, in the same order and similar words:*
    Col. iii. 18, iv. 1 = Eph. v. 22, vi. 9.

[1] See our note on ver. 9.

24. *The walk of sin:*
    Col. iii. 7 = Eph. ii. 2, iv. 17.
25. *The walk of holiness:*
    Col. i. 10, ii. 6, iv. 5 = Eph. ii. 10, iv. 1, v. 2, 8, 15.
26. *Redemption of opportunity:*
    Col. iv. 5 = Eph. v. 16.
The phrase is peculiar to these Epistles.
27. *Spiritual songs:*
    Col. iii. 16 = Eph. v. 19.
This precept is peculiar to these Epistles.
28. *Prayer and intercession:*
    Col. iv. 2 = Eph. vi. 18.
29. *The Mystery revealed:*
    Col. i. 26, 27, ii. 2, iv. 3 = Eph. i. 9, iii. 3, 4, 9, vi. 19.
30. *Riches:*
    Col. i. 27, ii. 2 = Eph. i. 7, 18, ii. 7, iii. 8, 16.
31. *Ages and generations:*
    Col. i. 26 = Eph. iii. 21.
"Generation" occurs, in St Paul, only in these Epistles and the *Philippians*.
32. *The word of truth:*
    Col. i. 5 = Eph. i. 13.
33. *Character and commission of Tychicus:*
    Col. iv. 7 = Eph. vi. 21.

Many other parallels, more or less exact, can be collected. Meanwhile it will be observed, from the above table, that the distribution of the points of likeness is complicated and, so to speak, capricious in many instances. There is no trace of a *systematic* expansion of the longer Epistle from the shorter, either by the author of the longer, or by a personator of the author. Rather, the phenomena perfectly fit the hypothesis of one author, of the richest possible power and individuality, and purity and nobility of purpose, dealing with two different but not unconnected sets of correspondents about the same time, and writing at once with a remembrance of their differences and with a mind preoccupied with one great department of Divine truth.

50 / Introduction

It will be observed (see above, p. 44) that the only important element of primary doctrine quite peculiar to the Colossian Epistle, as distinguished from the Ephesian, is the presentation of the Son of God as Cause and Head of the whole created Universe. (See further on this doctrine, Appendix C.) On the other hand one important omission appears, by comparison, in the Colossian Epistle. The Holy Spirit, whose work is prominent in *Ephesians*, is scarcely even alluded to here. The word "spirit" (πνεῦμα) occurs only twice, i. 8, ii. 5; and in ii. 5 the reference is probably not to the Holy Spirit, but to the human spirit. In iii. 16 we have "*spiritual* songs."

The following remarks are quoted from the memoranda already referred to (p. 22) of lectures by the late Dr Hort:

"The complexity of the problem of the special relations between *Ephesians* and *Colossians* is shewn by the endless variety of views held by competent critics. The great likeness and also the great unlikeness between the two is to be noticed. Much of the teaching of *Ephesians* recurs in *Colossians*, though sometimes in different combinations. On the other hand *Colossians* differs essentially in having a large portion controversial, the points of controversy being connected with Judaism, though not with the binding character of the Law. *Colossians* differs also from *Ephesians* by the personal matter of the last 12 verses.

"Other differences, less broad, but not less interesting, occur in many of the passages which shew most likeness.

"How can we best account for the combination of resemblances and differences?...No one supposes that the two Epistles are derived from a common original. If *Ephesians* is not genuine, the most obvious thought is that it is derived from *Colossians*, whether *Colossians* is genuine or not. *Ephesians*, with its purely general character, is less like St Paul's other Epistles than *Colossians*. But when critics work out the problem in detail, it is not so simple as it seemed. Holtzmann took endless pains with the comparison. The result which he reached was that *Ephesians* was written at the end of cent. i., with

Introduction / 51

borrowings from *an* Epistle to the Colossians, not *our* Epistle, but a much shorter one, now embedded in ours. Then, that this shorter *Colossians* was lengthened out by the author of *Ephesians* with interpolations in imitation of his own work. But this would be an extraordinary process.

"The only key to the intricacies is the supposition that the two are the work of *one* author, who in the corresponding parts of both was setting forth the same leading idea, needing to be modified in range and proportion in accordance with special circumstances, and to be variously clothed with language accordingly.

"In this case we can hardly speak of one as prior to the other; both might be products of the same state of mind. Practically, they were written together[1]. If the needs of the Colossians called for special warnings, yet these warnings needed, as the basis for a fuller faith, some of the doctrinal matter so prominent in *Ephesians*. If *Colossians* had been only controversial it would have been far less interesting.

"Holtzmann (*Introd.*, p. 293) suggests an excellent study. Compare Eph. iii. 8, 9 and 16, 17. Then put together Eph. i. 9 and 18. Then compare these two pairs, taken together, with Col. i. 26 and 27. We shall find a striking coincidence with variations. The Ephesian passages will appear as expansions of the Colossian in various directions. But the phrases are as much at home in their respective contexts in one Epistle as in the other...

"The prayer in Eph. i. 18 is for knowledge; the corresponding prayer in Col. i. 10 is that the Colossians may walk worthily, may bear fruit. But the apparent contrast is only a matter of proportion. The prayer in *Ephesians* has a no less practical goal in view...

"The idea of the Church as the body of which Christ is the Head is the same in *Colossians* as in Eph. iv. 15, 16. But the

---

[1] Still, we think that the literary phenomena are in favour of a free expansion of *Ephesians* from *Colossians* rather than otherwise. The fulness of the doctrine of the Holy Spirit in *Ephesians*, compared with the extreme brevity of *Colossians* on this point, is an illustration of our meaning. (Editor.)

idea of membership, only hinted at in *Colossians*, is worked out into an important passage in *Ephesians*.

"The more closely we scrutinize those parts of these Epistles which resemble each other, the more we find the stamp of freshness and originality *on both*. Whatever supports the genuineness, or the lateness, of either Epistle, does the same for the other. Evidence for *Colossians* becomes evidence for *Ephesians*.

"In *Ephesians* we find on examination no tangible evidence against St Paul's authorship; so it would be also if we examined *Colossians*. In both we have not merely the *primâ facie* evidence of his name, but also the evidence derived from the close connexion (of thought) with his other Epistles. Above all we find in both the impress of his wonderful mind."

Weiss (*Einleitung*, p. 267, *note*) writes: "The most careful examination of the parallel passages always leads to the conclusion that the appearance of dependence (*Abhängigkeit*) presented now in one Epistle, now in the other, is merely an appearance, which a more careful estimate of the context and purport of each several parallel passage destroys; and that the peculiar affinity of the two Epistles is cleared up only on the hypothesis that both are the independent but contemporaneous compositions of the same author."

These critical considerations are a good preparation for the fresh perusal of the Epistles, just as they stand. The study from without should always be accompanied by the study from within, which alone can bring home to the reader's whole inner man the self-evidencing moral greatness, as well as literary freedom, of the writings. Let him listen to them with at least some degree of sympathy with their matter and their manner, and he will hear through them both nothing less than the Voice of God, speaking direct to the mind, the conscience, and the will of man, alike to reveal eternal secrets and to prescribe the duties of a daily path of unselfish love.

Chapter 7

ARGUMENT OF THE EPISTLE

CH. i. 1—2. Paul, a divinely commissioned messenger of Jesus Christ, and Timotheus with him, greets the Christians of Colossæ, invoking blessing on them from God our Father.

3—8. He gives thanks to God, the Father of Christ, for the report he has heard [from their missionary pastor Epaphras] of their faith rested on Christ and their love exercised towards fellow Christians, a faith and love animated by the common hope [of the Lord's Return] from heaven, which was made known to them in the earliest, and truest, Gospel messages that had reached Colossæ, bringing with it, as it was bringing everywhere among men, its secret of fruitfulness and development; yes, so it was with them since first they had heard and spiritually understood God's gifts in their reality. It was that message [and not another] that Epaphras had originally carried to them—Epaphras, Paul's beloved fellow-servant and representative, who had [now come to him at Rome, and] told him of their loving spiritual life.

9—12. [His thanksgivings pass into petitions;] he prays that they may have the deepest possible spiritual insight into the will of God, in order to their meeting His wish in everything, as His saints should do; bearing the fruit of general practical holiness, and [so] advancing in that holy intimacy with Him [which active sympathy with His will infallibly developes]; and meanwhile gaining a fulness of strength proportioned to the forces flowing to them from God's revealed Self, and resulting in a life of perseverance and patience, full of joy, and of the thanksgiving prompted by the fact that the Father of their Lord has qualified them [in His Son] to enter into possession of the land of light, the Canaan of grace.

13—14. For indeed the Father *has* rescued them from the authority of the dark realm [of sin and death] into the kingdom of the Son whom He eternally loves, in whom we have the redemption of Divine forgiveness;

15—17 and Who is [Himself supremely great in Person and Function; for He is] the Manifestation of the Unseen God, eternally born of Him, and, as such, eternally antecedent to, and Lord over, all created being. In Him, [as the eternal Cause and Law,] all such being came to exist, in all its orders, and not least those angelic hierarchies [to which the Colossians were being tempted to transfer the trust and worship due to Him]. Yes, everything that *becomes*, was constituted through Him [as the Father's Divine Agent], and for Him [as its Reason and Goal]; He is the Antecedent of all things, He is the Bond of all things, [holding them fast in their cosmic union by His life and will].

18—20. He too, the same Person, is the Head of the Church, [the living Company of believing men], which thus forms His Body, [an organism animated by Him, and used as a vehicle of His action in the world]; He is the Origin, the Beginning, [of its life]; He, once dead, now risen again, is the Firstborn [of the family of immortality]; all He is and has done contributes to His unique preeminence in every respect [for us; no rival in our trust and worship is for a moment permissible]. In Him, [His Son incarnate and glorified,] it pleased the Father that the Plenitude [of Divine power and grace] should take up its abode; and, providing a sacred Propitiation in His Sacrificial Death, to receive into peace through Him, through Him [alone], His creatures, whether human or angelic, [whether fallen men, or angels needing in some mysterious sense a nearer approach to Him; let the Colossians remember this, when angel-worship is recommended to them].

21—23. [Now to come to their own case; as He had received other alienated beings into peace, so] He had received *them*, once estranged from Him and hostile to Him in their life-principles, (yet now, as a fact, [he cannot but gladly remind them,] brought back into peace by their Lord's Crucifixion-Death,) so as to present them to Himself [in the day of glory], perfect [in their Head's perfection], for His own approval. Only, let them adhere [for their very life] to the faith they had found, in the repose of a fixed reliance, not faltering in their hold on the hope of the Gospel, which had reached them as it had reached humanity at large, and of which he, Paul, was [an appointed] minister.

24—29. [In that ministry, as he thus reviews the glory of his Lord, and the grandeur of the Gospel and its work,] he rejoices to suffer [imprisonment, or whatever it may be,] and so to take his part in completing, in a life of toil and pain, those afflictions [of evangelization] which Christ [left incomplete, that His members might take them up;] afflictions in the interests of the Church, His body; that Church of which Paul was

Introduction / 55

constituted a minister, working on the lines of the stewardship entrusted to him by His Master, for the benefit of the Colossians [amongst others,] aiming always to unfold the Divine message to the full, even the Secret which was [comparatively] hidden since time and its developments began, but which is now unveiled to believers; to those, that is to say, whom God has been pleased to acquaint with the rich treasures included in the bright fact of this Secret opened now to Gentiles [as well as Jews,] and which is ["not It but He,"]—Christ, dwelling in His saints, [in a presence] which is the hope of glory [as the bud is the hope of the flower]. This Christ, [and no other, or others,] Paul and his friends, [whatever alien teachers may do,] proclaim, admonishing [not a select initiated circle, nor again merely the community, but] every individual believer, and teaching every individual believer, in the whole of Christian wisdom, [for they have no esoteric reserve in the matter,] that they may [at the Lord's Return] present to Him every individual full-grown through union and communion with Him. To this goal Paul toils onward, wrestling [with whatever may oppose, and now specially wrestling in prayer,] with a strength due to his indwelling Lord's power working in him.

CH. ii. 1—7. For they must understand that he *is* engaged in a great wrestle [of prayer] for them and their Laodicean neighbours, and the Christians [in general around them,] his [as yet] unvisited converts; he is praying that their hearts may be encouraged, and that they may be knit together in [the bond of] love, thus advancing into the enjoyment of the wealth found in a full conscious grasp [of the way of salvation], and into a full spiritual knowledge of God's supreme Secret, even Christ. It is in Christ that are found, [though they must be sought] as *hid* treasure, all the resources of [Divine] wisdom and knowledge. And he must insist on this, lest some [teacher or teachers] should lead them astray by specious and well-worded arguments. [He knows there is need to warn them of this], for, though absent bodily he is with them spiritually—[yes, near enough (he cannot but dwell on this brighter side)] to rejoice in, and take a fresh view of, their orderly array and solid front [against sin and error], due to their loyal trust in Christ. [But let this attitude be *maintained*;] at conversion they received [as Truth and Life, none other, none less, than] the Christ, even [the historic] Jesus, the Lord [Himself]; now let them [apply this truth to life], living daily in union with Him; as those who had been rooted into Him [as their soil], and were now being built up [individually

56 / Introduction

and together] in connexion with Him [their Corner Stone], and were being established [in spiritual health and power] by their faith in Him, along the lines of the first [and only true] teaching they had received. In that faith let them abound, [using it fully and freely], with thankfulness [as its attendant grace].

8—15. So let them beware, or they might be stripped, and led off spiritually captive, [by this or that teacher,] with his pretentious deceit of *a philosophy* [forsooth, rather than a Gospel], a speculative theory based not on Christ but on merely human tradition, and [at best] on [pre-Christian] institutions, merely introductory to the Gospel and in themselves non-spiritual. [Christ is all, for truth and liberty;] in Him dwells always the Fulness of the Godhead, manifested in His Incarnation; and in their union with Him they [by His Fulness] are filled full, [having in covenant possession all they need for peace and holiness,]—in Him, who is the Head of all those [unseen] powers and authorities [which some dream of as His rivals or substitutes]. In Him, [believing], they have actually received the true non-mechanical circumcision, [a death unto sin and a new birth unto righteousness, a better thing than its ancient type, which was now pressed upon them]; [for, coming to Him, they won a position of acceptance and power such that] they were [as it were] divested of the body as the vehicle of [victorious] temptation, thanks to this circumcision [of the soul] administered to them by Christ. In their Baptism [as the Divine Sign and Seal upon the faith which receives Him] they were [as it were so identified with Him the Crucified as to be symbolically] laid with Him in His grave; and [in the same sense, in that Baptism,] they rose with Him [to a life of acceptance and holiness in Him], through their faith in the working of God, who raised Him from death. [*They* were once in death, but were now alive. Spiritually] dead, in respect of their sins, and of their spiritually uncircumcised state by nature, they were raised to life [in Christ] by God, who forgave them all, and so cancelled that dread legal Bond, the Law's claim upon them, who had violated its rule of holiness. That Bond was [by their own fault] their deadly enemy, but even this their Lord took away from between [them and His Father], as it were rending it asunder with the nails of His Cross, and leaving it cancelled there. The unseen Powers of Evil, [these principalities and powers whose awful existence now haunted them,] He stripped of their spoils, [their human spoils,] and led them captive in open triumph, by virtue of that very Cross [which they thought His ruin].

16—23. So the Colossians were not to allow any teacher to take them to task for a neglect of ascetic rules of food, or of the festivals—annual, monthly, weekly—of the Old Law. These things were a shadow cast by a real Substance yet to come; but the Substance *has* come; it consists of Christ; [and they, in Him, are no longer in His shadow.] Let no teacher be allowed to have his misguided way and to rob them of their prize, [eternal life in Christ,] by teaching them an artificial humility and a worship of Angels [as mediators with the Supreme,] invading the spiritual world [with presumptuous speculation or assertion, as if he had seen it,] as he has *not;* inflated by the random thoughts of unspiritual speculation, and letting go his grasp of [Christ as] Head—that Head [with which every true limb is immediately and vitally connected,] and out of which [every part of the Body] through its joints and ligatures [of spiritual contact] is supplied, and [so] more and more [internally] compacted, and developed with a development of which God [is Cause and Law.] In their union with Christ they had [as it were] died to the introductory and mechanical religionism [of the past;] why then, as if [not dead to the world but] having their true life in it, did they let themselves be overrun with ascetic rules, *Handle not, nor taste, nor touch?* ([The things so forbidden were merely material, not moral;] their destiny was merely physical dissolution in the course of use.) All this was in the line of merely human precept and theory. True, it all had a specious look of reason; [there was a shew of sanctity and self-denial] in artificial observances and humility, and in ruthless severity towards the body; but it was of no value as a real barrier in view of the craving of the unregenerate element for the satisfaction of its desires.

CH. III. 1—4. As then they had risen with Christ, [in their union with Him the Risen One, entering in that union on a new life of acceptance and of moral power,] let them [use this wonderful position, meeting temptation not with a mechanical disciplinary routine, but] with a willing spiritual gravitation towards the life of heaven, towards the world where Christ was, seated [triumphant] on the Father's throne. Let them direct their bent of thought and will on that upper world, not on this world, [with its temptations, and its ineffectual remedies]. United to Christ, His death was as it were theirs, and now His life was theirs, a hidden life, [safe from the enemy's grasp, and from the world's eye,] for He is hidden in the Father's bosom. He is in fact their life, [the personal Cause and Source of their new peace and power;] and

58 / Introduction

when He shall again be manifested, [in His returning glory,] they shall be manifested in that glory with Him, [coming out finally and fully as "saints indeed"; a thought full of animation under present temptations].

5—12. So [let them apply *this* secret to their present needs. In *this* power] let them decisively put to death those sins which were, so to speak, the moving limbs of the unregenerate life; sins of lust, and greed, and idòl-worship, things which are bringing down the wrath of God upon those who [thus] disobey Him. In such practices they once moved and acted, when they found their life, [their interests,] in that miserable direction. But now, [as the case is, in their converted life,] they, like other believers, must divest themselves [as to toleration and practice] of absolutely all sins, [not only of specially fleshly sins but equally of] sins of temper, and of tongue. They must not lie to one another, for they have [as to covenant position] divested themselves of the condition of unregenerate man, [fallen in Adam,] with his practices of evil, and have been invested with that of regenerate man, [restored in Christ,] man who, [in Christ,] is ever being renewed [in spiritual life and power], so as to know his Lord truly, and to develope the moral likeness of the God who has thus [new-] created him. In this new human state the differences of race, privilege, civilisation, social status, all necessarily vanish; Christ is everything in all [His members, as they think of one another].

12—17. [Such was their ideal condition, such their covenant position. But on that very account it was now for them, in a life of watching and prayer, to realize the ideal, to act on the position. Had they "put on the new man"?] Then they must, [with a "new departure" of faith and purpose,] *clothe* themselves, as the chosen of God, on whom His special love is set, [(a "nobility" carrying "obligations" indeed!)] with practical kindness and sympathy, humility, patience; they must meet personal grievances, should such occur to them, with forbearance and forgiveness, the forgiveness to be looked for from those whom Christ has forgiven, [and who know it.] Above all, and as it were *upon* all, [like the girdle of grace,] they must put on holy love, the bond which holds the full Christian character together. The peace of Christ, [the inward calm caused by knowing Him as theirs,] is to arbitrate in every internal debate, [deciding, with the persuasive authority of His happy presence, *for* God and others, and *against* self;] for into this peace their conversion has brought them, [as their best secret

Introduction / 59

for the realization of] their corporate oneness in Him. And let them cultivate a thankful habit. Let the word of Christ, [the terms and truth of His Gospel,] dwell in them, [as a part of themselves, while they make full practical use of it] in holy wisdom. [Let them use it, among other ways,] in the warning and instructing exercise of holy song and music in their companies; singing [not with voice only but] with the regenerate soul to the Lord. In every part of their lives, let them act as the avowed servants of the Lord Jesus, blessing His Father, through Him, [for everything He appoints as their experience].

18—CH. iv. 1. [Let these holy principles be remembered above all in the Christian Home.] Let the wife live in that loving loyalty to her husband which their common union with Christ makes [more than ever] befitting. Let the husband love his wife, with an affection free [in Christ] from all tyrannous irritability. Let the child obey the parent in all things [where the Lord's express claims do not forbid;] for the Lord, [*the Son* of the Father,] delights in filial loyalty. Let parents renounce all unloving parental despotism, with its exasperation and its discouragement of the child's will. Let the slave be, [as a Christian, more than ever,] thoroughly loyal to his earthly master, [who, like him, is the slave of the heavenly Master;] let him serve not on the selfish principle of working only when watched, or only for his own comfort's sake, but with the simplicity of will of one who reverences his [always present] God. Whatever comes in "the daily round," let Him do it from the soul, as for his heavenly [and not only his earthly] Lord; being sure, [as he may be,] that from that Lord he shall get, in punctual recompense, His own "well done" in glory; for Christ is the Master whose slave he really is, [and who is indeed a benignant and mindful Master.] But [He is just and watchful too; and if the slave presumes on his conversion as an excuse] for wrongdoing, the true Master will requite *that* also, without partiality, [taking no apology for his violation of conscience from any supposed hardship of his lot. Lastly,] let the master provide carefully for his slave's interests; [above all, let him see that the slave is always sure of] domestic justice; remembering that his own Master watches him from heaven.

2—6. [In conclusion, let them all] persevere in prayer, and, in its habitual exercise, let them watch, [as those who are in a world of temptation,] and give thanks, [as those who have the Lord ever with them in it.] And in prayer let them not forget Paul and his friends at Rome, asking that for them God would open [new] opportunities for the preaching of the Gospel, that Secret of blessing bound up with Christ, on account of which he was now chained to his warder; let them ask that he might·make it a manifest reality around him, as he is bound to do. [For themselves,] let them live and behave with holy good sense in regard of the non-Christians round them, winning opportunities [for witness] at the cost of care and watchfulness. Let their conversation, [especially on such occasions,] be always animated by God's gracious presence, and made wholesome with the salt [of loving sincerity,] so as to give every questioner the fitting answer [of candour and conciliation].

7—9. As to Paul's own circumstances, a full account of them would be given by [the bearer of this Epistle,] Tychicus, his beloved brother, and faithful personal helper, and fellowservant in the Lord. Him he was sending for this very purpose, that [the Asian Christians, and now particularly] the Colossians, might know Paul's position, and might themselves be encouraged [in faith and love]. And with him would go Onesimus, a believing and beloved brother-Christian, one of themselves. These two friends would give a full report of things [at Rome].

10—14. He has greetings to send them; from Aristarchus, sharer of his prison; from Marcus, cousin to Barnabas, (let them remember a previous communication, and welcome him without reserve, should he visit them); from Jesus, better known as Justus;—three Hebrew-Christian friends, and the only [leading] members of their circle [at Rome] who were cooperating with him in the work of the Gospel, and [so] proving a solace to [his tired spirit, too often wounded by opposition from that quarter.] Epaphras, their own [evangelist,] added his greeting, that devoted servant of Christ, now always wrestling in his prayers for them that they might stand fast, mature and fully assured [of their ground and of their purpose] in every detail of God's will. Paul cannot but testify to the earnestness of this holy toil of Epaphras' for them and for their friends at Laodicea and at Hierapolis. Another greeting is that of Lucas, the beloved physician [well known to them by name;] and Demas adds his.

15—17. Let them send a greeting from Paul [down the valley] to the Laodicean Christians; particularly to Nymphas, in whose house the Laodicean congregation meets. And when the present Epistle has been read, let them take care to get it read also in that congregation, and let them also read [in their meeting] the Epistle which they will find coming to them by way of Laodicea. And let them say [in Paul's name and their own] to Archippus, [their lately appointed pastor,] "*Take heed to the ministry you received in the Lord, to do faithfully every part of it;* [*take heed to yourself, your teaching, and your brethren*"].

18. Lastly, here is Paul's autograph-farewell. Let them remember the chain [which he feels as he writes]. The Lord's presence and power be with them.

At the Name of Jesus every knee shall bow,
Every tongue confess Him King of glory now;
'Tis the Father's pleasure we should call Him Lord,
Who from the beginning was the mighty Word.

At His voice creation sprang at once to sight,
All the Angel faces, all the Hosts of light,
Thrones and Dominations, stars upon their way,
All the heavenly Orders, in their great array.

Humbled for a season, to receive a Name
From the lips of sinners unto whom He came,
Faithfully He bore it spotless to the last,
Brought it back victorious, when from death He pass'd;

Bore it up triumphant with its human light,
Through all ranks of creatures, to the central height;
To the throne of Godhead, to the Father's breast;
Fill'd it with the glory of that perfect rest.

Name Him, brothers, name Him, with love strong as death,
But with awe and wonder, and with bated breath;
He is God the Saviour, He is Christ the Lord,
Ever to be worshipp'd, trusted, and adored.

In your hearts enthrone Him; there let Him subdue
All that is not holy, all that is not true:
Crown Him as your Captain in temptation's hour;
Let His will enfold you in its light and power.

Brothers, this Lord Jesus shall return again,
With His Father's glory, with His Angel train;
For all wreaths of empire meet upon His brow,
And our hearts confess Him King of glory now.

Caroline Noel

COMMENTARY ON COLOSSIANS

PAUL, an apostle of Jesus Christ by the will of God, **1**
and Timotheus *our* brother, to the saints and faithful **2**

TITLE

THE oldest known form is the briefest, TO (THE) COLOSSIANS, or COLASSIANS (see note on ver. 1 below). So in the "Subscription" to the Epistle, which see. The title as in the Authorized Version agrees with that adopted in the Elzevir editions of 1624, 1633.

CH. I. 1—2   GREETING

1. *Paul*]   *Paulos.*   See Acts xiii. 9.   The Apostle probably bore, from infancy, both the two names, *Saul* (*Saoul, Saulos*) and *Paul.*   See on Eph. i. 1, and *Romans,* p. 8, in this Series.

an apostle]   Lit., **an envoy, a missionary**; in the Gospels and Acts always in the special sense of an immediate Delegate from the Saviour; except perhaps Acts xiv. 14, where Barnabas bears the title.   In Rom. xvi. 7 the sense is perhaps more extended; certainly so in 2 Cor. viii. 23 (Greek).   It always, however, in N.T. designates at least a *sacred* messenger, not excepting Phil. ii. 25 (Greek), where see note in this Series.—St Paul needed often to insist on the fact and rights of his divinely given apostleship; 1 Cor. ix. 1; 2 Cor. xii. 12; Gal. i. 1.— See further *Ephesians,* in this Series, Appendix F.

of Jesus Christ]   **Of Christ Jesus** is the better-attested order; an order of our blessed Lord's Name and Title almost peculiar to St Paul, and the most frequent of the two orders in his writings.   It is calculated that he uses it (assuming the latest researches in the Greek text to shew right results) 87 times, and the other order 78 times (see *The Expositor,* May, 1888).   The slight emphasis thus laid on the word "*Christ*" suggests a special reference of thought to our Lord in glory.—See further our notes on Rom. i. 1.

by the will of God]   So, in the same connexion, 1 Cor. i. 1; 2 Cor. i. 1; Eph. i. 1; 2 Tim. i. 1.—Lit., **by means of the will of God** (so too Rom. xv. 32; 2 Cor. viii. 5; besides the places just quoted).   The will

64 / Colossians 1

brethren in Christ which are at Colosse: Grace *be* unto

of God is regarded as *the means* of the Apostle's consecration, because with God to will implies the provision of the means of fulfilment.—See Gal. i. 1 for the deep certainty of a direct Divine commission which underlay such a phrase in St Paul's mind. *He knew* himself to be "a vessel *of choice*, to bear the name" (Acts ix. 15) of his Lord.

and Timotheus] Timothy is thus associated with Paul, 2 Cor. i. 1 (in the same words); Phil. i. 1; 1 Thess. i. 1; 2 Thess. i. 1; Philem. 1 (in the same words). The association (which in Philippians begins and ends with the first sentence) is here maintained throughout the opening paragraph, dropping at the words (ver. 23) "*whereof I Paul, &c.*" It is remarkable that Timothy is not mentioned in the contemporary Epistle to Ephesus; an omission probably to be explained by the more public and *circular* character of that Epistle (see *Introd.*, pp. 41, 42, and *Ephesians* in this Series, pp. 24—29), making it more suitable that it should go as from the Apostle of Asia alone.

Timothy is named 24 times in the N.T. See Acts xvi. 1 for his parentage and early home. For indications of his character as man and Christian cp. 1 Cor. iv. 17, xvi. 10, 11; 1 Tim. i. 2; 2 Tim. i. 4, 5, and esp. Phil. ii. 19—22. His association with St Paul was intimate and endeared. He appears oftenest in connexion with the Apostle's work in Europe; but he was himself an Asiatic by birth (xvi. 1), and we last see him as the delegate of St Paul at Ephesus (1 and 2 Tim.).

our *brother*] Lit., **the brother.** So he is called also 2 Cor. i. 1; Philem. 1. So too are designated Quartus (Rom. xvi. 23), Sosthenes (1 Cor. i. 1), Apollos (1 Cor. xvi. 12). Cp. 2 Cor. xii. 18; Eph. vi. 21; below, iv. 7. Strictly the term is the equivalent of "Christian;" but thus used it has a certain point and speciality, not as denoting an office or position, but known Christian worth and work.

2. *to the saints*] Holy ones; persons possessed of holiness, separated from sin to God. It is true that this is the language of "charitable presumption" (Pearson, *Exposition of the Creed*, Art. IX. p. 353); when a community is thus described St Paul does not thereby positively assert that each individual answers the description. But this presumptive use of the word "saint" does not lower the true sense of the word so as to make it *properly* mean merely a member of the baptized community, a possessor of visible Church privileges. "The saints" are *supposed* to be really separated to God, by purchase, conquest, and self-surrender.

faithful] The adjective is used of Christians frequently; see (in the Greek) Acts x. 45, xvi. 1; 2 Cor. vi. 15; Col. i. 2; 1 Tim. iv. 3, v. 16, vi. 2; Tit. i. 6. These and similar passages, and the contrast of the word "unfaithful" (*infidelis*, infidel), shew that as a designation of Christians it means not trustworthy but trustful; *full of faith*, in the Christian sense. The "faithful" are (see last note) *supposed* to be those who have really "believed unto life everlasting" (1 Tim. i. 16) and now "walk by faith" (2 Cor. v. 7).

brethren] Because "children of God by faith in Christ Jesus" (Gal. iii. 26; and see next note).

in Christ] See for parallels to this all-important phrase, Rom. viii.

you, and peace, from God our Father and the Lord Jesus Christ.

We give thanks to God and the Father of our Lord Jesus 3
1; 1 Cor. xv. 18; 2 Cor. v. 17; &c. And cp. the Lórd's language, Joh. vi. 56, xiv. 20, xv. 1—7, and the illustration given by e.g. Eph. v. 30.—These "brethren" are regarded as one with their Lord in respect of inseparable interest, holy dearness, and union by the life-giving Spirit (1 Cor. vi. 17); especially the latter. They are "brethren *in Christ*," brothers because "in" the Firstborn Son (Rom. viii. 29).—This phrase occurs some 12 times in the Epistle, and closely kindred phrases raise the number to about 20. It is likely that the special doctrinal perils of Colossæ led to this emphasis on the Christian's union with Christ.

Colosse] Properly *Colossæ* (*Colassai*), or *Colassæ*. On the spelling, see *Introd.*, p. 20, and on the topography of Colossæ and its neighbourhood, *Introd.*, ch. i. generally.—The older English Versions read *Colise* (Wyclif, 1380), *Colossa* (Tyndale, 1534, Cranmer, 1539, Rheims 1582), *Collossæ* (Geneva, 1557).

The verse thus far may perhaps be rendered more exactly, **To those who at Colossæ are holy and faithful brethren in Christ.** But the A.V. (and text R.V.) is grammatically defensible and is certainly *practically* correct.

Grace be *unto you, and peace*] So in the openings of Rom., Cor., Gal., Phil., Col., Thess., Philem., Pet., and Rev. In the Pastoral Epistles, and in 2 Joh., the remarkable addition "*mercy*" appears; in Jude, "*mercy, peace, and love.*"—In these salutations "*Grace*" is all the free and loving favour of God in its spiritual efficacy; "*Peace*" is specially the complacency of reconciliation with which He regards His people, but so as to imply also its results *in* them; repose, serenity of soul; happiness in its largest sense. See further on iii. 15 below.

from God our Father] To St Paul, God is the *Pater Noster* of Christians, in the inner sense of their union by faith with His SON. The Scriptures, while not ignoring a certain universal Fatherhood of God, always tend to put into the foreground the Fatherhood and Sonship of special connexion, of covenant, grace, faith. Among many leading passages see Joh. i. 12; Rom. viii. 14 &c.; Gal. iii. 26; 1 Joh. iii. 1, 2.—Cp. the Editor's *Outlines of Christian Doctrine*, p. 34.

and the Lord Jesus Christ] These words, present in the parallel passage Eph. i. 2, are probably to be omitted here, on documentary evidence.

3—8 THANKSGIVING FOR THE COLOSSIAN SAINTS

3. *We give thanks*] So Rom. i. 8; 1 Cor. i. 4; Eph. i. 16; 1 Thess. i. 2, ii. 13; 2 Thess. i. 3, ii. 13; Philem. 4.—Thanksgiving is the instinct of the life of grace.—These thanksgivings recognize God as the whole Cause of all goodness in His saints.

God and the Father] Better, with the more probable reading, **God, the Father.** Here, as often, the Father is called simply, and as it were

66 / Colossians 1

4 Christ, praying always for you, since we heard of your faith in Christ Jesus, and of the love which *ye have* to all the
5 saints, for the hope which is laid up for you in heaven,

distinctively, GOD. Not that He is more truly God than the Son, but that He is the Fountain of Godhead in the Son. Cp. Pearson, *Exposition*, Art. i., pp. 34, 35, 40.

praying always for you] Better perhaps, **always, when at prayer for you.**—The "prayer" here meant is prayer in its most inclusive sense, worship, of which thanksgiving is a part.—For St Paul's prayers for his converts cp. ver. 9; Eph. i. 16, 17, iii. 14; Phil. i. 9; 2 Thess. i. 1; 2 Tim. i. 3; and see below, iv. 12.

4. *since we heard*] More simply, **having heard.** He refers to the information given by Epaphras (ver. 7), probably quite recently. On the question whether he had ever visited Colossæ, see on ii. 1 below, *Introd.*, pp. 20, 21, and Appendix A. This verse gives no decisive evidence in the matter.

faith in Christ Jesus] Cp. Eph. i. 15 for a closely parallel passage. "The preposition ['in'] here...denotes the sphere in which their faith moves, rather than the object to which it is directed" (Lightfoot). But it is not easy to draw a clear distinction between "sphere" and "object" in this case. And surely Mar. i. 15 (Greek) (cp. Rom. iii. 25; Joh. iii. 15; and, in the LXX., Psal. lxxvii. (Heb. and Eng. lxxviii.) 22) proves the possibility of reference here to the Object of faith, on and in whom it reposes, as an anchor in the ground. On the other hand 2 Tim. i. 13 (quoted by Lightfoot) shews the possibility of explaining, "faith *maintained by union with* Christ." But this more recondite meaning scarcely fits this context, where the parallelism of clauses seems to suggest the saints' *regard towards* Christ first and then one another.

and of the love...saints] "This is His commandment, that we should *believe* on the name of His Son Jesus Christ, *and love* one another" (1 Joh. iii. 23). Divine faith, in true and full exercise, issues by its nature in a life and work of love towards men, regarded as either actual (as here) or potential brethren of Him who is faith's goal and rest.

all the saints] Doubtless not at Colossæ only, but everywhere. It was one of the earliest glories of the Gospel, illustrated everywhere in the N.T., to bind together in love a world-wide family. Cp. iii. 11 below.— The words **which ye have** are probably in the true text.

5. *for the hope*] I.e. **on account of the hope.** "That blessed hope," full of Christ, and the object of an intensely *united* expectation, gave special occasion, by its nature, for the exercise alike of the faith and the love just mentioned.

"Faith, love, hope," thus appear together, as 1 Cor. xiii. 13; 1 Thess. i. 3; and cp. 1 Pet. i. 3, 5, 22. Lightfoot compares also Polycarp, *Ep. to the Philippians*, c. 3: "Faith, which is the mother of us all, followed by hope, whose precursor is love." See Lightfoot's note on that place (*Apost. Fathers*, Pt. ii. vol. ii. sect. ii. p. 911).—The interaction of the three great graces has many different aspects. Faith, which alone

whereof ye heard before in the word of the truth of the gospel; which is come unto you, as *it is* in all the world; 6

accepts Christ, and so unites us to Him, is indeed the antecedent in the deepest sense to both the others, and their abiding basis. But in the experience of the life and walk of grace, faith itself may be stimulated by either or both of the sister-graces; and so on.

Meanwhile "*hope*" here, strictly speaking, is not the subjective grace but its glorious object, the Return of the exalted Lord to receive His people to Himself. See e.g. Phil. iii. 20, with our note; Tit. ii. 13; 1 Pet. i. 4—7; Rev. xxii. 20.

laid up for you in heaven] See for a close parallel, 1 Pet. i. 4; and cp. Heb. xi. 16, xiii. 14.

"*In heaven:*"—lit., **in the heavens**; as often in N.T. On this plural see our note on Eph. iv. 10. The hope is "*laid up*" there, because He who is its Essence (1 Tim. i. 1; cp. below ver. 27) is there, "sitting at the right hand of God" (below, iii. 1); and our final enjoyment of it, whatever *the details* of locality may prove to be, whatever e.g. be the destiny of this earth with regard to the abode of the Blessed, will take place under the full manifestation of His presence in *heavenly* glory. See our Lord's own words, Matt. vi. 20, 21; Luke xii. 34, xviii. 22; Joh. xiv. 3, xvii. 24.

ye heard before] He might have said simply, "*ye heard.*" But the expression "seems intended to contrast their earlier with their later lessons—the true Gospel of Epaphras with the false gospel of their recent teachers" (Lightfoot). On that "false gospel" see below, on ii. 8, etc., and *Introd.*, ch. iv.

the truth of the gospel] Not merely "*the true Gospel*," but that holy and mighty Truth, "Jesus and the Resurrection" (Acts xvii. 18), which is the basis and the characteristic of the one Gospel. The rivals of that Gospel could produce on the contrary only arbitrary assertions and *a priori* speculations, the cloud of a theory of existence and of observance instead of the rock of Jesus Christ.

The word "Gospel" (*euangelion*) occurs more than 60 times in St Paul's writings and addresses; elsewhere, 12 times in SS. Matthew and Mark together, once in the Acts, once in St Peter, once in the Revelation.—The expositor must never forget its true meaning; "*good tidings.*" Paradoxically but truly it has been said that the Gospel *as such* contains no precepts and no threatenings, though deeply and vitally related to Divine law and judgment. Its burthen is JESUS CHRIST as our perfect Peace, Life, and Hope, with a Divine welcome in His name to sinful man, believing.

6. *is come unto you*] Lit., "*is present to you;*" but the A.V. and R.V. are idiomatically right.

as it is *in all the world; and bringeth forth*, &c.] The word "*and*" here is textually doubtful; the adverse evidence though not decisive is considerable. If it is omitted, the rendering will be, **as also in all the world it is fruit-bearing**; and the meaning will be, practically, "it has reached you, as it reaches others everywhere, as a secret of fruit-bearing power."

and bringeth forth fruit, as *it doth* also in you, since the day ye heard of *it*, and knew the grace of God in truth:

"*In all the world:*"—"in all the *cosmos*," as Mar. xvi. 15. Cp. Matt. iv. 8, xxvi. 13; and, for a similar hyperbole, Rom. i. 8, and below, ver. 23. Here the *cosmos*, which sometimes means the universe at large (Acts xvii. 24), sometimes human society (1 Cor. v. 10), sometimes man as alienated with all his interests from God (Gal. vi. 14; 1 Joh. iii. 1, 13, etc.), is used by a perfectly lawful liberty of speech for space indefinitely large, places indefinitely many. The readers would well understand that Paul meant not that the Gospel had reached every spot of Europe, Asia, and Africa, but that *wherever*, in the already vast extent of its range among men, it had come, it proved always its proper power.

"*Bringeth forth fruit:*"—the Greek verb is (here only in Greek literature, apparently) in the middle voice, and this indicates specially *the innate, congenital*, fruit-bearing power of the Gospel. It is "essentially a reproductive organism, a plant whose seed is in itself" (Lightfoot). Hence the Christian is, if we may put it so, *nothing if not a fruit-bearer* (Matt. vii. 17—20; Luke xiii. 6; Joh. xv. 2—8, 16; Rom. vi. 22; Gal. v. 22; Phil. i. 11; Jas iii. 17).

Here add, with full MS. and other evidence, **and increaseth**, or, in view of the reading advocated above, **and increasing**. The noble and beautiful fact is thus given us that the Gospel's fruit-bearing does not exhaust its source but rather developes the outcome. Transferring the imagery from the Gospel to its believing recipients, we gather that the more freely the Christian yields, as it were, his soul and his life to the fruitful energy of the Spirit (Gal. v. 22) the stronger will he become for always ampler production. And so it is with the believing Church as a whole.

as it doth *also in you*] "The comparison is thus doubled back, as it were, on itself" (Lightfoot). He returns, careless of literary symmetry, to the thought closest to his heart, the fruitful and growing life of faith *at Colossæ*, which is now his bright example and illustration of the blessing experienced "in all the world."

since the day] From the very first hour of intelligent faith the Divine secret of fruit and growth had worked; as it was, and is, always meant to do.

ye heard of it, *and knew*] Better, **ye heard and knew**.

"*Knew:*"—the Greek verb is a strong one, *epignôscein*. It, or its kindred noun *epignôsis*, occurs e.g. Matt. xi. 27; Rom. iii. 20; 1 Cor. xiii. 12; Eph. i. 17, iv. 13; below, ver. 9, 10, ii. 2, iii. 10; 2 Tim. ii. 25, iii. 7; Heb. x. 26; 2 Pet. i. 8, ii. 20. The structure of the word suggests *developed* knowledge; the N.T. usage tends to connect it with *spiritual* knowledge. The Colossians had not only heard and, in a natural sense, understood the Gospel; they had *seen into it* with the intuition of grace (cp. 1 Cor. ii. 12, 14).

the grace of God] His free and loving gift of Christ to the believing soul, and Church, to be "all in all;" "righteousness, sanctification,

as ye also learned of Epaphras our dear fellowservant, who 7

and redemption" (1 Cor. i. 30). This they had "heard" as Gospel, and "known" as life and peace.

For the phrase, cp. Acts xi. 23, xiii. 43, xiv. 26, xv. 40, xx. 24; Rom. v. 15; 1 Cor. i. 4, iii. 10, xv. 10; 2 Cor. i. 12, vi. 1, viii. 1, ix. 14; Gal. i. 15, ii. 21; Eph. iii. 2, 7; 2 Thess. i. 12; Tit. ii. 11; Heb. xii. 15; 1 Pet. iv. 10, 12, and cp. v. 10.

in truth] The words, grammatically, may refer to the reality of either the reception or the thing received. Order and connexion, and the drift of the whole Epistle, with its warning against a visionary and illusory "other Gospel," favour the latter. So we render, or explain, **in (its) reality**; in its character as the revelation of eternal fact and pure spiritual truth. Cp. Eph. iv. 21, and our note.

7. *as ye also learned*] In the word "*as*" he refers to the "truth" just spoken of (Lightfoot). *So*, and not otherwise, had Epaphras phrased his message.

The word rendered "*also*" should certainly be omitted, on documentary evidence. As it stands, it simply emphasizes the fact; "*as you* actually *learned from Epaphras*." But its omission leaves the English reader less likely to misunderstand the sentence, as if it implied *some other* informant of the Colossians, *besides* Epaphras.

Epaphras] Named also below, iv. 12, and Philemon 23. The name is an abbreviation of *Epaphroditus*, and it has been guessed that the Epaphroditus of Phil. ii. 25, iv. 18, and this Epaphras, are the same person. But both name-forms were very common at the time; and *nothing but the name* tends to an identification in this case, unless indeed the warm and devoted Christian character indicated in both Phil. ii. and Col. iv. does so. And this happily was not so rare in the Church as to make an argument.

From the notices in this Epistle and in Philemon we gather that he was a Colossian by birth, or at least by abode; that he had been the first, or at least chief, evangelist of Colossæ (see further, *Introd.*, p. 21), and that he was now at Rome, arrived from Asia, and was St Paul's "fellow-prisoner of war;" i.e. either actually imprisoned with him on some charge connected with the Gospel, or so incessantly with him in his captivity as practically to share it. The latter is more probable.— For his character, see further, on iv. 12.—Tradition makes Epaphras first bishop of Colossæ, and a martyr there.

fellowservant] Strictly, **fellow-bondservant, fellow-slave.** He uses the word again, of Tychicus, iv. 7, and not elsewhere. It occurs Rev. vi. 11, xix. 10, xxii. 9; and, of non-spiritual servitude, Matt. xviii. 28—33, xxiv. 49.—To the Christian, in a life of humble surrender to his Lord, the fact of his own holy bondservice is inexpressibly dear; and so the thought of his association in it with others is an endearing and uniting thought.

for you] Another reading is **for us, on our behalf** (so R.V.). For this there is weighty documentary evidence, though it cannot be called overwhelming. It is however supported internally by the evidence in

70 / Colossians 1

8 is for you a faithful minister of Christ; who also declared unto us your love in the Spirit.

9 For this cause we also, since the day we heard *it*, do not cease to pray for you, and to desire that ye might be filled

the context that Epaphras was, so to speak, *vice-evangelist* "for" St Paul at Colossæ.

minister] Greek, *diâconos;* so Eph. vi. 21, and below, *vv.* 23, 25, iv. 7. The word essentially implies activity and subordination. In Phil. i. 1; 1 Tim. iii. 8—12; the word denotes holders of a subordinate and active office in the organized Christian ministry (and cp. Rom. xvi. 1). See our notes on Phil. i. 1, and Appendix C. to that Epistle. But such a reference here is unlikely, if only because of the wording, "diaconos *of Christ.*" Epaphras, whatever his church-office, was the loving *worker under Christ* for Paul and Colossæ. For such a use of the word cp. Joh. xii. 26; 1 Cor. iii. 5 (a close parallel); 2 Cor. vi. 4, xi. 23; 1 Thess. iii. 2.—The Latin Versions render, *minister.*

8. *also*] "As he preached to you from us, so *also* he brought back from us to you the tidings, etc." (Lightfoot.)

your love] See on ver. 4 above.

in the Spirit] "In" Whom they were (Rom. viii. 9).—Cp. Rom. xv. 30, where probably "the love" spoken of is that quickened in the hearts of the saints by the Holy Ghost. (See our note there. Cp. also 2 Tim. i. 7).—"Love" is the first and ruling ingredient in the "fruit of the Spirit" (Gal. v. 22), by Whom "the love of God hath been poured out in our hearts" (Rom. v. 5), sure prelude and secret of a regenerate love to others.

9—12 THANKSGIVING PASSES INTO PRAYER THAT THEY MAY WILL AND WALK WITH GOD

9. *For this cause*] In view of the whole happy report from Colossæ.

we also] The "*also*" means that the news of the loving life at Colossæ was *met* by the loving prayer of Paul and his friends.

since the day, &c.] The phrase used above of the Colossians, ver. 6. This (as Lightfoot remarks) gives a point to the "*also.*"

do not cease to pray] So Eph. i. 16; and see Acts xx. 31. An "affectionate hyperbole" (Ellicott); and such hyperboles are absolutely truthful, between hearts in perfect sympathy. On St Paul's prayers, see above on ver. 3.

to desire] The word defines the more general idea conveyed by "*pray*" just above. "*Prayer*" (in the Greek, as with us) may include many directions of thought in worship; "*desire*" fixes the direction, that of petition.—On the verbs used for praying, asking, and the like, in the Greek Scriptures, see Grimm's *Greek-Eng. Lex. to N.T.* (ed. Thayer), under αἰτεῖν.

"*Desire,*" as very often in the English Bible, here means "*make*

Colossians 1 / 71

with the knowledge of his will in all wisdom and spiritual understanding; that ye might walk worthy of the Lord unto 10

request" (A.V.). See e.g. 2 Kings iv. 28; Psal. xxvii. 4; Matt. xvi. 1; Acts vii. 46; 2 Cor. viii. 6; 1 Joh. v. 15. This meaning is still not uncommon.
filled] A word and thought often occurring in similar connexions in St Paul. Cp. Rom. xv. 13, 14, 29; 2 Cor. vii. 4; Eph. iii. 19, v. 18; Phil. i. 11, ii. 2, iv. 19, below, ii. 10; 2 Tim. i. 4.—Nothing short of the total of what God can and will give to the saints satisfies his inspired desire.
knowledge] *Epignôsis;* more than *gnôsis*. See above on ver. 6.
of his will] Cp. Eph. v. 17, and our note there.—"*Thou sweet, beloved will of God*,"[1] is meant by the Gospel to be the Christian's always underlying and ruling thought and choice. And such an attitude of soul, if genuinely taken, will lead direct to an active enquiry "*what the will of the Lord is.*" Mme. Guyon, on this verse (*La Sainte Bible*) writes characteristically and truly: "All perfection consists in doing the will of God...the works which seem greatest are nothing if they are not in the will of God....The more the soul does the will of God in all things, the more it knows God."
spiritual] As due to the gift and teaching of *the Spirit*. The adjective should be placed before "*wisdom*" (as R.V.), qualifying both it and "*understanding*."
understanding] A narrower and more precise word than "*wisdom*." The man spiritually "wise" brings that characteristic habit of thought to bear on special questions, and spiritually "understands" them. Cp. for a partial parallel Eph. i. 17. And for the Apostle's desire that his converts should (under the Holy Spirit's guidance) "think for themselves," see 1 Cor. xiv. 20; Eph. iv. 14.
10. *walk*] A very frequent word in St Paul; most frequent in Eph., where see iv. 1 for a close parallel. See 1 Thess. ii. 12 for one still closer verbally. The word denotes life in its action and intercourse.— The spiritual knowledge which he asks for them is thus sought for the most sacredly practical of purposes—in order to their closer conformity to the will of God *in real life*.
worthy of the Lord] Lit., **worthily** &c.; so R.V. But all previous English versions read as A.V., perhaps using the adjective adverbially.— Ideally, of course, no human "walk" is "worthy of the Lord." But practically it can and should be so, in the sense of being governed at every step by the Divine motive of His love and presence, and so presenting a true correspondence to that motive.
" *The Lord:*"—"St Paul's common, and apparently universal, usage requires us to understand ['the Lord'] of Christ." (Lightfoot). The "*worthy of God*" of 1 Thess. ii. 12 thus gives to the phrase here a deep significance in relation to the Godhead of Christ. Such alternative expressions indicate how truly for St Paul the Father and the Son are

---

[1] See the hymn beginning, *Liebwerther, süsser Gottes-Wille*, in Tersteegen's *Blumengärtlein*; translated in *Hymns of Consecration and Faith*, No. 257.

72 / Colossians 1

all pleasing, being fruitful in every good work, and increas-
11 ing in the knowledge of God; strengthened with all might,

Persons of the same Order of being. Cp. for similar indications (among very many passages) Rom. viii. 35 with 39; Eph. ii. 22 with iii. 17.

unto all pleasing] "So as to aim at, and go the length of, *meeting every wish* (of the Lord's)."—The word rendered "pleasing" is most instructive. In classical Greek it denotes a cringing and subservient habit, ready to do or say anything to please a patron; not only to meet but to anticipate his most trivial wishes. But when transferred to the spiritual region, and the believer's relations to his Lord, the word at once rises by its association. *To do anything* to meet, to anticipate, His wishes, is not only the most beneficial but the most absolutely right thing we can do. It is His eternal and sacred due; it is at the same time the surest path to our own highest development and gain.—See Lightfoot's excellent note.—For a close parallel to the wording here, see 1 Thess. iv. 1, where the cognate verb is used.

fruitful] See above on ver. 6. The verb here is in the active, not middle, and so somewhat less pregnant in meaning.

every good work] Observe the characteristic impartiality and wholeheartedness of Christian obedience; as just above, "*all* pleasing."

increasing] See above on ver. 6; and cp. below ii. 19; 1 Pet. ii. 2; 2 Pet. iii. 18.

in the knowledge] The Greek, in the best-attested reading, is capable also of the rendering "*by the knowledge;*" and so Ellicott, Lightfoot, and margin R.V. But the text R.V. renders as A.V., though using this other and better-attested Greek, which gives *epignôsis* in the dative, without preposition. This is quite good grammatically; cp. *e.g.* the Greek of Rom. iv. 20; Phil. ii. 8. The dative is used as the case of reference; the growth is growth *with regard to* spiritual knowledge of God; that is, it is a development of that knowledge in the believer, a growth in it.—The other (and we think inferior) rendering meanwhile conveys an undoubted and important truth.

"*The knowledge of God:*"—which "is life eternal" (Joh. xvii. 3). "You must needs know that to enjoy God and His Christ is eternal Life; and the soul's enjoying is in knowing" (Baxter, *Saint's Everlasting Rest*, Part i. sect. vii.).

11. *strengthened*] "*made powerful;*" R.V. marg. The same verb occurs in the LXX. of Psalm lxvii. (Heb. and Eng. lxviii.) 28, and some other O.T. passages, and in Heb. xi. 34. A compound of it occurs Acts ix. 22; Rom. iv. 20; Eph. vi. 10; Phil. iv. 13.—The three last reff. are a full spiritual commentary on the word here.—The Lat. Versions have *confortati;* Wyclif, "*counfortid.*"—Observe that the Greek participle is in the present or continuing form, and suggests a maintained and abiding strengthening.

with] Lit., **in.**

all might] Greek *dunamis;* the cognate noun to the verb just rendered "*strengthened.*" The strengthening was to meet "all" sides and kinds of spiritual need with a corresponding completeness.—For the word in such a connexion, cp. especially Luke xxiv. 49; Acts i. 8 in the Greek.

according to his glorious power, unto all patience and long-suffering with joyfulness; giving thanks unto the Father, 12

according to his glorious power] Lit. and far better, **according to the power** (or **might**, R.V.) **of His glory**; in a way worthy of the forces springing from that "glory" of God which is in fact His supreme and blessed Nature in manifestation.—The word *"glorious"* (in the A.V.) represents similar Greek in the following passages; Rom. viii. 21; 2 Cor. iv. 4; Phil. iii. 21; 1 Tim. i. 11; Tit. ii. 13; and these all gain greatly in significance by the literal rendering.
unto all patience] The "all" of result answers to the "all" of Divine supply.
"Patience:"—the Greek word rises above, while it amply includes, the thought of uncomplaining suffering. It is a noble word, denoting the *endurance* of the soul in the path of faith, hope, and love; *perseverance*, under trials, in the will of God. Cp. (in the Greek) especially Matt. x. 22; Luke viii. 15, xxi. 19; Rom. ii. 7; Heb. xii. 1, 7.
longsuffering] Latin Versions, *longanimitas*, a beautiful and literal equivalent for the Greek. The word "longanimity," formed on this, and used by the Rhemish translators (1582), was adopted by Bp Jeremy Taylor (cent. 17), but has never taken root in English.—The temper indicated is the opposite to that *haste* of spirit which gives the man no time, under pressure of pain or (particularly) of *wrong*, to remember what is due to others, and to the Lord. Cp., for the use of the word and its cognates, Matt. xviii. 26; 1 Cor. xiii. 4, &c.; and, for a soul-moving reference to the "longanimity" of the Lord Himself, 1 Tim. i. 16.—The two words, "*patience*," "*longsuffering*," occur together, 2 Cor. vi. 4, 6; 2 Tim. iii. 10; Jas. v. 10, 11.
with joyfulness] **with joy.** Cp. esp. Isai. xxix. 19; Hab. iii. 17, 18; John xvi. 20—24, xvii. 14; Acts xiii. 52 (a good illustration here from facts); Rom. xiv. 17, xv. 13; 1 Thess. i. 6; Heb. x. 34; Jas i. 2; 1 Pet. i. 8. Nothing like the Gospel can open the secret of a joy, perfectly real and unaffected, under sufferings and sorrows, and that without the least tendency to blunt sensibility.
Observe the holy paradox of the thought here. The fulness of Divine power in the saints is to result primarily not in "doing some great thing" but in enduring and forbearing, with heavenly joy of heart. The paradox points to one deep characteristic of the Gospel, which prepares the Christian for service by the way of a true abnegation of himself as his own strength and his own aim.
12. *giving thanks*] as the disciple is to do "in everything" (1 Thess. v. 18). So would the deep-felt "joy" be specially expressed. See on ver. 3 above.
unto the Father] Who is always revealed as the ultimate Object of thanksgiving, the eternal Fountain of the whole Redemption. Cp. e.g. Matt. xi. 25; Joh. iii. 16, xvii. 1, 4; 2 Cor. i. 3; Eph. i. 3; Phil. ii. 11; 1 Pet. i. 3.—He is here viewed as the Father of the Son, not *immediately* as "*our* Father;" see ver. 13.

74 / Colossians 1

which hath made us meet to be partakers of the inheritance
13 of the saints in light: who hath delivered us from the power

which hath made us meet] **Who qualified us**, or (Lightfoot), **made us competent**; i.e., gave us, as His redeemed ones in the Son (ver. 14), title to and entrance on our spiritual possessions.—The time-reference is, from one point of view, to the moment of the Lord's finished work; from another, to the moment of each believer's personal union with the Lord.—The same verb occurs 2 Cor. iii. 6 (only), "He qualified us to be ministers, &c." In the Old Latin Version we find *qui vocavit nos, etc.* This represents a various reading of the Greek, "who *called* us."— But the evidence for "*qualified*" is decisive. Another various reading, not to be adopted, is "*you*" for "*us.*"

to be partakers, &c.] Lit., **unto the portion of the lot of the saints in the light.** "The kingdom" (ver. 13) of the Son of God is the realm of light, the light of spiritual knowledge, purity, and joy; the mystical Canaan of the redeemed; the "*lot*" or inheritance of the "peculiar people," in which each one has his "*portion.*" In other words, the saints, possessed by Christ, themselves possess Christ as their riches and light, and are "*qualified*" to do so by the grace of the Father who gave the Son for them and to them.—The reference is not immediately to the coming glory, but to the present grace. Cp. Luke xvi. 8; Joh. viii. 12, xii. 36; Eph. v. 8; 1 Thess. v. 5; 1 Joh. i. 7, &c.; for the imagery of "light" in such a connexion.

It is questioned, whether we are to understand the Apostle to speak of "*the lot in the light,*" or of "*the saints in the light*"? Probably the words "*in light*" qualify *all* parts of the thought. The mystical Canaan is "in the light," and so are its inhabitants therefore.

"*Saints:*"—see on ver. 2 above.

13—14. THE THOUGHT PURSUED: THE GREATNESS OF THEIR REDEMPTION, AND OF THEIR REDEEMER

13. *hath delivered*] Better, **delivered, rescued.** The time-reference is the same as that of "*qualified us,*" explained in the last note but one. The verb is that used in the Lord's Prayer (Matt. vi. 13), and e.g. 1 Thess. i. 10; 2 Tim. iii. 11, iv. 17, 18.

the power of darkness] Lit., **the authority of the darkness**; Latin Versions, *de potestate tenebrarum.* The exact phrase recurs, in our blessed Lord's lips, and in the very crisis of His work for our "rescue," Luke xxii. 53.—The word rendered "authority" (*exousia*) is distinguished from mere "force" (*dunamis*), and denotes some sort of recognized *dominion*, whether lawful (e.g. Matt. x. 1; Rom. xiii. 1, &c.) or unlawful. In secular Greek (as Lightfoot shews) it has a slight tendency to denote excessive or tyrannous dominion. This must not be pressed in the N.T., as a Concordance will shew; but in this Epistle (ver. 16, ii. 15) and its Ephesian companion (ii. 2, iii. 10, vi. 12), it certainly takes that direction, referring to evil spiritual powers and their sphere of dominion.

of darkness, and hath translated *us* into the kingdom of
his dear Son: in whom we have redemption through his 14

Man, in the Fall, so *surrendered himself* to the Usurper that, but for
the action of his Divine King and Deliverer, he would now lie not
merely under the force but under the dominion of his enemy. Cp. Eph.
vi. 12 and our note.

"*The darkness:*"—cp. again Eph. vi. 12. Here the idea presented
is the antithesis to that of the holy "light" of ver. 12; a (moral) region
of delusion, woe, pollution, and death, in which the "Antipathist of
Light"[1] rules over those who "*are darkness*" (Eph. v. 8) and "do its
works" (Eph. v. 11; cp. 1 Joh. i. 6). On the whole expression here,
cp. 1 Pet. ii. 9.

hath translated] Lit. and better (as above) **translated, or transferred.**

the kingdom] Rescued from a tyranny, they stepped not into a "no
man's land" but at once under the righteous, beneficent sovereignty and
protection of the true King. The "kingdom" here is, immediately,
our *present* subjection, in grace, to the Son of God; to be developed
hereafter into the life of glorified order and service (Rev. xxii. 3). See
on Eph. v. 5 in this Series.

Lightfoot, in an interesting note here, says that St Paul uses this
positive language about the actual deliverance of the Colossians,
inasmuch as "they are [in St Paul's view] *potentially* saved, because
the knowledge of God is itself salvation, and this knowledge is within
their reach...He hopes to make them saints by dwelling on their
calling as saints." True; but the meaning put on the word "*calling*"
is, we think, inadequate. On the general phenomenon of "inclusive"
apostolic language see above on ver. 2.

his dear Son] Lit. and far better, **the Son of His love.** Lightfoot,
following Augustine, takes this most precious phrase to mean, in effect,
the Son of the Father who is (1 Joh. iv. 8, 16) *Love*; the Son who
accordingly manifests and as it were embodies the Father's Love (1 Joh.
iv. 9, 10). But surely the more probable meaning is that the Son is
the blessed Object of the Father's love (so Ellicott); the supremely
Beloved One (cp. the parallel passage, Eph. i. 6, where see our note).
Far from "destroying the whole force of the expression" (Lightfoot),
this interpretation is full of ideas in point here. The "kingdom" is
what it is to its happy subjects because its King is the Beloved Son, in
whom the subjects are therefore not subjects only but sons, and beloved.
See Eph. i. 6 and 7, in connexion, for a strong suggestion in this
direction.

14. *redemption through his blood*] Omit the words "*through His
blood,*" on clear documentary evidence.—They stand unchallenged in
the parallel verse, Eph. i. 7. And the truth they express comes out
explicitly below, *vv.* 20, 22.

"*Redemption:*"—lit., "*the redemption,*" here fairly represented by
our redemption, as R.V. The word "redemption" (like its Greek

---

[1] So Coleridge, *Ne plus Ultra*.

76 / Colossians 1

15 blood, *even* the forgiveness of sins: who is the image of the

equivalent) points by derivation to the idea of a *rescue by ransom*, whatever the ransom may be. This meaning often in usage vanishes, or at least retires, as where a deliverance by *mere power* is called a redemption (e.g. Exod. vi. 6). But it is always ready to reappear when the context favours; and certainly does so here, in view of the parallel passage in Eph. and ver. 20 below. Cp. esp. Rom. viii. 23; and for illustration Matt. xx. 28; Heb. ix. 15; 1 Pet. i. 18, 19. And see our notes on Eph. i. 7.

the forgiveness of sins] Lit., **of the (our) sins.**—Eph. i. 7 has "(*our*) *trespasses.*"—Observe this account of our Redemption in Christ. It is primarily Forgiveness, Remission. It involves indeed immensely more both for soul (Tit. ii. 14) and body (Rom. viii. 23); but all else is so inseparably bound up with Forgiveness as its *sine quâ non* that the whole is expressed by this great part. See further on Eph. i. 7.

Bp Lightfoot thinks that the "studied precision" both here and in Eph. of this description of Redemption may "point to some false conception of Redemption put forth by the heretical teachers." And he shews that "the later Gnostics certainly perverted the term, applying it to their own formularies of initiation." With them it would mean a "redemption" as remote as possible from ideas of forgiveness; a release of the mystic from the bondage of matter into the liberty of esoteric "knowledge." Lightfoot asserts no direct connexion between these later Gnostics and the Colossian heretics; but he sees in the later teaching a hint of possible similar aberrations earlier. See further, *Introd.*, ch. iii..

Before quitting ver. 13, observe the phrase, "*in* whom," not "*through*, or *by*, whom." The idea thus given is that of union with Christ (see on ver. 2 above). The Remission, won by the Redeemer's dying Work, is for those who by faith are incorporated into the Redeemer's mystical Person.—The editor ventures to refer to his *Thoughts on Union with Christ*, pp. 104, 124, etc.

15—17 THE THOUGHT CONTINUED: GREATNESS OF THE REDEEMER AS HEAD OF CREATION

15. *who is*] Here opens, in closest connexion with the preceding matter, a confession of truth and faith about the Person of the Redeeming Son of God, the King of the redeemed. He appears in His relation to (*a*) the Eternal Father, (*b*) the created Universe, especially the Universe of spirits, (*c*) the Church of redeemed men. Every clause is pregnant of Divine truth, and the whole teaches with majestic emphasis the great lesson that the Person is all-important to the Work, the true Christ to the true salvation.

the image] So 2 Cor. iv. 4. The Greek word (*eicôn*) occurs often in Biblical Greek, most frequently (in O.T.) as a translation of the Hebrew *tselem*. Usage shews that on the whole it connotes not only similarity but also "*representation* (as a *derived* likeness) and *manifestation*" (Grimm's *N. T. Lexicon*, ed. Thayer; and see Lightfoot's note,

invisible God, the firstborn of every creature: for by him 16

or rather essay, here). An instructive passage for study of the word is Heb. x. 1, where it is opposed to "*shadow*," and plainly means "*the things themselves, as seen.*" Thus the Lord Christ, in the mystery of His Person and Natures, is not only a Being resembling God, but God Manifest. Cp. Joh. xiv. 9, and Heb. i. 3.

"Christian antiquity has ever regarded the expression 'image of God' as denoting the eternal Son's perfect equality with the Father in respect of His substance, power, and eternity...The Son is the Father's Image in all things save only in being the Father" (Ellicott; with reff. *inter alia* to Hilary *de Synodis*, § 73; Athan. *contra Arian.* i. 20, 21).

the invisible God] For the same word see 1 Tim. i. 17; Heb. xi. 27. And cp. Deut. iv. 12; Joh. i. 18, v. 37; 1 Tim. vi. 16; 1 Joh. iv. 20. This assertion of the Invisibility of the Father has regard to the *manifesting* function of the Image, the Son. See Lightfoot here. The Christian Fathers generally (not universally) took it otherwise, holding that the "Image" here refers wholly to the Son in His Godhead, which is as invisible as that of the Father, being indeed the same. But the word "Image" by usage tends to the thought of vision, in some sort; and the collocation of it here with "the Invisible" brings this out with a certain emphasis. Not that the reference of the "Image" here is directly or primarily to our Lord's visible Body of the Incarnation, but to His being, in all ages and spheres of created existence, the Manifester of the Father to created intelligences. His being this was, so to speak, the basis and antecedent of His gracious coming in the flesh, to be "seen with the eyes" of men on earth (1 Joh. i. 1). In the words of St Basil (*Epist.* xxxviii. 8, quoted by Lightfoot) the creature "views the Unbegotten Beauty in the Begotten."

the firstborn of every creature] Better perhaps, **Firstborn of all creation** (Lightfoot and R.V.), or, with a very slight paraphrase, **Firstborn over all creation**; standing to it in the relation of priority of existence and supremacy of inherited right. So, to borrow a most inadequate analogy, the heir of an hereditary throne might be described as "firstborn to, or over, all the realm." The word "*creature*" (from the (late) Latin *creatura*) here probably, as certainly in Rom. viii., means "creation" as a whole; a meaning to which the Greek word *inclines* in usage, rather than to that of "a creature" (which latter Ellicott and Alford however adopt). See Lightfoot's note.

"*Firstborn:*"—cp. Psal. lxxxix. 27; and the Palestinian Jewish application, thence derived, of the title "Firstborn" to the Messiah. A similar word was used of the mysterious "Logos" among the Alexandrian Jews, as shewn in the writings of St Paul's contemporary, Philo. Studied in its usage, and in these connexions, the word thus denotes (*a*) *Priority of existence*, so that THE SON appears as antecedent to the created Universe, and therefore as belonging to the eternal Order of being (see the following context); (*b*) *Lordship over* "all creation," by this right of eternal primogeniture. See Psal. lxxxix. 27, and cp. Heb. i. 2.

were all *things* created, that are in heaven, and that are in

"*Of all creation:*"—so lit. The force of the Greek genitive, in connexion with the word "*first*" (as here "*first*born"), may be either *partitive*, so that the Son would be described as first *of* created things, or so to speak *comparative* (see a case exactly in point, Joh. i. 15, Greek), so that He would be described as first, or antecedent, *in regard of* created things. And the whole following context, as well as the previous clause, decides for this latter explanation of the grammar.

On the theological importance of the passage see further Appendix C.

16. *for*] **because.** Now follows the proof, given in the creative action of the Son, of His priority to and lordship over created being.

by him] Lit. and far better, **in Him.** "The act of creation is supposed to rest in Him, and to depend on Him for its completion and realization" (Ellicott). In other words, the mighty fact that all things were created was *bound up with* Him, as its Secret. The creation of things *was in* Him, as the effect *is in* its cause.

A meaning so to speak more recondite has been seen here. The text has been taken to mean that the Son, the Logos, is as it were the archetypal Universe, the Sphere and Summary of all finite being as it existed (above time and temporal development) in the Eternal Mind; and accordingly that, when it came into being in time, its creation was "in" Him who thus summed it up. We venture to think that such a view is rather "read into" the words of the Christian Apostle, from non-Christian philosophies, (see Appendix C), than derived from the words.

were...created] A real event, or real events, in time. The Son is seen to have been "First with regard to creation" by the fact that He produced it; Himself existing before (or rather above) time, above all succession, all becoming.

"*Created:*"—the Greek verb denotes the making, constituting, of a new state of things. As a *Divine* operation, such "creation" is the ordering by sovereign will of the material (of whatever kind) which by that will exists. See on Eph. ii. 10; and cp. Joh. i. 3; Heb. i. 2, 10—12, iii. 3, 4.

The "Creator" here in view is properly the Father, working "in" the Son. But such, in the light of the context, is the Son, that, being from one point of view the Instrument, He is also from another the eternal Co-Agent of the Father's will.

that are in heaven, and that are in earth] In all regions of finite being; in the whole created universe. Cp. Gen. i. 1, and a long chain of passages down to Rev. xxi. 1.

visible and invisible] Belonging to all orders of finite being. The division is not precisely between "material" and "spiritual;" for e.g. human beings might be classed under both these. It practically emphasizes the fact that personal powers of the Unseen Universe were as truly "created in" the Son of God as existences (of any kind) that

earth, visible and invisible, whether *they be* thrones, or dominions, or principalities, or powers: all *things* were created

could be seen. Here, as through the whole passage, the errors current at Colossæ are in view; errors which put "Christ" and the unseen Powers in a very different relation. See *Introd.*, ch. III.

thrones, or dominions, or principalities, or powers] More strictly, **thrones, or lordships, or governments, or authorities.** See Eph. i. 21 for a close parallel. The word *"thrones"* is absent there, as *"powers" (dunameis)* is absent here. For similar language cp. Rom. viii. 38; below, ii. 15; Eph. iii. 10, vi. 12; 1 Pet. iii. 22. See further our notes on Eph. i. 21 (partially quoted below, Appendix D).

Lightfoot remarks here: "No stress can be laid on the sequence of the names, as though St Paul were enunciating with authority some precise doctrine respecting the grades of the celestial hierarchy....He does not profess to describe objective realities, but contents himself with repeating subjective opinions....His language here shews the same spirit of impatience with this elaborate angelology as in ii. 18." We venture to dissent, in measure, from this statement. It is most certain that St Paul is not here directly and as a main purpose teaching a doctrine of angels. But he is glorifying the Son of God by a view of His relation to created being; and assuredly this would not be best done by alluding to phases of created being which might all the while be figments of the imagination. Passingly, but distinctly, so we hold, he does affirm the existence both of angels and of angelic orders, "the powers that be" of the invisible world, "created in" the eternal Cornerstone of order, the Son of God.—In Eph. iii. 10, beyond question, "the principalities and powers" are regarded as *facts* of the unseen world.

all things] From the details of his allusion to the hierarchies he returns to the universal statement.

were created] Lit. **have been created, stand created.** (Not so in the first clause of this verse.)

by him] Quite precisely, **through Him**; the phrase of e.g. Joh. i. 3, 10; 1 Cor. viii. 6; Heb. i. 2. It teaches that the Son, in creation, while Himself a true Divine Origin (*"Beginning,"* Rev. iii. 14) of finite being, is the Divine Instrument of the Father's supreme Origination.— The phrase alone does not *quite* fix this meaning, for in a very few passages (e.g. Heb. ii. 10) it is used of a supreme Agent's action. But phrase and context together, as here, are decisive.

for him] "The Word is the final cause as well as the creative agent of the Universe...the goal of the Universe, as He was the starting-point. ...This expression has no parallel, and could have none, in the Alexandrian phraseology and doctrine" (Lightfoot). Thus interpreted, this wonderful phrase points to that "far-off Divine event" shadowed out by 1 Cor. xv. 28; when all finite existence, even all existence which *from its own side* is "hostile" to God, shall be "put under the feet" of the Son, made the footstool of His throne, contributing with a harmony perfect *from the side of God* to the glorification of the Son, and the realization of the Father's eternal purpose in Him. Meanwhile the words surely refer not to the mysterious future only, but to the present,

80 / Colossians 1

17 by him, and for him: and he is before all *things*, and by

to all periods and moments. From one side or another all finite being is, consciously or not, willingly or not, always subserving the glory of the Son of God, and of the Father in Him.

We gather from 1 Cor. xv. 28 that the "event" of the final subjection of all things to the Son will open up, in eternity, a mysterious "subjection" of the Son to the Father. What that means we cannot enquire here. Whatever it is, it is no dethronement of the Son (Rev. xxii. 3); most surely no *revolution* in the inner and eternal Relations of Godhead; rather, a mighty Manifestation of Sonship and Fatherhood. It is instructive in this direction to remember that the present passage was written some years later than 1 Cor. xv., and that thus the course of inspiration did anything but *lower* the Apostle's language about the glory and eternity of the Son.

In the light of this phrase deep is the significance of, e.g., Rom. xiv. 8, and of every Scripture in which Christ appears as the Lord and God of the believer's life and being.

17. *he*] Emphatic in the Greek; HE, and no other who could even seem to rival or obscure His sublime eminence.

is before all things] *ante omnes*, Latin Versions. The Greek genitive form is ambiguous; it might be either masculine or neuter. But the mention in the last clause, in the unambiguous nominative, of "all things," decides for a similar reference here.

Lightfoot prints his rendering here, "*and* HE IS *before all things*," comparing Joh. viii. 58, and Exod. iii. 14, and adding, "The imperfect ['*was*'] might have sufficed,...but the present ['*is*'] declares that this preexistence is absolute existence." He quotes Basil of Cæsarea (*adv. Eunom.*, iv.) as emphasizing the special force of "*is*" (as against e.g. "*was*" or "*became*") in this very passage: "(the Apostle) indicates thus that He ever *is* while the creation *came to be*."

"*Before:*"—i.e., as the whole context shews, in respect of priority of existence; the priority of eternity.

by him] Lit. and better, **in Him**; see above on ver. 16.

consist] I.e., literally, **stand together, hold together**. The Latin-English "*consist*" (Latin versions, *constant*) exactly renders the Greek. "He is the principle of cohesion in the Universe. He impresses upon creation that unity and solidarity which makes it a cosmos instead of a chaos" (Lightfoot). And Lightfoot quotes Philo to shew that the "Logos" of Alexandrian Judaism was similarly regarded as the "Bond" of the universe.

"Christ was the conditional element of their *creation*, the causal element of their *persistence*...The declaration, as Waterland observes, is in fact tantamount to 'in Him they live, and move, and have their being'" (Ellicott).

Natural philosophy, after all observation and classification of phenomena and their processes, asks necessarily but in vain (so long as it asks only "Nature"), what is their ultimate secret, what *is*, for instance, the last reason of universal gravitation. Revelation discloses that reason in the Person and Will of the Son of God.

him all *things* consist. And he is the head of the body, the 18

Thus far the Apostle has unfolded the glory of Christ as the Cause and Bond of all being in the sphere of "Nature," material and otherwise. Now he turns to the sphere of Grace.

18—20   THE THOUGHT CONTINUED. GREATNESS OF THE REDEEMER AS HEAD OF THE CHURCH, BEARER OF THE DIVINE PLENITUDE, AND ATONING SACRIFICE

18. *And he is*] The same words as just above, and a solemn echo of them. *He*, the same Person, *is* also, necessarily, all that is now to be stated. The Head of Nature is the Head of Grace; the Person one, the operations analogous though differing.

the head] A word combining the thought of supremacy with that of the origination and conveyance of life and energy. The Son of God presides over His Church, but more—He is to it the constant Cause and mighty Source of spiritual vitality. "Because He lives, it lives also." Its organization is rooted in Him, grows from Him, and refers to Him. Cp. 1 Cor. xi. 3; Eph. i. 22, iv. 15, v. 23; and below, ii. 10, 19. The idea, it will be seen, appears in this precise form (the Headship of *the Body*) only in Eph. and Col.; but cp. Rom. xii. 5; 1 Cor. x. 17, xii. 21.

the body] Cp. Rom. xii. 5; 1 Cor. x. 17, xii. 27; Eph. i. 23, ii. 16, iv. 4, 12, 16, v. 23, 30; below, ver. 24, ii. 19, iii. 15. This side of the imagery is strictly correlative to that of "the Head." It presents the believing Company as an Organism subject to the Lord, dependent vitally on Him for its being, cohesion, and energy, and forming an animated vehicle for the accomplishment of His will. And it indicates of course the mutual relations of "the members" (see on this esp. 1 Cor. xii.) in their widely differing functions of life and service.

"To know, to do, the Head's commands,
For this the Body lives and grows:
All speed of feet, all skill of hands,
Is for Him spent, and from Him flows."

the church] The Greek admits the rendering, "*of the body of the Church;*" i.e., of the Church defined, or described, as a body; viewed as being a body. The difference between this rendering and that of A.V. and R.V. is however almost imperceptible; and ver. 24 below, and Eph. i. 23, incline the rendering in their direction.

The word "Church" here appears in its highest reference, denoting the society of human beings "called out" (as the word *ecclêsia* implies) from the fallen world into vital union with the glorified Christ as Head. It occurs again ver. 24, and nine times in Eph. (i. 23, iii. 10, 21, v. 23, 24, 25, 27, 29, 32), always with the same reference. See also Heb. xii. 23; and cp. Acts xx. 28; 1 Cor. xv. 9.—As presented here, the idea rises above the level of "visibility;" it transcends human registration and external organization, and has to do supremely with direct spiritual relations between the Lord and the believing Company.

church: who is the beginning, the firstborn from the dead;
19 that in all *things* he might have the preeminence. For it

It is in fact "the Bride, the Lamb's Wife," of Rev. xxi., only not yet manifested in bridal splendour. It is the "called, justified, and glorified" of Rom. viii.; "the Church of the firstborn" of Heb. xii.; "the royal priesthood, the people of possession," of 1 Peter. All other Christian meanings of the word Church are derived and modified from this, but this must not be modified by them. See Hooker, *Eccl. Polity*, iii. 1, quoted below, Appendix H.

who is] **Seeing He is** (Ellicott).

the beginning] The Origin, the Principle and Secret, of the life of the living Body. Cp. Rev. iii. 14, where the probable reference is not (as here) to the spiritual creation specially but to created existence generally. Perhaps also (as Wordsworth suggests) the word (*Archê*) points also to the Son's *governing* primacy, supreme above all possible angelic "Governments." But this would be a secondary reference.

the firstborn from the dead] Not merely "*of* the dead," but "*from* them;" passing in a supreme and unique sense "from death unto life;" rising in "the power of an indissoluble life" (Heb. vii. 16), a life-originating life (cp. 1 Joh. v. 11, 12).—The word "*Firstborn*" here echoes ver. 15, where the Son appears as (by right of *nature*, "First-*born*,") antecedent and supreme with regard to the whole natural creation. Here He is such, by a similar right, as to the whole spiritual creation. But now comes in the great paradox that He is this, in the sphere of grace, through the process of *death*, not through Incarnation alone apart from death. As *slain and risen* He enters, by right and in fact, on His position as living Head of Grace for His Church; "declared to be THE SON of God with power" (Rom. i. 4), in order to our adoption and re-generation. Not as if He could be thus "born" a new Personality; but as being thus constituted actually the Second Adam of the new Race He is not only the "First-fruits" but the "First-Born" in His resurrection.—For the term in this connexion cp. Rev. i. 5.

in all things] Of grace as of nature, of new life as of old.

he] Emphatic in the Greek; HE, the same, and without partner or rival.

have the preeminence] Lit., and better, **might become (the) First, might take the first place** (so Ellicott).—The thought here of "*becoming*," as distinguished from "*being*," must not be lost; what He "is" eternally to finite existence at large He "becomes" actually to His new Creation in His finished and victorious Sacrifice and risen Life. Nor must the echo from clause to clause (in the Greek) of the word "*first*" be lost.

"With this clause the predications respecting Christ seem to reach their acme" (Ellicott); an acme of calm but rapturous ascription and confession concerning the all-beloved Son of the Father, Secret of Creation, Life and Lord of His happy Church.—No passage in the N.T. more fully, perhaps none so fully, witnesses to the Divine "Nature, Power, and Eternity" of the Saviour of mankind.

pleased *the Father* that in him should all fulness dwell;

19. *For it pleased* the Father, &c.] "*The Father*" is supplied by the translators (A.V. and R.V., and the older versions from Tyndale (1534) downwards, except the Roman Catholic Rhemish (1582) which reads "*in Him it hath well pleased al fulnes to inhabite.*" The Old Latin reads *in ipso complacuit omnis plenitudo inhabitare;* the Vulgate, *in ipso complacuit omnem plenitudinem inhabitare.*—Grammatically, the Greek admits three possible explanations: (*a*) "*For in Him all the Plenitude was pleased to take up Its abode;*" (*b*) "*For He* (*the Son*) *was pleased that all the Plenitude should take up Its abode in Him;*" (*c*) "*For He* (*God, the Father*) *was pleased that all the Plenitude should take up Its abode in Him* (*the Son*)." What decision does the context, or other side-evidence, indicate? The explanation (*b*) is discredited as assigning to the Son a determining choice which the whole context leads us to assign to the Father. The explanation (*a*), adopted and ably defended by Ellicott, is that of the Old Latin Version. It is grammatically simple, and it is capable of doctrinal defence; "the Plenitude" of the Divine Nature being taken to include the actings of the Divine Will as the expression of the Nature, and so to *signify* the Divine Personality (here, of course, that of the Father). But it is in itself a surprising and extremely anomalous expression; and it becomes still more so when we read on, and see what are the actions attributed to the same Subject, and that the Subject appears in the masculine gender in the word rendered "*having made peace*" (see note below), while the word *Plerôma* (*Plenitude*) is neuter. On the whole we believe (*c*) to be the true explanation, with Alford, and Lightfoot, who compares Jas. i. 12, iv. 6 (the better supported reading in each case); "*the crown which He* (unnamed) *promised;*" "*the Spirit which He* (unnamed) *caused to dwell in us.*" He points out also that the noun (*eudokia*) kindred to the verb here is often, and almost as a habit, used of God's "good pleasure" where God is not named.

all fulness] Lit. and better **all the Fulness, all the Plenitude**. Cp. below ii. 9; "all the Fulness of *the Godhead;*" a phrase of course explanatory of this which is so nearly connected with it. Lightfoot (pp. 323—339) discusses the word with great care and clearness, and brings out the result that the true notion of it is *the filled condition of a thing*, as when a rent is mended, an idea realized, a prophecy fulfilled. He shews that the word had acquired a technical meaning in St Paul's time, in Jewish schools of thought, a meaning connected especially with the eternally realized Ideal of Godhead; the Divine Fulness; "the totality of the Divine Powers and Attributes."—See further our note on Eph. i. 22, where the Church is called "the Plenitude of" the Son.

dwell] The verb denotes permanence; **should take up its lasting abode**. Does this "taking up the abode" refer to Eternity, or to Time? to the time-less communication of Godhead from the Father to the Son, or to a communication coincident with the completion of the Incarnate Son's redeeming work? We think the latter, in view of the following context. From eternity, eternally and necessarily, the Plenitude "took up," "takes up," Its abode in Him as to His blessed Person. But not

84 / Colossians 1

20 and, having made peace through the blood of his cross, by him

till His Work of death and resurrection was accomplished was He, historically, so constituted as that It "took up Its abode" in Him as Head and Treasury for us of "all grace." This now He is, lastingly, everlastingly.

20. *having made peace*] Between Himself, the Holy Judge and King, and His subjects. He is thus now "the God of Peace" (Rom. xv. 33; 1 Thess. v. 23; Heb. xiii. 20); and "we, justified by faith, have peace with God through our Lord Jesus Christ" (Rom. v. 1).

The Subject of the statement is, as before, the Father. While the Crucified Son is the immediate Agent, the Father "who spared not His own Son" (Rom. viii. 32), because He "loved the world" (Joh. iii. 16), is the remoter Agent, Eternal Source of all salvation.

through the blood of his cross] The Cross of the Son. Here first the sacred Atoning Death is explicitly mentioned; its fact and its mode.

"*The blood:*"—i.e. the Death, viewed as the Ransom-price. Some expositors find in "*the blood* of Christ" (in the N.T. generally) a reference different from that of "*the death* of Christ," connecting it rather with life than with death; with surrender to God, and impartation to man, of the Lord's vivifying life rather than with the immolation of His life as (because of His undertaking for us) forfeited to the Law. But certainly in this passage, at least, the thought not of vivification but of propitiation is prominent. See the notes just below.—On the subject of "the Blood of Christ" generally the Editor may refer to his *Outlines of Christian Doctrine*, pp. 85, &c., and to *The Blood of the New Covenant*, by W. S. Smith, D.D., Bishop of Sydney.

by him] Christ. Lit., **through Him.**

to reconcile] The Greek verb here rendered "*reconcile*" occurs elsewhere (in exactly the same form) only in the next verse and Eph. ii. 16. Its form emphasizes the thought of conciliating *back again*, after breach of loyalty or amity. Ideally, the whole Church and each individual was (in Adam unfallen) originally at peace with God; then came revolt, and now *re-*conciliation. On such an ideal view (very different from that of personal conscious experience) see our note on Eph. ii. 12 ("*being aliens.*")

A simpler form of the same verb occurs e.g. Rom. v. 10; 1 Cor. vii. 11; 2 Cor. v. 18—20. The main notion of both verbs is the propitiation of an alienated superior, so that he accepts offending inferiors, who are thus and then "reconciled" to him. And the superior "reconciles them" so far as he acts on the provided propitiation. Here the Father "reconciles" by constituting His Son the all-sufficient and all-acceptable Lord of Peace. See further our note on Eph. ii. 16.

all things] For similar language cp. Matt. xvii. 11 ("*Elias... restoreth all things*;") Acts iii. 21, ("*the times of the restoration of all things which God spake by...His holy prophets;*" i.e. the bringing back of Paradise, and of the Theocracy, in their heavenly and eternal reality). The word "*all*" is at once glorified and limited by the words, in apposition, just below, "*whether the things on the earth or the things in the heavens:*" see note there. The human and angelic "worlds"

to reconcile all *things* unto himself; by him, *I say*, whether they be things in earth, or *things* in heaven.

are the objects of the "reconciliation" in view here; not "all things" apart from those limits, but "all things" within them. See the closely parallel passage, Eph. i. 10.

unto himself] Lit., "*unto Him.*" But the reflexive English pronoun rightly represents the Greek non-reflexive, in the light of N.T. *usage*. See Lightfoot's note.

Here the "reconciliation" of the "all things" is seen to be not (as some expositors, ancient and modern, take it) a reconciliation to one another, so that e.g. angels, alienated by man's sin, shall again be perfectly harmonized with man. It is a reconciliation of the "all things" *to God*, in the way of propitiation.

by him, I say] An emphatic resumed reference to the Reconciling Son, standing alone and "preeminent" in His wonderful work.

whether they be things *in earth, or* things *in heaven*] Lit., "*whether the things*," &c. He refers back to the "*all things*" just above; see note there.—It is significant that "*the things under the earth*" are not mentioned in this great phrase. It is surely revealed (1 Cor. xv. 28) that all created existence, in the amplest sense, shall in some supreme way be "*subdued* unto" the Son and unto the Father in Him; there shall be *order* before the Throne in all the depths as well as heights of being. See Phil. ii. 11, and our note there. But this is another thing from "reconciliation" and "peace." The universalism of this passage is no negation of the awful warnings of Scripture about the final and irremediable exclusion from "peace" of the impenitent creature.

What then do the words here actually import? We answer with Alford (see the whole of his careful note here): "No reconciliation [of angelic beings] must be thought of which should resemble *ours* in its process—for Christ...paid no propitiatory penalty [for angels] in the root of their nature, as including it in Himself. But, forasmuch as He is their Head as well as ours...it cannot be but that the great event in which He was glorified through suffering should also bring them nearer to God...That such increase [of blessedness] might be described as a *reconciliation* is manifest: we know from Job xv. 15, that 'the heavens are not clean in His sight,' and ib. iv. 18, 'His angels He charged with folly.' In fact every such nearer approach to Him may without violence to words be so described, in comparison with that previous greater distance which now seems like alienation; and in this case even more properly, as one of the consequences of that great propitiation whose first...effect was to reconcile to God, in the literal sense, the things upon earth, polluted and hostile in consequence of man's sin. So that our interpretation may be thus summed up: all creation subsists in Christ: all creation therefore is affected by His act of propitiation: sinful creation is, in the strictest sense, *reconciled*, from being at enmity: sinless creation, ever at a distance from His unapproachable purity, is lifted into nearer participation...of Him, and is thus *reconciled*, though not in the strictest, yet

86 / Colossians 1

21 And you, that were sometimes alienated and enemies in *your* mind by wicked works, yet now hath he reconciled

in a very intelligible and allowable sense."—The implied need, even in *the angelic* world, of the Son's Work of peace, would have a special point for the Colossians.

Observe, in leaving ver. 20, the order of the words in the Greek: **And through Him to reconcile all things to Himself, making peace through the blood of His cross—through Him, whether the things,** &c.

21—23 THE SUBJECT PURSUED: THE SPECIAL CASE OF THE COLOSSIANS WITH REGARD TO REDEMPTION

21. *you*] In the Greek "*you*" is accusative, and (in the best supported reading) the only verb to govern it is "*to reconcile*" in ver. 20. (See note on "*hath He reconciled*" just below.) Thus the *construction* runs unbroken from ver. 20 into this verse. But there is a break, a paragraph, practically, in *the thought and treatment*.

As in Eph. i. 13, so here, the Apostle moves from the general case of the "all things" to the particular case of the Colossian believers, included among "the things on the earth." Cp. also Eph. ii. 1; a close parallel.

sometimes] Ideally, before Christ's work; biographically, before their conversion to Him.

alienated] **Estranged**, Lightfoot.—Cp. Eph. ii. 12, iv. 18, and our notes there. Here, as there, the unregenerate man, and now particularly the heathen man, is viewed as (*ideally*) once in covenant and peace with God, and recipient of His "life," but "fallen" thence.—See note above on "*to reconcile*," ver. 20.

enemies] Not, as some render, "*hated*." The Greek *does* mean "*hated*" Rom. xi. 28; but scarcely so anywhere else in N.T.—For the truth, cp. Rom. viii. 7. In its inmost essence, sinfulness is *hostility* to the nature, will, and claims of the Holy One. He therefore on His part must be *judicially adverse* to the sinner, apart from the propitiation He has provided. But this side of the fact is less prominent here.

in your *mind*] The word rendered "*mind*" commonly denotes the rational powers in general; cp. e.g. Eph. iv. 17; 1 Pet. i. 13. The Colossians in their heathen state had shewn their "enmity" "*in* those powers," inasmuch as the *approved principles* of their lives were contrary to the will of God.

by wicked works] More lit., **in your wicked works**; the orbit, so to speak, traced by their life of "enmity." For the truth, cp. 1 Cor. vi. 9—11; Eph. ii. 1—3; Tit. iii. 3—7.

now] "*As the fact is*," in the actual provision of mercy and gift of grace. "Comp. e.g. ver. 26, Rom. v. 11, vii. 6, xi. 30, 31, xvi. 26; Ephes. ii. 13, iii. 5; 2 Tim. i. 10; 1 Pet. i. 12, ii. 10, 23." (Lightfoot.)

hath he reconciled] More lit., **did He reconcile**, in the finished work of Christ. But the somewhat better supported reading gives the

in the body of his flesh through death, to present you holy 22

passive; **you were reconciled.** Thus (see note on "*you*" just above) we have here a new sentence, grammatically, although the order of thought *practically* justifies the rendering of the A.V. Reading thus, we may regard the words from "*yet now*" to "*through death*" as a parenthesis in the construction.

22. *in the body*] Cp. for this word in a similar connexion Rom. vii. 4; Heb. x. 10. And see Matt. xxvi. 26 (and parallels); 1 Cor. x. 16, xi. 27; 1 Pet. ii. 24. In all these passages the thought is of the blessed Body not generally, as regarding the Incarnation, but particularly, as regarding the Propitiation. "He *partook of flesh and blood, that by means of death* he might...deliver" (Heb. ii. 14, 15).—The phrase "*in* the body" has relation to *the Union* of the Redeemer and redeemed. His dying work actually availed for them as they became "*members of* His body, of His flesh and of His bones" (Eph. v. 30).

of his flesh] His "natural" Body, as distinguished from His "mystical" or non-literal Body, the Church. It has been thought that these words aim at the *Docetic*, or *phantasm*, heresy; the belief that the Body of the Lord was but a semblance. But Lightfoot observes that Docetism does not appear in history till later than St Paul's time[1], and that were it otherwise the phrase here is too passing for the supposed purpose.

through death] Better, perhaps, having regard to MSS., **through His death.** See note on "*in the body*," just above, and "*the blood of His cross*," ver. 20.—The mysterious glory of the Atoning Death, dealt with as the central topic of teaching in Romans and Galatians, is never far from the foreground in these later Epistles, though their main work is to unfold other aspects of the truth. Cp. e.g. Eph. i. 7, ii. 16, v. 2, 25; Phil. ii. 8, iii. 10, 18; below, ii. 14.

Here probably ends the parenthesis indicated in the last note on ver. 21.

to present you] The construction is continuous with, "*It pleased [the Father]...to reconcile...all things...and you*" (*vv.* 19—21), supposing our view of a parenthesis of the words just before these to be right. (Otherwise, the construction is continuous with the "*He reconciled*" of the A.V. in ver. 21.)—The infinitive is *illative*, carrying out into details of purpose the previous statement. The Father was "pleased to reconcile them" so that His purpose for them was to "present them to Himself" (see Eph. v. 27 for similar language about the work of the Son), in the great day of triumph and welcome (2 Cor. iv. 14), when the "justified" shall be the "glorified" (Rom. viii. 30).

holy and unblameable and unreproveable] **holy, and without blemish, and unaccusable.** Does this mean, spiritually perfect as to their condition, or judicially perfect as to their position? We may perhaps reply, both; for in both respects the glorified will be complete. But we think the main reference is to perfectness of acceptance in

[1] Jerome however (*adv. Lucif.*, § 23) says that the "Lord's Body was said to be a phantasm" "while the Apostles were yet in Judæa" (*Apostolis adhuc apud Judæam*).

88 / Colossians 1

23 and unblameable and unreproveable in his sight: if ye continue in the faith grounded and settled, and *be* not moved away from the hope of the gospel, which ye have heard,

Christ, perfectness of "reconciliation" "in the body of His flesh through death." The language of Rom. viii. 33 is much in point here; there the saints are "unaccusable" ("*who shall accuse the elect of God?*") *because Christ died, rose again, and intercedes*. In His merits they are welcomed as He is welcomed Himself. See further our notes on Eph. ii. 4.—Meantime the concurrent and related prospect of the personal spiritual perfectness of the saints, as "Christ in them" is at length fully developed in the world of glory, lies close to the other reference.

in his sight] **before Him.** So Eph. i. 4; and cp. Jude 24, "*before His glory.*"

23. *if*] With a certain emphasis in the Greek, *pressing* on the saints the need of watching and prayer; a need which leaves untouched in their proper sphere the sure promises of the "final perseverance" of the saints.

"If we look to stand in the faith of the sons of God, we must hourly, continually, be providing and setting ourselves to strive...To our own safety our own sedulity is required. And then blessed for ever and ever be that mother's child whose faith hath made him the child of God." (Hooker, *Sermon of Faith*, at the end; see the whole Sermon.) See our notes on Phil. iii. 11, iv. 3.—The emphatic caution here has manifest reference to special dangers at Colossæ.

continue in] **Abide by, adhere to.** So Lightfoot, having regard to the special construction of the Greek.

the faith] So A.V. and R.V. Lightfoot says "perhaps '*your* faith' rather than '*the* faith'." And the contrast-parallel Rom. xi. 23 ("if they abide not still *in unbelief*") is distinctly in favour of this. The Colossians were to persist, for their very life, in the Divine simplicity *of believing*.

grounded] Lit., **founded, built on a foundation**; a perfect participle. Cp. Eph. iii. 17, where the basis is "love;" and Matt. vii. 25, where it is "a rock," the truth of Christ. Eph. iii. 17 offers an instructive parallel, connecting (as this passage does) "*faith*" with "*foundation.*" It is as believing that the Christian *enjoys the fixity* of the word, and of the love, of God.

settled] The Greek appears elsewhere only 1 Cor. vii. 37, xv. 58. Usage suggests the special thought of settled *purpose;* resulting here from a settled rest on eternal truth. Cp. 1 Pet. ii. 6—9.

be *not moved away*] Omit '*be.*" The Greek ("*moved away*") is a present participle, and suggests a state of chronic or frequent unsettlement, as new allurements away from the truth beset them. Cp. Eph. iv. 14.

the hope] "*That blissful hope, even the appearing of the glory, &c.*" (Tit. ii. 13); "*the hope of glory*" (below, ver. 27).

of the gospel, which ye have heard] So connect. "The hope" revealed *and* which was preached to every creature which is under heaven; whereof I Paul am made a minister; who now 24 rejoice in my sufferings for you, and fill up that which is

in the message of apostolic truth, brought them by Epaphras in the power of the Spirit,—this, and no rival to it, was to be their anchorage. Better, **which ye heard**, when you were evangelized and converted.

and *which was preached*] Omit "*and*." **Which was proclaimed**; lit., "*heralded.*"—Cp., for this verb with "*the gospel,*" e.g. Matt. iv. 23; Gal. ii. 2; 1 Thess. ii. 9.—The time-reference of "*was*" is, so to speak, ideal; it "*was*" done when the Saviour, in His accomplished victory, bade it be done (Mar. xvi. 15).

to every creature which] More lit., **in all the creation which**, &c. "The expression...must not be limited to man," says Lightfoot. But it is difficult to accept this. "All creation," in the largest sense, shall indeed in its way share the blessings of our salvation (see e.g. Rom. viii. 19—22; and cp. Rev. v. 13). But the thought here, and Mar. xvi. 15, is of *proclamation*, and *reception by faith*; in view of which we cannot, in any intelligible sense, bring in "rocks and stones and trees." Context surely limits the word to " our *fellow-creatures*," in the human sense.

under heaven] An hyperbole, in the technical sense; a *verbal* but not therefore *real* exaggeration, the excess of the phrase being meant only to leave a just impression of the surprise of the fact. See above on ver. 6 ("*in all the world*").—After all, if our remark on "*was preached*," just above, is right, this phrase like that is ideal, and in that respect not hyperbolical.

For the exact phrase cp. e.g. Gen. i. 9, vi. 17, vii. 19; Deut. ii. 25; Acts ii. 5, iv. 12.

whereof I Paul am made, &c.] **Became**, when the Lord called me to it. The same phrase occurs Eph. iii. 7. He emphasizes *his own* part and lot in the ministry of the Gospel, as he has just emphasized that Gospel itself as the veritable message of God, alone authentic amidst all false Gospels. So he asserts his own commission, authentic amidst all false evangelists. Cp. for instances of a similar emphatic *Ego*, 2 Cor. x. 1; Gal. v. 2; Eph. iii. 1 (with note in this Series); Philem. 19.

a minister] *Diáconos*. See above on ver. 7.

24—29 THE APOSTLE'S JOY, AND LABOUR, IN HIS MINISTRY

24. *Who*] This word is undoubtedly to be omitted, on the evidence of documents. Read, **Now I rejoice.**

now] as I review the glory of our Redeemer in His Person and His Work, the scope of His Gospel, the blessedness of His service.

rejoice in my sufferings] Cp. Eph. iii. 1, 13; Phil. ii. 17, 18.

"A pastor should always regard himself as the representative (*vicaire*) of the love of Jesus Christ towards His Church, not only for teaching, but also for suffering" (Quesnel, on this place).

behind of the afflictions of Christ in my flesh for his body's
25 sake, which is the church: whereof I am made a minister,

fill up.. afflictions of Christ] Lit., **fill up, as required, the lackings of the tribulations of Christ.** The verb rendered "*fill up*" by A.V. is a double compound (found here only in the Greek Scriptures) conveying the thought of a supply *occasioned by, fitted to, a demand.* (See Lightfoot's quotations.) The word rendered "*sufferings*" is better "*afflictions,*" or more exactly "*tribulations,*" "*troubles.*" It is nowhere else in N.T. used of our blessed Lord's experiences, though it occurs in the Psalm of the Crucifixion, xxii. (xxi. in the LXX.) 11. Its ordinary reference is not to the pains of *death* but to the toils and anguish of persecution, and generally to the trials of a burthened *life.*

Thus there is no suggestion here of any supplement added by Paul to the unique Sufferings of the Propitiator in His atoning Death; a sorrow and labour in which the Lord stood absolutely alone, unapproachable for ever by any or all of His people, " bearing their sins," " made a curse for them." The reference is to the toils, shame, and persecution of the Lord's life and labour as "*the Apostle* of our profession " (Heb. iii. 1), our supreme Evangelist and Pastor. In *these* "troubles," though indeed preeminent, He was not unique. He only "*began* to do and to teach " (Acts i. 1) personally what through His members He was to carry on to the end, and what was in this respect left incomplete when He quitted earth. Every true toiler and sufferer for Him and His flock contributes to the " filling up " of that incompleteness, so far as he toils and bears *in Christ.*

"The idea of expiation or satisfaction is wholly absent from this passage " (Lightfoot).

"The Apostle entered deep into the spirit of his suffering Master when he wrote those words, so embarrassing for the commentators, so edifying for the simple, where the sufferings of the disciple are made almost as necessary for the instruction of the Church as those of the Saviour for its redemption." (Ad. Monod, *Saint Paul, Cinq Discours,* p. 55.)

in my flesh] Connect these words with "*fill up,*" not with "*afflictions of Christ*" as some expositors. True, "in all their affliction He is afflicted" (Isai. lxiii. 9); and so in a tender sense He was "afflicted in " His servant's " flesh," his sensibilities and powers in bodily life. But, as Lightfoot points out, this explanation here is out of harmony with the verb "*fill up as required.*" The thought is of tribulations necessary for the practical ends of gathering in and building up the Church.

for his body's sake, &c.] Cp. 2 Tim. ii. 10, a close parallel. For the sake of the glorious Head, the spiritual Body becomes Paul's absorbing interest.

On the words "*body*" and " *Church* " see above, on ver. 18.

25. *whereof*] That is, of the Church; on behalf of it, serving its holy interests.

Colossians 1 / 91

according to the dispensation of God which is given to me
for you, to fulfil the word of God; *even* the mystery which 26
hath been hid from ages and from generations, but now is
made manifest to his saints: to whom God would make 27

according to] His "ministry" was *conditioned* and *guided* by the terms of "the dispensation" just about to be mentioned.
the dispensation] Better, **the stewardship.** So Eph. iii. 2, a close parallel. For the figure see 1 Cor. iv. 1, 2, ix. 17; 1 Pet. iv. 10. And cp. Matt. xiii. 52.—On Eph. i. 10, where the word occurs in a somewhat different phase of meaning, see note in this Series.
It is almost needless to say that the N.T. use of the figure of stewardship has regard to the minister's duty to *provide* the household of God with the food of truth, and not to any supposed right or duty to *reserve* that food.
fulfil the word of God] I.e. in the light of the context, not to "accomplish His promise," but to "develope, unfold, His message to the full." Cp. Rom. xv. 19; "I have fully preached (lit., *fulfilled*) the Gospel of Christ."
26. *the mystery*] I.e. as always in N.T., a truth undiscoverable except by revelation, a holy *secret;* whether or no, when revealed, it is what we can or cannot understand. See our note on Eph. i. 9. We have this "secret" unveiled and described just below. Lightfoot points out that the Greek word *mustêrion*, "*mystery*," is "not the only term borrowed from the ancient mysteries [rites of special and secret initiation, lying, in a sense, apart from and behind the popular heathen worship] which St Paul employs to describe the teaching of the Gospel." He gives instances from ver. 28 below, Phil. iv. 12, and perhaps Eph. i. 14. "There is this difference however, that whereas the heathen mysteries were strictly confined to a narrow circle, the Christian mysteries are freely communicated to all. There is therefore an intentional paradox in the employment of the image by St Paul."— And this may have had regard here to the suggestion by the alien teachers at Colossæ that they had *esoteric* truths to tell to their disciples.
hid] Cp. esp. 1 Cor. ii. 7—10; Eph. iii. 9. And see for cognate truth Matt. xi. 25; Luke x. 21.
from ages and from generations] Cp. "*from the beginning of the world*," Eph. iii. 9; where lit., "*from the ages.*" Here lit., **from the ages,** &c., or, as well paraphrased in R.V., **from all ages,** &c. "*From*" is here a preposition of time; "*ever since ages and generations were;*" through all developments of the history of intelligent creation, whether longer ("*ages,*" *æons*), or more limited ("*generations*"). See our note on Eph. iii. 9.
now] "When the fulness of the time was come," Gal. iv. 4. Cp. Eph. iii. 5, 9, 10.
revealed] Historically, in the Incarnation, Sacrifice, and Triumph of Christ; personally and spiritually (1 Cor. ii. 10), by the Holy Ghost dealing with the man.
27. *would*] Lit., **willed,** or (as R.V.) **was pleased.** All was sovereign mercy. Cp. Matt. xi. 27.

known what *is* the riches of the glory of this mystery among the Gentiles; which is Christ in you, the hope of glory:

the riches of the glory] "*Riches*" is a favourite term with St Paul, in reference to Divine things. Cp. Rom. ii. 4, x. 12, xi. 12, 33; 1 Cor. i. 5; 2 Cor. viii. 9, ix. 11; Eph. i. 7, ii. 4, 7, iii. 8; Phil. iv. 19; below, ii. 2. For this exact phrase, so pregnant with light and joy, "*riches of glory*," see Rom. ix. 23; Eph. i. 18 (a close parallel), iii. 16.

"*Glory:*"—the word so used gives us the thought not only of greatness, wonder, and bliss, but of GOD as the secret of it all.

among the Gentiles] Lit., "*in the Gentiles.*" i.e., this "wealth of glory" in the disclosed mystery is now shewn to the saints as realized in Gentile as well as Jewish believers. The "Mystery" is, in fact, the Divine plan of a Church gathered from all mankind, and filled, in its every member, and in the resulting total of its life and power, with Jesus Christ. For commentary, see the Ep. to the Ephesians, esp. ii. 11—iii. 21.

which is] "The mystery passes into the living Christ" (Bp Alexander, in *The Speaker's Commentary*).

Christ in you] The rendering "*among you*" (A.V., margin) is equally good grammatically. Alford and Ellicott adopt it, while remarking that it includes and implies "*in you.*" Lightfoot, not without hesitation, thinks "*in you*" more probable. R.V. retains "*in you*," without marginal alternative. This surely is right. The deeply kindred passage in Eph. ii. culminates with the wonderful possibility and fact of the "dwelling of Christ *in our hearts* by faith;" it makes this the central sanctuary, so to speak, of the work and experience of grace. In this briefer but equally intense passage it seems congruous that the climax of thought should be the same.—We would say rather that "*in you*" includes and implies "*among you*" than *vice versâ*. This appears to be, on the whole, Lightfoot's view. He compares (besides Eph. iii.) Rom. viii. 10; 2 Cor. xiii. 5; Gal. iv. 19. And see Gal. i. 16, ii. 20; Rev. iii. 20.

True, "Christ *in you*" is a thought not identical with "Christ *dwelling in the heart.*" The latter (see our notes on Eph. iii. 17) is so to speak the development and full realization of the former. But we mean that the tone of these words, in the light of the fuller kindred (Ephesian) passage, leads us rightly to see *here* the richest possible meaning in the briefer phrase.

the hope of glory] See again Eph. iii. for commentary. The Indwelling of the Lord in the saints, received by faith, in the power of the Holy Ghost, is connected by indissoluble links of truth and thought with the foreview of blessings "in the Church, in Christ Jesus, throughout all ages."

Who shall discuss and analyse such a statement? It is a matter for adoring wonder, simplest faith, and a most blessed and genuine experience, now as when it was written. While our justification in Christ is, from one all-important point, the sure reason and pledge of our coming "glory" (Rom. v. 1—2), Christ's most true and living presence

Colossians 1 / 93

whom we preach, warning every man, and teaching every 28
man in all wisdom; that we may present every man perfect

as the Risen One in us is, as it were, the very bud of the celestial flower, the actual dawn of the eternal day. Cp. 1 Tim. i. 1.

"*Glory:*"—undoubtedly, in connexion with the word "*hope,*" the word points to the heavenly Future, in which alike in the saint and in the Church of the saints the unveiled Face of God will develope an eternity of holy bliss and power, all drawn from Him and all spent for Him. Cp. Psal. lxxiii. 24; Acts vii. 55; Rom. v. 2, viii. 18, 21; 2 Cor. iv. 17; Eph. i. 18; Phil. iii. 21; below, iii. 4; 1 Thess. ii. 12; 2 Thess. ii. 14; 2 Tim. ii. 10; 1 Pet. v. 1, 4, 10; Jude 24; Rev. xxi. 11, 23.

28. *we*] Emphatic. He has the alien emissaries in mind.

preach] Slightly better, as R.V., **proclaim.** The Greek word recurs with Christ as its living Object, Acts xvii. 3; Phil. i. 16, 18.

warning] Better, as R.V., **admonishing**; a word which is rather more general in its scope. The kindred noun occurs Eph. vi. 4.

every man...every man...every man] Perhaps this solemn emphasis has a double reference; (*a*) as Lightfoot, to the universality of the Gospel, whose "counsels of perfection" are not (as the false teachers would have it, in *their* "Gospel") for a privileged inner circle of votaries but for every one without exception who comes to Jesus Christ; and (*b*) to the fact that in this universality the individual is never lost or merged in the community; *each soul, each life,* as if there were no other, is to be "perfect in Christ."

in all wisdom] In the whole field of that holy "wisdom" which is not a mere mass of knowledge but the principles and secrets of a life of faith and love. It is better to explain this phrase thus than as meaning that "we" teach with perfect wisdom. This would less fully bring out the emphasis (so strong in the Greek) of "*every,*" "*all,*" in this verse. The point is that *every* disciple may and should learn *every* secret of grace. There are no spiritual secrets *behind the Gospel.*

that we may present] when the Lord returns, and the pastor "gives his account" (Heb. xiii. 17). See for another side of the same prospect, Eph. v. 27.

perfect] *Teleion.* In this word Lightfoot sees a technical term of the pagan "mysteries," borrowed and adapted for the Gospel. In the mysteries, the *teleios,* or "perfect," was the man who had passed his novitiate and was fully instructed. The term was certainly used by the Gnostics of the sub-apostolic age to denote the man who had passed from mere "*faith*" (so called) into "*knowledge*" (so called). See Lightfoot's full and instructive note, in which he further remarks that the word "*perfect*" is early used in Christian literature to distinguish the baptized man from the catechumen. But we doubt whether the word here can with any certainty be viewed as quasi-technical, or however whether such can be its *main* bearing. It appears in e.g. Matt. v. 48, with the apparent meaning of spiritual entirety, whole-heartedness, in the life of love; and cp. 1 Cor. xiv.

94 / Colossians 2

29 in Christ Jesus: whereunto I also labour, striving according to his working, which worketh in me mightily.

2 For I would that ye knew what great conflict I have for

20; Heb. v. 14; where it is "full-grown," adult, as different from infantine. So Eph. iv. 13, and perhaps Jas. iii. 2; 1 Joh. iv. 18. Not initiation so much as developed maturity of conscience, faith, life, experience is the thought of this passage.

in Christ Jesus] vital union with whom is the *sine quâ non* of growth and maturity, because of spiritual life altogether.—The word "*Jesus*" is to be omitted, by documentary evidence.

29. *also*] i.e. "*actually*," "as a matter of fact."

labour] The Greek verb denotes *toil even to weariness*. It (or its cognate noun) occurs e.g. 1 Cor. xv. 10, 58; Gal. iv. 11; Phil. ii. 16; 1 Thess. i. 3, v. 12; 1 Tim. iv. 10; 2 Tim. ii. 6; Rev. ii. 2, 3.

striving] The Greek verb (our word "*agony*" is the descendant of a cognate) occurs e.g. Luke xiii. 24; 1 Cor. ix. 25; below, iv. 12; 1 Tim. vi. 12; and a cognate, Phil. i. 30 (see note); below, ii. 1 (see note); 1 Thess. ii. 2; Heb. xii. 1 ("*race*" A.V.). By usage, the word gives the thought of the strife and stress of the athletic arena; a thought conspicuous in e.g. 1 Cor. ix. 25; 1 Tim. vi. 12. It thus conveys an impression of contest *with obstacles* in view of a definite *goal*.

See our note on a similar phrase, Phil. i. 27.

according to, &c.] Observe the intimation, at once restful and animating, that the presence and movement within him of the power ("*working*," *energeia*) of God were the force behind all his apostolic activity. "By Him he moves, in Him he lives;" while yet the man's "moving" and "living" is none the less genuinely personal. Cp. 1 Cor. xv. 10; 2 Cor. iii. 5, iv. 7, xii. 9, 10; Phil. ii. 12, 13, iv. 13; and above, ver. 11.

mightily] Lit. and better, **in power**. Cp. above ver. 11, and note.

"*Christ in him*" was for St Paul not only "the hope of glory" but also the mainspring of action; the secret of a "power" which was anything but violence, or disorder, but which brought with it a wonderful victory and an inexhaustible energy of life and love. For every "recipient of Christ" (Joh. i. 12) the same secret is to do the same work, as it is reverently recognized and welcomed, according to each one's path of duty and service.

CH. ii. 1—7 HIS LABOUR OF PRAYER FOR THE COLOSSIANS AND OTHER UNVISITED CONVERTS: THERE IS NEED, FOR ERRORS ARE IN THE AIR

1. *For, &c.*] He takes up the word "*striving*," just used, and justifies it by telling them of a certain special "*strife*" of his on their behalf.

I would that ye knew] Lit. and better, **I wish you to know**. So 1 Cor. xi. 3; and cp. e.g. Rom. i. 13; 2 Cor. i. 8.

Colossians 2 / 95

you, and *for* them at Laodicea, and *for* as many as have not seen my face in the flesh; that their hearts might be ² comforted, being knit together in love, and unto all riches

conflict] *Agôn.* See note on i. 29 ("*striving*").—Here is the present special form of his pastoral "wrestling" on their behalf. It is (see next verse) the "strife" of prayer; "I will not let Thee go except Thou bless" *them* (Gen. xxxii. 26). See, for the efforts of another similar "wrestler," iv. 12 below.

Laodicea] Cp. iv. 13, 15, 16; Rev. iii. 14. "The rich, commercial city of Laodicea, formerly called Diospolis, afterwards Rhoas, and subsequently Laodicea, in honour of Laodice, wife of Antiochus II. [261—246 B.C.], was situated on the river Lycus, about eighteen [eleven?] English miles to the west of Colossæ and about six miles south of Hierapolis, which latter city is not improbably hinted at in ['*as many as,*' &c.]" (Ellicott). "The ruins at the present day are of vast extent, and indicate the importance of Laodicea" (Lewin, *Life and Epp. of St Paul*, i. 357; see an engraved view, *ibid.*, opposite p. 360). See further, *Introd.*, p. 13.

and as many as have not seen, &c.] These words, *taken with the context*, naturally mean that St Paul had never personally visited Colossæ, Laodicea, and their district. The opposite view has been maintained, as e.g. by Mr Lewin (who however withdrew his argument later; see his work just quoted, i. 172 note). No doubt the mere phraseology here is ambiguous; "*and as many, &c.*" may denote equally either *a different* class of persons from those just named, or *the rest of the same* class. But the latter alternative is strongly favoured both by the simplicity of reference natural in a passage so fervent and so passing, and by the history. See further *Introd.*, p. 20.

my face] "*My parson*" (*persona*), Tyndale, Cranmer; "*my person*," Geneva. Tyndale no doubt follows Luther's *meine Person.*

2. *comforted*] *Ut consolentur*, Latin Versions. But the Greek verb means more than to console; it is rather to hearten, to encourage. *Confortatio*, the (late) Latin original of our "*comfort*," is "to make *fortis, strong;*" and "*comfort*" long retained this meaning in English. Wyclif here has "*counfortid;*" and in his version of Isai. xli. 7 he actually writes "*he coumfortide hym with nailes*, that it shulde not be moued" (*Bible Word-Book*, p. 117).

being] Better, **they being**; the Greek participle agrees not with "*hearts*" but with the owners of the hearts.

knit together] Cp. below ver. 19, and Eph. iv. 16 (a suggestive parallel). The Greek verb always in the LXX. means "*to instruct*"; and the Latin Versions here have *instructi* (hence Wyclif, "*taughte*"); which however *may* mean "*drawn up*," "*marshalled,*" and so may be nearly the same as A.V. The parallels just quoted are decisive for A.V.

in love] "which is *the bond* of perfectness," iii. 14. Cp. Eph. iv. 2, 3; Phil. ii. 1—4.

and unto all riches] The saints, drawn together *in* love, would by

of the full assurance of understanding, to the acknowledgement of the mystery of God and of the Father, and of

the loving communication of experience and by other spiritual aid, all advance *to* a fuller knowledge of the Lord and His grace.—On "*riches*" see note on i. 27.

the full assurance] "*Fulness*" R.V. margin; Latin Versions, *plenitudo, adimpletio*. The Greek word recurs 1 Thess. i. 5; Heb. vi. 11, x. 22; and nowhere else in Biblical or classical Greek. In all these passages the word "*fulness*" would give an adequate meaning. But the cognate verb, which is more frequent, appears by usage to convey the idea of, so to speak, *an active* fulness, a fulness having to do with consciousness. This is an argument for retaining (with Ellicott, Alford, Lightfoot, R.V. text) the A.V. rendering.—He prays that they may more and more enter into the "wealth" of *a deep and conscious insight* into "the mystery of God."

understanding] See on i. 9 above.

to the acknowledgement] This clause is the echo and explanation of the last; "*unto* all the riches &c., *unto* the acknowledgement &c."

"*Acknowledgement*":—*epignôsis;* see on i. 9 above.

the mystery of God, and of the Father, and of Christ] "The ancient authorities vary much in the text of this passage" (margin, R.V.).—The chief variants are as follows: (*a*) "*the mystery of God*"; adopted by Tischendorf in his 7th (last but one) edition of the N.T., and by Alford: (*b*) "*the mystery of God*, even *Christ*," or, as the same Greek may be rendered, "*the mystery of the* (or, *our*) *God Christ*"; adopted, with the first alternative translation, by Tischendorf in his 8th (last) edition, Tregelles, Wordsworth, Lightfoot, Westcott and Hort, and R.V.: (*c*) "*the mystery of God, which is Christ*": (*d*) "*the mystery of God the Father of Christ*": (*e*) the reading represented by A.V., which is that of most later MSS. Lightfoot in a long and careful note (pp. 318, 319) reasons for the high probability of reading (*b*), and for regarding all others as formed from it either by explanatory addition or by cutting a knot of supposed difficulty by omission. Dr Scrivener (*Introd. to N.T. Criticism*, pp. 634—6) also discusses the case, with Lightfoot's reasoning among other things before him, and inclines to the same *reading*, though apparently preferring the other *rendering* given above. His only difficulty lies in the small documentary support given to a reading in itself otherwise so likely. And he says, "The more we think over this reading, the more it grows upon us, as the source from which all the rest are derived. At present, perhaps, ['*of God the Father of Christ*'] may be looked upon as the most strongly attested, ...but a very small weight might suffice to turn the critical scale."

Adopting the reading thus accepted by Lightfoot and favoured by Scrivener, how shall we render it? Shall we say, "*the mystery of the God Christ*"? The phrase would convey eternal truth; but *as a phrase* it has no precise parallel in St Paul. To him Christ is indeed absolutely Divine, Coequal in Nature with the Father; but this truth is always seen, so to speak, through His Sonship, so that He is designated rather

Christ; in whom are hid all the treasures of wisdom and 3

"the Son of God" than simply "God." (See however Acts xx. 28; Tit. ii. 13.) Shall we say "*the mystery of the God of Christ*"? Here a near parallel appears Eph. i. 17. But the preceding context here (esp. i. 27) distinctly inclines to our connecting "*the mystery*" with "*Christ*," so that He shall be the Father's "Secret" of "all spiritual blessing" (Eph. i. 3) for His people; their all-blessed Resource, hidden yet open, for "pardon, and holiness, and heaven." Cp. 1 Cor. i. 30, where "*wisdom*" is in a certain sense equivalent to "*mystery*" here.
So we render, **the mystery of God, even Christ**.

3. *in whom*] Christ, the Secret of God, is now *characterized* as such; the Secret is—*Christ as the Treasury of wisdom and knowledge*.

are hid &c.] Better, regarding the order of the Greek, **in whom are all the treasures,** &c., **hidden (there)**. The thought that they are "hidden" is emphasized.—See below, note on "*wisdom* &c."

all] So that He is absolutely sufficient, and supposed supplies from elsewhere are a delusion. So "*all riches*" just above; and i. 19.

the treasures] A rich (and frequent) plural.

wisdom and knowledge] Words recurring together Rom. xi. 33; 1 Cor. xii. 8. In such a passage they are scarcely perhaps to be minutely distinguished[1] (as they must be in 1 Cor. xii.); they blend into the one idea of the resources of the Divine Mind. For surely here, as in Rom. xi. (a near parallel), it is the wisdom and knowledge *of God* which are in view; a point not noticed by Ellicott, Alford, or Lightfoot. (There is doubtless a *reflected* reference here to human speculation, exercised upon the treasures of Divine thought.)

The treasures of this Divine "wisdom and knowledge" are in Christ "*hiddenly*" (Ellicott), inasmuch as they are (*a*) to be found in Him alone, (*b*) to be found therefore only by entrance into Him, (*c*) never, even so, to be "found out unto perfection."—The Greek word, as Lightfoot shews, is in all likelihood borrowed from the heretical vocabulary, and transfigured. The embryo "Gnostic" of St Paul's days probably, as his successors certainly, gloried in an alleged possession of inner, esoteric, secrets of being and of knowing, treasured in books thence called *apocryphal* (*secret, hidden*); a word identical with the Greek adjective here (*apocruphoi*). (So that, in the Fathers, by "apocryphal" books are not meant the Jewish religious books we commonly call so, but the "secret" literature of the heretical sects.)

Christ is thus the glorious "Apocrypha" (if we may dare to say so) of the Christian; our "esoteric wisdom" is only an ever-deepening

---

[1] Where wisdom (*sophia*) and knowledge (*gnôsis*) have to be distinguished, the essential difference appears to be that *sophia* is a moral-mental term, *gnôsis* a term purely mental, or rather one which fixes attention on the cognition of truth simply as such. Conceivably, the man of "knowledge" *may* stop with a mere sight of truth; the man of "wisdom" reflects upon it, receives it, in a way affecting character and action. The words "wise," "wisdom," in the Greek, are thus "never in Scripture ascribed to other than God or good men, except in an ironical sense" (Trench, *N.T. Synonyms*, 2nd Series).

4 knowledge. And this I say, lest any *man* should beguile
5 you with enticing words. For though I be absent in the
flesh, yet am I with you in the spirit, joying and beholding
6 your order, and the stedfastness of your faith in Christ. As

insight into HIM revealed.—"Jesus Christ is a great Book. He who can indeed study Him in the word of God will know all he ought to know. Humility opens this Divine Book, faith reads in it, love learns from it" (Quesnel).

4. *And this I say, lest* &c.] He states the precise practical occasion of such a general statement of truth. It is, the danger now surrounding the Colossians, and of which Paul, though absent, is keenly and lovingly cognizant.

beguile you] Lit., "*reason you aside*," "*lead you astray by reasoning.*"

enticing words] Almost, "*a persuasive style*," as distinguished from the power of solid facts truly presented and received. The pretensions of speculative heresy, always flattering man rather than humbling him, would answer this description exactly.—R.V., **persuasiveness of speech.** —"The subtlety of human reasonings has always been the stumbling-block of faith" (Quesnel).

5. *For*] He means that he knows the need of such warning, though he is so far away. He is close to them "*in spirit.*"

in the spirit] Is this the human spirit or the Divine? 1 Cor. v. 4 (with 3) appears to decide for the former. It is scarcely enough to say (as Lightfoot) that this is "the common antithesis of flesh and spirit, or body and spirit;" for in many important passages (e.g. Gal. v. 16—18) the antithesis to "*the flesh*" is precisely the Divine Spirit dwelling in the man. And here the meaning might well be (cp. 2 Cor. xii. 2, 3) that in some way supernatural the Holy Spirit gave him, in spite of bodily absence, a mysterious presence of intuitive consciousness. But the tone of the context is in favour of a simpler meaning; and "*flesh*," here used evidently in its most literal sense, points the same way. And so the words "*my spirit*" (1 Cor. v. 4) present a true parallel and explanation; though even there a certain mystery seems to be indicated. He is *present* in the sense of spiritual love and influence.—Jerome compares Elisha and Gehazi (2 Kings v. 26).

joying and beholding] The "*joy*" of what he hears of them leads him more vividly to "*behold*" them, as if in actual view.—Observe his loving wish to dwell even here on their brighter side.

order...stedfastness] Both words are military; Lightfoot renders them **orderly array** and **solid front** respectively. "The enforced companionship of St Paul with the soldiers of the Prætorian Guard at this time (Phil. i. 13) might have suggested this image. At all events in the contemporary Epistle (Eph. vi. 14 sq.) we have an elaborate metaphor from the armour of a soldier" (Lightfoot).

"*Stedfastness* (*solidity*) *of your faith*":—cp. Acts xvi. 5 (lit., "*grew solid in* (or *by*) *their faith*"); 1 Pet. v. 9 (lit., "*whom resist, solid in* (or *by*) *your faith* ").—The "solidity" in all these places implies at once the compact spiritual steadiness of the community and (the true and neces-

ye have therefore received Christ Jesus the Lord, *so* walk
ye in him : rooted and built up in him, and stablished in 7

sary condition to such steadiness) the simplicity and thoroughness of the
individual as a believer.

6. *As ye have therefore* &c.] As if to say, "I see with joy your
present stedfast faith and consequent holy union; therefore I entreat
you at once to stay there and to grow there, for you will be tempted
towards a very different region otherwise."

"*Have received*":—somewhat better, **did receive**, at their conversion.—
The Greek word rendered "*receive*" is frequently used of the reception
of *teaching*,—learning; and no doubt the reference is mainly to their
"reception" from their missionary (i. 7) of the revealed *truth*. See
further just below. But Ellicott well says that "the object [Christ] is
so emphatically specified" as to imply that "they received...Christ
Himself, in Himself the sum and substance of all teaching." Cp. Joh.
i. 12; 1 Joh. v. 11, 12.

Christ Jesus the Lord] Lightfoot punctuates and renders, **the Christ,
even Jesus the Lord**; taking the reference to be to their having learned
and welcomed as the true *Christ* (Messiah) not the speculative "Christ"
of the heretics but the historic *Jesus* of the Incarnation and the Cross.
This rendering (in view of the Greek) strongly commends itself to us,
though R.V. retains A.V. In any case, however, the solemn emphasis
of the whole phrase points in the direction of thought indicated by
Lightfoot.

"*The Lord*":—doubtless in the highest sense of the word. Cp.
Phil. ii. 11.

walk ye in him] "Let your *actual life* as believers be guarded and
guided by this Lord thus received." He warns them of the danger, amidst
heretical surroundings, of an *unapplied* orthodoxy. If they would be
both firm and vigorous they must put truth into life.—On the word
"*walk*" see above on i. 10. It occurs often in these Epistles of the
Captivity; eight times in Eph., four times in Col., twice in Phil.

"*In Him*":—see on i. 2 above.

7. *rooted*] A perfect participle. It recurs Eph. iii. 17, the only
other place in which St Paul uses precisely this metaphor, which combines the thought of fixity with that of derived and developing life from
a genial source. There, as here, the metaphor of *building* (more frequent with St Paul) appears, in the Greek, beside this other.

built up] See the last remark. The Greek is a present participle, to
be expressed in (not quite classical) English by, **being built up**. See for
a close parallel Eph. ii. 22; and cp. i. 23 above.—The compound verb
here gives the thought of *building upon*, and the reference might be
taken to be to Christ as the Foundation (1 Cor. iii. 11). But the
phrase "*in* Him" just below suggests here another of the many sides of
His relation to the "building"; and leads us to explain this of the
internal "building up" of the community as new members join it and
cohere with it; and also of the individual, as layers (so to speak) of experience and spiritual character accrue in his life and walk. The *present*
participle is thus clearly suitable.

the faith, as ye have been taught, abounding therein with thanksgiving.

8 Beware lest any *man* spoil you through philosophy and

in Him] as He is the "Stone of the angle" (Eph. ii. 20) "in" which the converging lines of structure hold together. Cp. i. 17.—But this imagery must not be pressed too far, for "*in Him*" relates here to "*rooted*" as well as "*built up.*"

stablished] Again a present participle.

in the faith] Omit "*in*," and render, with Lightfoot, and R.V. margin, **by your faith**. Their faith, their submissive personal reliance on their Lord, would "strike their *root* downward" and compact their spiritual *structure*; and so it would make them continuously more stable. "Faith is, as it were, the cement of the building" (Lightfoot).

as ye have been taught] Better, **as ye were taught**, when Epaphras evangelized them. Then they learnt *Whom* to believe in, and *how* to believe in Him, for righteousness and life.

abounding] A favourite word with St Paul. It occurs five times in Philippians. Nothing short of spiritual wealth, and its full employment, ever satisfies him.

therein] In your faith, regarded as "the sphere" of the sense of "abundance." Loyal reliance on the all-sufficient Christ was to be largely, fully, exercised.

with thanksgiving] Lit., "*in thanksgiving.*" Thanksgiving was to attend, to surround, this large exercise of faith. It would do so as a matter of *reason*; for the possession of such an Object of faith was indeed ground enough for holy gratitude. And it would do so also as a matter of *experience*; for there is no surer secret for a glad thankfulness than full habitual reliance on the Christ of God.

"The words ["*thankful, give thanks, thanksgiving*"] occur in St Paul's writings alone of the apostolic Epistles. In this Epistle especially the duty of thanksgiving assumes a peculiar prominence by being made a refrain, as here and in iii. 15, 17, iv. 2; see also i. 12" (Lightfoot).

8—15. WARNING AGAINST ALIEN TEACHINGS : CHRIST IS ALL FOR PEACE AND LIFE

8. *Beware* &c.] Quite lit., "*See lest any one shall be your spoiler*"; the positive and imminent risk being indicated by the future tense ("*shall be*"), quite anomalous in such constructions.

any man] "This indefinite [expression] is frequently used by St Paul, when speaking of opponents whom he knows well enough but does not care to name" (Lightfoot). Cp. Rom. iii. 8; 1 Cor. xi. 16, xiv. 37, xv. 12; 2 Cor. iii. 1, x. 2, 12, xi. 20, 21; Gal. i. 7, 9; above, ver. 4, below ver. 16; 2 Thess. ii. 3, iii. 10, 11; 1 Tim. i. 3, 6, vi. 3, 21.

spoil you] Better, with R.V., **maketh spoil of you**. The Greek word is not known in earlier Greek literature, but its form leaves no doubt of its meaning.—The false teachers would not merely "despoil"

vain deceit, after the tradition of men, after the rudiments

the Colossians of certain spiritual convictions and blessings, but would lead *them* away captives, as their deluded adherents and devotees. Lightfoot compares 2 Tim. iii. 6.

through philosophy...deceit] We may fairly represent the Greek, sacrificing precise literality, thus: **through his empty deceit of a philosophy.** No doubt the false teachers posed as great intellectualists, and took care to present their "gospel" as something congruous in kind with existing speculations, Greek or Eastern, about knowing and being. They would say little or nothing like " *Thus it is written*, and thus it behoved Christ to suffer and to rise......and that repentance and remission...should be preached in His name " (Luke xxiv. 46, 47); but rather " Thus the finite stands related to the Infinite; thus spirit is eternally differenced from matter, and thus it secures its emancipation from its material chain."

Lightfoot in an interesting note traces the word "*Philosophy*" from its alleged origin in the modesty of Pythagoras (cent. 6 B.C.), who declined the title of "*wise*" (*sophos*), preferring that of "*wisdom-lover*" (*philosophos*), to its later association with "subtle dialectics and profitless speculation," as in St Paul's age. And he remarks on two different views about pagan Philosophy represented among the Fathers; that of e.g. Clement of Alexandria (cent. 2—3), who regarded it as "not only a preliminary training...for the Gospel, but even as in some sense a covenant...given by God to the Greeks"; and that of e.g. Tertullian (at the same date) who saw a positive antithesis between "the philosopher" and "the Christian." Lightfoot remarks that St Paul's speech at Athens "shows that his sympathies would have been at least as strong" with Clement as with Tertullian. Can we go quite so far? Surely the *main drift* of his teaching emphasizes the tendency of independent speculation—not to discover facts destructive of the Gospel; no such timid misgivings beset him; but—to foster mental habits hostile to a submissive welcome to the Gospel. Cp. esp. 1 Cor. i. 17—iii. 23.

"Folly indeed it is," says Quesnel, "to seek to establish a science wholly Divine on foundations wholly human. And this is what they do who seek to judge of the things of faith by the principles of philosophy."

tradition] *Paradosis.* Cp. 1 Cor. xi. 2; 2 Thess. ii. 15, iii. 6; for this word used in a good sense, that of apostolic teaching and precept. Strictly, it means what is "*handed on*," and so may mean, by connexion, either (as here) an esoteric "*deposit*," passed down as it were along the line of the initiated, or simply "*teaching*," the conveyance of opinion or knowledge in any way from one mind to another.—It is remarkable that in this latter sense, very commonly, the word "tradition" is used by the Fathers to mean simply Scripture; "*evangelic*" or "*apostolic tradition*" denoting respectively *the teaching* of *the Gospels* and *the Epistles*.—Here, however, obviously the word inclines to its worse reference; the more or less esoteric teaching about things unseen, "handed on" in the heretical circles, not published in the daylight.

102 / Colossians 2

9 of the world, and not after Christ. For in him dwelleth all
10 the fulness of the Godhead bodily. And ye are complete

of men] Whereas the Apostle's mission and Gospel was "not of men, neither by man" (Gal. i. 1) nor "according to man" (*ibid.*, 11). He "neither received it of man, nor was taught it, but by revelation from Jesus Christ" (*ibid.*, 12). Nothing is more emphatic in St Paul than this assertion of the strictly and directly superhuman, Divine, origin of the Gospel as a message.

rudiments] Cp. Gal. iv. 3.—The Greek word means a first beginning, or principle (see Liddell and Scott's *Greek Lexicon*, under στοιχεῖον), for instance, as a simple vocal *sound* (that e.g. of the letter *r*) is a first element in speech. Hence it comes to mean "*an element*" in knowledge, or instruction; and hence, elementary instruction. The same word also denoted the *heavenly bodies*, regarded as the *first grounds* of measurement of time; and many ancient expositors saw this meaning here, as if the Apostle had in view the observance of "days, and months, and seasons, and years" (Gal. iv. 10). But Lightfoot points out that (*a*) the reference here is to some *mode of teaching*, (*b*) the observance of "times" was too subordinate a factor in the errors in question to be thus named as a part for the whole. See his note here and also on Gal. iv. 3.—The Apostle has in view the pre-Christian ordinances of e.g. sacrifice and circumcision, regarded as temporary, introductory to the Gospel, and now therefore to be laid aside. *In their place*, they were Divine; *out of their place*, they are "of the world."

On the word στοιχεῖον see further Grimm's *N.T. Lexicon*, ed. Thayer.

of the world] Belonging to an order not spiritual but only mechanical, material. See the last words of the previous note. For such a reference of the word *cosmos* cp. 1 Cor. i. 20.

not after Christ] "Christ is neither the author nor the substance of [this] teaching" (Lightfoot). The holy and necessary exclusiveness of the Gospel cannot admit such "traditions" and "elements" even as subordinate allies. They must absolutely give way before it.

9. *For*] He is about to shew that "Christ" is the antithesis of this false gospel in two respects; (*a*) His glorious Person is all in all as the substance of the true Gospel; (*b*) His code of resulting observance appears not in an ascetic rule but in a life of liberty and purity in union with the Risen Lord Himself.

in him dwelleth &c.] See above on i. 19.

the Godhead] The Greek word (*theotēs*) stands here alone in the N.T. It is as strong as possible; *Deity*, not only *Divinity*, which is a word much more elastic and inclusive.—The Latin Versions have *divinitas* here; and the word *deitas* was coined later, on purpose to express the true force of *theotēs*. See Lightfoot, who quotes Trench's *Synonyms*.

bodily] "'Bodily-wise,' 'corporeally'; with a bodily manifestation" (Lightfoot).—From all eternity the Divine Plenitude had "dwelt" in the Son of the Father. But in the Incarnation of the Son this in-

Colossians 2 / 103

in him, which is the head of all principality and power:
in whom also ye are circumcised with the circumcision 11
made without hands, in putting off the body of the sins

dwelling had been, "for us men and our salvation," conditioned by the fact of the Lord's true human Body. In that Body, and through it, was manifested His union with us, and was wrought out His work for us in life and death. From Him now exalted, not only as the Son but as the Son Incarnate, Slain, and Risen, radiates to all His members the Holy Ghost (Rev. v. 6). So, for us, the Divine Plenitude dwells in Him "bodily-wise"; not circumscribed by His holy human Body, which "is in heaven and not here" (see the last Rubric of the Communion Office), but eternally conditioned, as to our fruition of It, by the fact of His Incarnation.

10. *And ye are complete in him*] Lit. and better **And ye are** (emphatic) **in Him filled full**; or perhaps, with Lightfoot, **And ye are in Him, filled full**—two statements in one; you *are in* Him, and you are *filled full* in Him. You are in immediate union with Him, and in that union you possess, potentially and as you need it, all grace, as possessing Him in whom is all the Fulness. Cp. Eph. i. 23 and our notes.—The word rendered "*complete*" is a grammatical echo of the word just above rendered "*Fulness*" or "*Plenitude*."

Such are the resources of the believer, and of the Church, in their wonderful union with the Lord. What need then of alien and lower secrets of succour and strength?

which is the head &c.] See on i. 19 above. All the personal Powers of the Unseen, however real and glorious, are but limbs (in their order of being) of this Head; therefore no nearer to Him than you are, and no less dependent on Him. Live then on the Fountain, not on Its streams; use to the full the fulness which in Christ *is* yours.

11. *in whom*] The truth of the holy Union of members and Head is again in view. What he is about to speak of was done by the fact of, by virtue of, their oneness with Christ.

are circumcised] Better, **were circumcised,** when you entered "into Christ." They already *had* that Divine Reality, the sacred but obsolete type of which the new teachers now pressed upon them. As regarded order, ceremonial, deed and seal of conveyance, they acquired this in their Baptism; as regarded inward and ultimate reality they acquired it by believing on the name of the Son of God. See Joh. i. 12; cp. 1 Joh. v. 1.—Baptism is the Sacrament of Faith, and *never*, in principle and idea, to be dissociated from its Thing (*Res*), as if its work was done where the Thing is not truly present.

made without hands] It is a thing of the spiritual, eternal, order, the immediate work of the will of God.—Cp. 2 Cor. v. 1.—Is this "circumcision" simply holy Baptism? No, surely, but that "inward and spiritual grace" of which Baptism is the sacramental Seal, "a death unto sin and a new birth unto righteousness" (Church Catechism). It is vital union with Christ, through faith, by the Holy Spirit (see 1 Cor. vi. 17), viewed as our separation from the condemnation (Rom. vi. 11) and power (*ib.*, 12,

12 of the flesh, by the circumcision of Christ: buried with him

13) of sin, and so our real entrance into a position of covenanted peace (Rom. v. 1) and a condition of covenanted grace. In both these aspects it is the Antitype of the type Circumcision, and the Reality under the seal Baptism.

the putting off] The Greek is one strong compound word; "*the entire stripping off.*" It was, in principle and as regarded the call and grace of God, *a total break* with the old position and condition; not a reform but a revolution of the man's standing and state.—The physical imagery is drawn of course from the severe Abrahamic rite.

the body of the sins of the flesh] Omit, on good evidence, the words "*of the sins,*" which appear to be a (very intelligible) gloss or comment.

What is "*the body of the flesh*"? Elsewhere in St Paul the word "*body*" appears never to mean anything but the physical frame, save in passages referring to the Church; but (in passages at all akin to this) it is that frame viewed as in some sense the vehicle of sin, or rather of temptation. Cp. Rom. vi. 6, vii. 24, viii. 10, 11, 13. As God's handiwork, the body is good, and on its way, in Christ, to glorification. As the body of man in the Fall, and as man's means of contact with a sinful external world, if in no other way, it is so conversant with and affected by evil as to be (*in that respect*) an evil. As such it is "the body of the flesh," that is, the body conditioned by, and reacting upon, our nature fallen and unregenerate.—See our notes on Rom. viii. 4 and Eph. ii. 3, on the word "*flesh*."

In Christ, "by the Spirit," the Christian is empowered to "mortify the practices of the body" (Rom. viii. 13). In Christ, "the body is for the Lord, *and the Lord for the body*" (1 Cor. vi. 13). In this respect the man, while still liable to physical weakness and weariness, and truly capable of temptation, and as a fact never so using his "fulness" in Christ as to be wholly free (whatever his consciousness) from the burthen of evil in and through "the body of the flesh," yet stands on such a ground of vantage over the power of that body as to find by faith a noble practical reality in the strong words of this verse.—See further, on the other hand, notes on iii. 5.

by the circumcision of Christ] Lit., **in** &c.; "*as united to, interested in.*"—What is this circumcision? that given by Christ, or that undergone by Christ? Much may be said for the latter. Our Lord was "circumcised for man," as the sacramental Seal of His "subjection to the law for man"; and so His historical Circumcision has a deep connexion with our possession, through Him, of acceptance and sanctification, the fruit of His Righteousness and Merits. But in this context the other reference is preferable. We have but just read of a "*circumcision not made with hands*"; surely the same is in view here. Christ, Messiah (the word here is not Jesus, which might have better suggested the historical reference), *gives us* spiritual circumcision when He joins us to Himself (see notes above), and so the circumcision is "His."

12. *buried with him*] Cp. Rom. vi. 4; the only parallel.—Union with Christ is primarily union with Him as the Dead and Buried, because His Death (consummated as it were and sealed in His Burial) is

in baptism, wherein also you are risen with *him* through the faith of the operation of God, who hath raised him from the dead. And you, being dead in *your* sins and the uncircum- 13

the procuring cause of all our blessings in Him, as it is our Propitiation and Peace. The Christian, joined to Him, shares as it were the atoning Death and the covering, swallowing, Grave of his blessed Representative; he goes to the depths of that awful process with and in his Lord.

in baptism] The form of the Greek word (*baptismos* not *baptisma* in the best reading) perhaps emphasizes the action rather than the abstract institution; it recalls the decisive "Rubicon" which his sacramental Washing was to the convert. See Lightfoot here.

The immersion of the baptized (the primeval and ideal form of rite, but not invariable as a literal action; see *Teaching of the Apostles* (cent. 1), ch. vii.) is undoubtedly here in view. The plunge beneath the water signified identification with the buried Lord, and sealed it to faith. Lightfoot quotes from the *Apostolic Constitutions* (a book heretical in doctrine but valuable as a witness to usages; cent. 3) the words (iii. 17), "the plunge is our dying with Him, the coming up, our rising with Him."

It must be said again (see above on ver. 11) that, in the ultimate reality, not the Sacrament but faith in God's promises joins us to the Lord in His death. But the Sacrament so seals the faith that the terms appropriate to faith attach to the Sacrament, naturally though secondarily. Cp. Gal. iii. 26, 27, in the significant connexion of the verses. And see Beveridge on Artt. xxv., xxvii.; and Lombard, quoted in Appendix K.

ye are risen with him] Better, **ye rose with** Him.—The state to which baptism was your sacramental admittance is a state of union with Christ as the Risen One; fellowship in His supreme Acceptance and in His possession of the full wealth of the Spirit as our Mediator and Surety. Baptism seals to faith all our possessions in the now glorified Redeemer.

through the faith of &c.] Better, **through your faith in the working** (*energeia*) **of God**. Observe the reference to faith in connexion with the Sacrament; and see next note.

who hath raised him] Better, **who raised Him**. Cp. 1 Pet. i. 18—21 (especially 21) for a close and instructive parallel.—Faith rests upon God as He is viewed specially as the Raiser of the Lord from the dead, because in that character we see Him as reconciled and as actively gracious to us. See further Heb. xiii. 20, 21.

13. *And you*] It is as if the Apostle would have written, "*and you with Him*," carrying on the last sentence. But he pauses on the word "*you*," and makes a new statement.

dead in your *sins*] See Eph. ii. 1, and 5, for a close parallel written about the same time.

"*Dead*":—devoid of spiritual and eternal life, in its Christian sense. For the truth that unregenerate man is thus "dead" see Eph. v. 14; Joh. v. 24; 1 Joh. iii. 14, v. 12; and cp. Joh. iii. 3, vi. 53. See also Gen. ii. 17. The state indicated is one not of dormancy, or imperfect development, but one in which a living principle necessary for organization, growth and energy, in reference to God and holiness, is entirely

cision of your flesh, hath he quickened together with him, 14 having forgiven you all trespasses; blotting out the handwriting of ordinances that was against us, which was con-

lacking, and in which there is no innate tendency to develop such a principle. The "life eternal" must come *ab extra*.

in your sins] Better, **in respect of your trespasses**; the conditions and the symptoms of the "death."—On the word rendered "*trespass*" see Trench, *N. T. Synonyms*, on ἁμαρτία, and our note on Eph. ii. 1. It has a slight tendency by usage to denote sin in its less grievous aspects; but this must not be pressed here.

the uncircumcision of your flesh] A phrase explained by the previous passage (ver. 11) where the spiritual circumcision is in view, and "the body of the flesh." It is the unregenerate state, in which man is separated neither from the guilt of sin nor from its power.

hath he quickened] Better, **He quickened, He raised to life**; ideally, when your Lord rose, actually when you came into union with Him by faith.

The word "*you*" should be repeated after "*quickened*," by the best documentary evidence.

having forgiven] Better, **forgiving**; at the moment, in the act, of the "quickening." The Lord's Resurrection was the expression of the fact of His acceptance by the Father; our entrance on union with Him as the Risen One was the expression of our acceptance in Him.

you] Better, **us**; all believers, not Gentiles only. "St Paul is eager to claim his share in the transgression, that he may claim it also in the forgiveness" (Lightfoot).

all trespasses] Lit., **all the trespasses**; with reference to the recent mention of "your trespasses" (see last note but three).—Observe the Divine *fulness* of the remission.

14. *blotting out*] **cancelled** (Lightfoot).—The act of "forgiving" is described under vivid imagery. Cp. Acts iii. 19; and see Psal. li. 1, 9, cix. 14; Neh. iv. 5; Isai. xliv. 22; Jer. xviii. 23.

the handwriting] **The bond, note-of-hand.** The original word, *cheirographon*, meaning an autograph, is used often in this sense, and oftener (transliterated) in Latin than in Greek. So here the Latin Versions have *chirographum decreti*.—What is "*the bond*"? The question is best answered under the next words.

of ordinances] Lit., "*with relation to ordinances*"; based on them, conditioned by them. "*The bond written in ordinances*"; R. V.—These "ordinances" (*dogmata*) are not *rites* but, as the Greek word always means in the N.T., *orders, decrees*. The reference cannot be solely to the "decrees" of the *Jewish Law*, for here the case of *all* believing sinners is in view. The decrees are rather that of which that Law was only one grand instance, the Divine precept of holiness, however conveyed, whether by revelation or by conscience (see Rom. ii. 12—15). Man's assent, however imperfect, to the rightness of that precept, is as it were his signature of obligation to "the bond"; a bond which his sin has made to be a terribly *adverse* engagement.

trary to us, and took it out of the way, nailing it to *his* cross; *and* having spoiled principalities and powers, he 15

Lightfoot points out that the Greek commentators "universally" interpret the words rendered "of ordinances" quite differently; "*by the dogmata*, or *doctrines* (*of the Gospel*)"; the Gospel being the means of the abrogation of the Law. But this, as he shews, is (*a*) alien to the context, (*b*) out of harmony with an important parallel word in ver. 20 below (see notes on that verse), (*c*) not supported by the usage (elsewhere in N.T.) of the Greek word *dogma*.

contrary] **directly opposed** (Lightfoot). The Greek is a single compound word, giving by its form the thought of a close and grappling opposition. The broken Law becomes an active enemy of the transgressor.

and took it out of the way] Quite lit., **and it** (emphatic) **He hath taken out of the midst**; from between us and God, as a barrier to our peace.—"*He hath taken*":—the tense indicates the lasting and present result of the decisive act of atonement.

nailing it to his *cross*] Lit., **to the Cross.**—See i. 20 for a previous allusion to the Cross.—The Lord was "made a curse for us" (Gal. iii. 13), "made sin for us" (2 Cor. v. 21), in other words, treated as Transgression personified, in His atoning death. He there discharged our bond, and thus cancelled it, tore it up as it were; and the tearing up is vividly described as the piercing of it with the nails which had affixed Him, our Satisfaction, to the Cross.—There seems to be no evidence for the existence of any legal custom, such as the nailing up an abrogated decree in public, which could have suggested this language. It comes wholly from the Crucifixion.

Observe carefully the free use in Scripture of legal and commercial imagery to convey great aspects of the truth of our salvation.

15. *having spoiled*] "*Having put off from Himself*" (R.V.).—The Greek verb is apparently unknown before St Paul; classical illustration is impossible. Its literal meaning is "*to strip off*"; and its voice is middle. This voice, it is alleged, compels us to explain it of the Lord's stripping off something *from Himself, divesting Himself*. And explanations vary between (*a*) that given in margin R.V., ("having put off from Himself *His body*"), supported by the Peshito Syriac version and (among other Fathers) by Ambrose, Hilary, and Augustine (see Lightfoot); and (*b*) that given in text R.V., advocated by Lightfoot, and supported by Chrysostom, Theodore of Mopsuestia, and other Fathers. In this last, the thought would be that the powers of evil swarmed, so to speak, around Him who had taken our place under "the curse of the Law," and that He in His triumph, stripped or cast them off.

The objection to (*a*) is that it brings in an alien and isolated idea, and in obscure terms. The objection to (*b*) seems to us to be that it presents to us an image very peculiar in itself, and not obviously proper to the next words. *To cast off* enemies and then at once *to exhibit* them are not quite congruous ideas.

And why should we reject the A.V. rendering as if ungrammatical? The lawful force of the middle voice would be as well represented by

made a shew of *them* openly, triumphing over them in it.

"stripping *for Himself*" as "stripping *from Himself*"; it makes the subject of the verb to be also in some degree the object of the action. And the Lord did "strip His foes *for Himself*": "He *taketh from him the armour*, and *divideth the spoils*" (Luke xi. 22). The imagery is then congruous; the disarmed and despoiled foes are then appropriately, as captives, "*shewn*" *in triumph*. We recommend accordingly the A.V.[1]

The Old Latin Version has *exuens se*, following explanation (*b*). The Vulgate renders the verb *exspolians*—the immediate original of the A.V.

principalities and powers] Lit., **the governments and the authorities,** the *recognized* enemies of Redemption and the Redeemer. These made their dire hostility supremely felt in that "hour" which He Himself called "the authority of the Darkness" (Luke xxii. 53). The personal adversaries (under their Chief; see the intimations of Luke iv. 13; Joh. xiii. 2, xiv. 30), who had crossed His path so often as the "demons" of possession, now directly assailed Himself, as they are still permitted in measure to assail (Eph. vi. 12) His followers, who meet them in Him the Conqueror.—See further above on i. 16.

made a shew of them] Nearly the same Greek verb as that used Matt. i. 19; "*make her a public example.*" The Latin Versions have *traduxit*, "*led them along*," as the captives in a Roman triumph.

openly] Rather, **boldly** (Lightfoot). The "openness" indicated by the Greek phrase (quite literally, "*in*, or *with, outspokenness*") is the openness of *confidence*. It is used Joh. vii. 4 (where Lightfoot explains it to mean "*to assume a bold attitude*"); Eph. vi. 19; Phil. i. 20.

triumphing over them] The Greek verb (*thriambeuein*) occurs elsewhere (in N.T.) only 2 Cor. ii. 14; where it is variously explained "*to make to triumph*" or "*to lead in triumph.*" Here it is of course the latter.—Philologically it is probably akin to the Latin *triumphus*.

in it] The Cross. The margin A.V., "*in Himself*" is quite untenable, though it is countenanced by the Latin, (*in semetipso*), and by Wyclif, Tyndale ("*in his awne persone*"), Cranmer, and Rheims. The Genevan version has "*in the same* crosse."

The Lord's atoning Death, the apparent triumph of His foes over *Him*, was His absolute and eternal triumph over *them*, when it was seen, in His Resurrection, to be the mysterious Ransom of His Church from the curse and from sin, and so His own glorification as its Head. *Vicit qui passus est; cui gloria in æternum.*

This whole passage while pregnant with primary and universal truth has doubtless a special reference all the while to the "Colossian heresy" with its angelology and angelolatry. He who is King of all orders of good Angels is here presented as Conqueror of their evil counterpart; HE, from both points of view, fills the field.

---

[1] It is objected that below, iii. 9, we have the same verb in the same voice used where the meaning clearly is "to strip *from oneself*." But classical parallels exist to such a varying use of the middle in neighbouring contexts. See Sophocles, *Ajax*, 245, 647 (Dindorf). (Note by the Bishop of Worcester.)

Let no *man* therefore judge you in meat, or in drink, or 16 in respect of a holyday, or of the new moon, or of the sabbath days: which are a shadow of *things* to come; but 17

16—23 CHRISTIAN LIBERTY AND THEORIES HOSTILE TO IT

16. *therefore*] Such is the Christian's position in this sacrificed and triumphant Saviour. He stands possessed of the full inheritance of which the Mosaic ritual institutions were at once the shadow and the veil. Now therefore, so far as those institutions are presented to him by any school of teaching as an obligation and bond on Christian practice, he must decline to receive them.

judge you] **Take you to task** (Lightfoot). Cp. Rom. xiv. 3, 4, for a close parallel, full of the principles of both liberty and duty in Christ. See also 1 Cor. x. 29.

in meat, or in drink] Rather better, **in eating and in drinking.** For the Mosaic laws about food cp. Lev. xi., xvii.; Deut. xiv., &c. Of allowed or forbidden *drinks* little is said in the Old Law; Lightfoot notices Lev. x. 9 (the prohibition of wine to the priests at special times); xi. 34 (the prohibition to drink liquid from an "unclean" vessel); and the law of the Nazirite, Numb. vi. 3. Cp. with the text, Heb. ix. 10.—Possibly the Colossian misleaders forbade wine *in toto;* not at all on modern philanthropic principles, but as a token of abjuration of social life.

in respect of] Lit., "in *the portion* of;" i.e. "in, or under, *the class* of;" and so, idiomatically, **with regard to.** The Latin Versions render literally, *in parte diei festi;* and so Wyclif, "*in part of feest dai;*" Tyndale, Cranmer, Geneva, "*for a pece* (*peece*) *of an holy daye.*"

holy day] **feast day,** R.V.—The Greek word denotes the *yearly* Jewish festivals; Passover, Pentecost, Atonement, Tabernacles, &c. It is used by the LXX. to translate the Hebrew *mô'êd,* rendered in A.V. (e.g. 1 Chron. xxiii. 31) "*set feast;*" see Chronicles just quoted for an example of such a threefold enumeration as this of holy times.— Lightfoot refers to Gal. iv. 10 ("*days, and months, and seasons, and years*") as a true parallel here; it only adds a fourth observance, the (sabbatic) *year.*

new moon] See Numb. x. 10, xxviii. 11, 14, 16; and cp. 1 Sam. xx. 5; 2 Kings iv. 23; Psal. lxxxi. 3; Isai. i. 13, 14.

sabbath days] Better, **sabbath.** The original (*sabbata*) is a Greek plural in form and declination, but only as it were by accident. It is a transliteration of the Aramaic singular *shabbâthâ* (Hebrew, *shabbâth*).

It is plain from the argument that the Sabbath is here regarded not as it was primevally (Gen. ii. 3) "made for man" (Mar. ii. 27), God's benignant gift, fenced with precept and prohibition only for His creature's bodily and spiritual benefit; but as it was adopted to be a symbolic institution of the Mosaic covenant, and expressly adapted to the relation between God *and Israel* (Exod. xxxi. 12—17); an aspect of the Sabbath which governs much of the language of the O.T. about it. *In that respect* the Sabbath was abrogated, as the sacrifices were abrogated, and the New Israelite enters upon the *spiritual realities*

110 / Colossians 2

18 the body *is* of Christ. Let no *man* beguile you of your

foreshadowed by it as by them. The Colossian Christian who declined the ceremonial observance of the Sabbath in this respect was right. An altogether different question arises when the Christian is asked to "secularize" the weekly Rest which descends to us from the days of Paradise, and which is as vitally necessary as ever for man's physical and spiritual well-being.

17. *a shadow*] Cp. Heb. viii. 5, x. 1. The word suggests the idea of "an image cast by an object and representing its form." (Grimm's *N.T. Lexicon*, ed. Thayer.)

things to come] from the point of view of the Old Dispensation. The Epistle to the Hebrews is a large apostolic expansion, so to speak, of this sentence; giving us at full length the assurances that the Mosaic ordinances were adjusted with a Divine prescience, to the future of the Gospel; and that the fulfilment of their true import in Christ abrogates their observance.—Render exactly, **the things to come.**

the body is *of Christ*] The Fulfilment, the shadow-casting Substance, is "*of Christ*," is "*Christ's*," because it *consists of* Him in His redeeming Work. His atoning Sacrifice, His Gift of the Spirit, His Rest, are the realities to which the old institutions pointed.

18. *Let no* man] Another parallel but distinct caution after that of ver. 16.

beguile you of your reward] **Rob you of your prize**, R.V. The verb is compounded with the noun *brabeion* (used Phil. iii. 14), an athletic prize. Here, as in Philippians, it means the life eternal, "the crown of life" (Jas. i. 12; Rev. ii. 10). The Colossians were tempted to forsake their position and privilege in Christ, found and retained by faith; and, so far, they were tempted to lose their "hold on the eternal life" (1 Tim. vi. 12, 19) which is in Him alone (1 Joh. v. 12). Cp. Rev. iii. 11.—What their Lord would do to save them from the fatal step was altogether another matter; their one duty was not to take the step.

The alien teachers are represented here (having regard to the classical usage of the verb) "not as umpires, nor as successful rivals, but simply as persons frustrating those who otherwise would have won the prize" (Lightfoot).

Tyndale and Cranmer curiously render, "*Let no man make you shote at a wronge marke*," probably influenced by Luther, who has *Lasset euch Niemand das Ziel verrücken*; an untenable paraphrase. Geneva, "*Let no man...beare rule over you.*"

in a voluntary humility] The Greek means, quite literally, "*willing in humility*"; and some questions arise about the construction. These may be reduced to two main alternatives. (*a*) Is "*willing*" to be connected with the verb just previous, and to be rendered, "let no one rob you of your prize *willingly*," "*meaningly*," "*of malice prepense*"? (*b*) Is "*willing*" to be connected with the words just following, and explained, "*taking pleasure in* humility"? Of these (*a*) is easier grammatically, but Ellicott urges the grave objection that it attributes a Satanic and almost incredible malice to the teachers in question. It may be answered that St Paul need not be charging them with "mean-reward in a voluntary humility and worshipping of angels,

ing" to rob their followers of heaven, but with "meaning" to rob them of a faith with which as a fact the hope of heaven was bound up. Lightfoot advocates (*b*), and proves that it is a construction supported by the LXX., where it is not used "only with personal pronouns" (as Ellicott says), but with ordinary nouns; see Psal. cx. (Heb. and Eng. cxi.) 1, cxlvi. (Heb. and Eng. cxlvii.) 10. The strong Hebraism, without any N.T. parallel, is certainly startling, however; and we recommend (*a*), though doubtfully, with the explanation given above. The rendering would be somewhat thus, in paraphrase: **Let no man have his own way in robbing you** &c.

humility] "Humility is a vice with heathen moralists but a virtue with Christian Apostles....In this passage which (with ver. 23) forms the sole exception to the general language of the Apostles, the divergence is rather apparent than real" (Lightfoot). An artificial, gratuitous, humility is not humility but its parody. And such was the thing in question; an abasement of man before unlawful objects (see next words) of worship; a prostration self-chosen, and also self-conscious.

worshipping of angels] A practice highly developed in later Judaism, while entirely absent from the apostolic teaching, and indeed clearly condemned here, and Rev. xix. 10, xxii. 9, and implicitly in Heb. i.— It is noticeable that the Council of Laodicea (A.D. 394), so near Colossæ, forbids (c. 35) Christians to leave the Church and go away "to name angels" in secret assemblies, calling this a "secret idolatry," and apparently connecting it with Jewish influences. Theodoret in his Commentary here speaks of the existence in his time (cent. 5) of Oratories (*euctêria*) to the Archangel Michael in the region of Laodicea and Colossæ, and of their popularity, apparently as rivals to the regular Churches. At this day in Abyssinia Michael has his holyday *every month*.—See further *Introd.*, pp. 15, 31, 33.

"Angels," says the saintly Jansenist Quesnel here, "will always win the day over Jesus Christ despised (*anéanti*) and crucified, if the choice of a mediator between us and God is left to the vanity of the human mind."

For a (doubtful) early sanction of angel-worship see a difficult sentence in Justin, *Apology*, I. c. 6. Irenæus, Justin's contemporary, says (ii. 57) that the Church "does nothing by the invocation of angels."

Whatever its origin and details, such a worship inevitably beclouds the Christian's view both of the majesty and of the nearness and tenderness of Christ his living HEAD.

"*Worshipping*":—*thrêskeia*; a word akin perhaps in etymology to "*tremble*," and denoting religious devotion mainly in its external aspect; a *cultus*. The word or its cognate occurs elsewhere in N.T. Acts xxvi. 5; Jas. i. 26, 27. Lightfoot quotes a sentence from Philo, the Jewish contemporary of the Apostles, where it is expressly distinguished from piety (*hosiotês*); and he says that "generally the usage of the word exhibits a tendency to a bad sense." Such a sense is quite in point here; an unauthorized and abject *cultus* was the natural expression of a counterfeit "humility."

intruding into *those things* which he hath not seen, vainly
19 puft up by his fleshly mind, and not holding the head, from

intruding into those things *which he hath not seen*] *Quæ vidit ambulans* (Old Latin); *Quæ non vidit ambulans* (Vulgate); "*Dwelling in the things which he hath seen*" (R.V.). Here are serious differences of reading and translation, which must be briefly discussed.

(*a*) Shall we render "*Intruding into*," or, "*Dwelling in*"? Classical usage of the Greek verb favours the latter rendering; the word is used e.g. of a god's *haunt* in a region or a spot. The usage in LXX. and Apocrypha slightly favours the former rendering; the word is used there of the invasion or new occupation of a country (Josh. xix. 51; 1 Macc. xii. 25, xiv. 31). The balance must be struck by our conclusions on the rest of the phrase.

(*b*) "*Things which he* hath not *seen*": "*Things which he* hath *seen*." Is the negative to be omitted or not? "Many authorities, some ancient, insert '*not*'" (margin, R.V.). Ellicott approves the insertion of "*not*"; Lightfoot advocates the omission. It is difficult to discuss the evidence in a note, and we have attempted to state it in outline in Appendix J. Here it must suffice to say that we venture to recommend the reading **which he hath not seen**. It seems to us more likely, on a view of the facts, that the negative should have dropped out early than that it should have been deliberately inserted.

If we reject "*not*," the meaning will most probably be that the erring teacher "*dwells in*, or *dwells on*, what he has seen," his alleged visions and revelations, the "manifestations" which he says, and perhaps thinks, he has witnessed, and which he prefers to the apostolic Gospel. If we retain "*not*," the meaning will be that he *invades* the region of the Unseen with a presumptuous confidence of assertion, as if he *had* seen it. In either case he might *assert* his enjoyment of angelic or other visions; but in the latter case the Apostle denies such a claim if made. Cp. Ezek. xiii. 3; " Woe unto the foolish prophets, that *follow their own spirit, and have seen nothing.*"

vainly] The Greek word means "*at random*," without reason or cause. Cp. Rom. xiii. 4; 1 Cor. xv. 2. (This meaning in some passages glides into that of "*without result*"; Gal. iii. 4, iv. 11.) The true Gospel is not so; its loftiest assertion springs from deepest fact and truth.

puft up] A present participle, indicating habit and development. For the word in a similar connexion cp. 1 Cor. viii. 1.

by his fleshly mind] Lit., "*by the mind of his flesh*."—"*The mind*" (*nous*) here is the merely reasoning faculty as distinguished from spiritual intuition. " *The flesh* " is, as often in St Paul, the unregenerate state, in which the sinful principle dominates. See Eph. ii. 3 and note there in this Series.—In that verse "*flesh*" and "*mind*" are somewhat similarly collocated; but the word rendered (in A.V.) "*mind*" is lit. "*thoughts*"; "the mind" in particular action.—He is "puffed up" by an exercise of thought characteristic of the unregenerate state.

19. *holding*] **Holding fast** (R.V.). The word is used Acts iii. 11

which all the body by joints and bands having nourishment
ministered, and knit together, increaseth *with* the increase

of the healed cripple's *grasp* of the Apostles who had healed him.—The
erring teacher is said "not to hold" the Head, not only as a man but as
a teacher.

the head] "Regarded as a title, so that a Person is at once suggested"
(Lightfoot). Angel-worship, and all its ways, was *ipso facto* a slackening
of the soul's contact with Christ.

On this sacred word "*Head*" see i. 18 and notes; and cp. the close
and full parallel, Eph. iv. 15, 16.

from which] Better, **out of Whom**. The relative pronoun is masculine,
while the Greek word for "*head*" is feminine.

"*Out of*":—so in Eph. iv. 16. The thought conveyed is at once of
vital connexion and derivation.

all the body] Verbatim as Eph. iv. 16.—The emphasis is on the
"*all.*" No part, no member, must be for a moment out of *direct* life-
contact with the Head.

by joints and bands] Better, **through the (its) joints and ligatures.**
The phrase is closely akin to that of Eph. iv. 16, where "*compacting*"
and "*joints*" are mentioned. Here as there (see our notes) the
thought is of the direct coherence of every part of the Body *with the
Head*. The other cognate thought, of the cohesion of the parts and
limbs *with each other*, is not present, at least not prominent. The
Christian has here to be warned that nothing must make him lose or
loosen his own direct communion with Christ his Head.—The physical
imagery must not be pressed. In our body, doubtless, the central forces
of the organism affect the remoter structures through the nearer. But
the mystical Body is such that, while it is a true organism as a whole,
yet all the while individually "the Head of *every man*" (in Christ) "is
Christ" (1 Cor. xi. 3; cp. *ibid.* vi. 17). And this was what the
Colossian errors tended to obscure.

having nourishment ministered] Better, simply, **being supplied**
(R.V.).—The cognate noun to the (one) Greek word here, a present
participle, appears Eph. iv. 16; "every joint of *the supply*." The
thing "supplied" is all the Virtue of the Head; grace in all its forms.

knit together] Another present participle, indicating a continuing and
developing process. The Greek is identical with that rendered "*compacted*," Eph. iv. 16.—The constant "supply" of the life and power of
the Head tends to a constant closer and firmer internal cohesion of the
body, in its spiritual development.

increaseth with *the increase of God*] Lit., **groweth the growth of
God.**—The growth contemplated may mean in part the numerical
growth, the attraction of new converts to the manifestly living and holy
community. But the more immediate reference is to development from
within; the individual's and the community's "growth in the grace and
knowledge" (2 Pet. iii. 18) of the Head.

"*The increase of God*":—His, because He is its Origin, and Secret,
and as it were Atmosphere. The brief pregnant phrase conveys this
truth with a peculiar grandeur and force.

20 of God. Wherefore if ye be dead with Christ from the rudiments of the world, why, as though living in the world, 21 are ye subject to ordinances, (touch not; taste not; handle

> Lightfoot suggests that we have here also an implied caution against the Jewish errors. "Thus the finite is truly united with the Infinite"; not through intermediate orders of being, but in Christ. In an interesting note he goes on to explain the perfect fitness of St Paul's imagery of the Head and Body, in the light of modern physiological discoveries. "The volition communicated from the brain to the limbs, the sensations of the extremities telegraphed back to the brain, the absolute mutual sympathy between the head and the members, the instantaneous paralysis ensuing on the interruption of continuity, all these add to the completeness and life of the image." He then gives instances of ancient scientific speculation on the seat and distribution of vital power in the human body; and concludes: "Bearing in mind all this diversity of opinion among ancient physiologists, we cannot fail to be struck in the text not only with the correctness of the image but also with the propriety of the terms; and we are forcibly reminded that among the Apostle's most intimate companions at this time was one whom he calls 'the beloved physician' (iv. 14)."—Such subsidiary assistance, if used by the Apostle, would leave untouched the authority of inspiration in the resulting language.

20. *Wherefore*] The word is certainly to be omitted on documentary evidence. A new and separate theme is now in view, the doctrines of the intruding teachers about duty and morals.

if ye be dead] Lit. and better, with R.V., **if ye died.** See on vv. 11, 12.—"*If*" assumes the "death" as a fact.

with Christ] To whom they were vitally joined, through faith, sealed by baptism, for all the purposes of His redeeming work.

from the rudiments of the world] See above on ver. 8.

living in the world] Not merely "*being*," but "*living*;" having your life-power and life-interests of and in the world. Their true "life was hid with Christ" (iii. 3), and so could not be truly thus conditioned.

are ye subject to ordinances?] R.V. "*do ye subject yourselves to ordinances?*" Lightfoot, "*are ye overridden with precepts, ordinances?*" The latter rendering is slightly too strong; but both indicate the main point of the Greek. The religion of the Colossians was becoming one of mechanical rule and measure, a round of ordered "practices," imposed by directors, to expiate or purify by their performance. The life of faith and love was giving way to an arbitrary discipline, far different from the obedience of the heart to the will of God in Christ.

21. (*touch not; taste not; handle not;*] Better (discarding *the bracket* here), **Handle thou not, nor taste, nor touch.** This rendering represents exactly the construction of the Greek, and is truer to the shades of meaning of the first and last of the three Greek verbs. The last verb denotes a lighter and less deliberate touch than the first, and so here conveys *a climax* of prohibition.

The prohibitions in question would be those of the Mosaic law,

not; which all are to perish with the using;) after the com- 22
mandments and doctrines of men? which *things* have in- 23
deed a shew of wisdom in will worship, and humility, and

developed and exaggerated by the Pharisaic schools. Schoettgen (*Horæ Hebr. in N. T.*) quotes from the Talmud just such precepts: "*Touch not a vessel, till thou hast washed hands and feet from* (*its*) *brim;*" "*They say to a Nazirite, Drink not...shave not...*&c." "The Latin commentators, Hilary and Pelagius, suppose these prohibitions to be the Apostle's own, thus making a complete shipwreck of the sense" (Lightfoot). In much more modern comments the same mistake appears.

Our Lord's teaching (e.g. Matt. xv. 1—20) takes the exactly opposite direction to this system of prohibitions, and is a lasting warning to His Church on all kindred subjects. Cp. also 1 Cor. viii.; 1 Tim. iv. 3.

22. *which all are to perish with the using;*)] Lit., **which are all for corruption in the consumption.** I.e., the things which are thus forbidden as soul-tainting are things merely material, not moral, and this is evidenced by their merely material destiny—physical dissolution in the course of natural use. Cp. Matt. xv. 17.—This clause should be bracketed apart, as in R.V.

Observe St Paul's instructive opposite use, in an opposite connexion, of the same consideration, 1 Cor. vi. 13. There an assertor of a distorted "liberty" is met by the thought that alike "meats" and "belly" are to cease to exist with the present order of things; then why for their sake violate real claims of purity?

after the commandments, &c.] The thought returns to the prohibitive formulas; these are not utterances of God's will, but "*according to*," of the kind of, on the scale of, merely human rule and principle. Obviously, so far as any of them were Mosaic, St Paul would fully recognize their Divine authority *in their own period and for their own purpose*. But the period was over, the purpose was fulfilled in Christ. To impose them now was to put God's edict to man's arbitrary use.

"*Of men:*"—cp. Matt. xv. 9; Mar. vii. 7; and see Isai. xxix. 13, the passage quoted by our Lord, and doubtless here in St Paul's mind. The LXX. there agrees almost verbatim with the words here, more so than with the quotations in the Gospels.

23. *which* things] More precisely, if the word may be tolerated, **which-like things**; the prohibitions given above, ver. 21, and all others which depend on the same principle.

have indeed] More precisely, **do indeed have**, with a slight emphasis on the admission. There was a specious and seductive "reasonableness" in the theory.

a shew] Greek, *logos*; "*word, speech,*" and so "*repute;*" with an implied contrast here between such repute and *reality* (*ergon*).

of wisdom] It was a characteristic of Jewish thought at the time to attempt to throw a glamour of philosophic fitness over Pharisaic doctrine and practice. See *Introd.*, p. 32.

will worship] The Greek compound noun denotes a self-chosen,

neglecting of the body, not in any honour to the satisfying of the flesh.

self-imposed, service (in the religious sense); a round of *supererogatory* observance; a parody on the genuine reverence and obedience of the Gospel.—The element in the compound represented by "*worship*" is the noun used Jas. i. 27 (and see 26), and rendered "*religion*" in our Versions.

humility] See above, on ver. 18. The special direction of this false humility here would be, perhaps, that of abject submission to Pharisaic "directors," mistaken for a true surrender to the will of God.—"Who can submit our will to the will of God, save the Spirit of God?" (Quesnel).

neglecting of the body] Lit., **unsparing (treatment) of the body**; a severe and active physical asceticism.—Something of Oriental *dualism* may well have influenced this ascetic practice. Scarcely anywhere outside Scripture itself is the true *honour of the body* recognized in religious systems; the tendency to regard it as merely the burthen, or prison, of the soul appears almost everywhere. And this is a fruitful source of the asceticism which rather attacks than disciplines the body.—Cp. Wisdom ix. 15: "The corruptible body presseth down the soul." The Pharisee Josephus (*contra Apion*., ii. 24) says that "the soul, by its union with the body, is subject to miseries." The Alexandrian Philo, a coeval, like Josephus, of the Apostles (as perhaps the author of Wisdom also was) calls the body, "a loathsome prison." Twelve centuries later Francis of Assisi called his body, "my brother, the ass." See Dr F. W. Farrar's note on Wisd. ix., in the *Speaker's Commentary*.—Contrast 1 Cor. vi. 13; 1 Thess. v. 23, etc.

not in any honour to the satisfying of the flesh] Better, as R.V., **not of any value against the indulgence of the flesh**. This explanation, fully sustained by the Greek grammar, was long ago advocated by Mr Conybeare (C. and Howson, *Life etc. of St Paul*, ch. xxv., in a note to the translation of the Epistle), and had been suggested still earlier (as he says) by Abp Sumner. It satisfies the context as no other does, supplying just such a counterpart as might be expected (from the use of the word "*indeed*," μὲν) to the admission that the system had "a shew of wisdom." See Lightfoot's note for full proof that the Greek preposition (πρὸς) is rightly rendered (perhaps we may better say *explained*) "*against*" in such a context.

Other interpretations are as follows; (*a*) "*to satisfy the (reasonable) wants of the body*." But this gives a *good* meaning to the Greek word rendered by A.V. "*satisfy*," whereas it has by usage a meaning of excess and indulgence.—In this explanation, the words "*not in any honour*" are taken as a clause apart, parallel with the words just previous; "not (*holding the body*) in any honour."—(*b*) An explanation which supposes St Paul to put the case from his opponent's view-point: "*it being no worthy thing to regard the satisfaction of the flesh*." This is the hesitating exposition of Theodore of Mopsuestia (cent. 4—5).—(*c*) An explanation which, like (*a*), breaks the last clause into two: "*not of any (real) value, (but) tending only to gratify the flesh*," *i.e.*, to inflate the

If ye then be risen with Christ, seek those *things* which 3 are above, where Christ sitteth on the right hand of God.

pride of unregenerate man. So, on the whole, many modern expositors. But the sentence is thus unnaturally dislocated, and a meaning given to the word "*flesh*" improbable in this context.

As explained above, the words are a pregnant warning against the delusive but specious hope that the human spirit is to be transfigured into moral harmony with the Divine purity through inflictions on the body. The sublime true secret of that transfiguration is given us in e.g. Rom. viii. 13; "If ye *by the Spirit* mortify the practices of the body, etc." And see below on ch. iii. 4, 5.

CH. III. 1—4   THE SUBJECT CONTINUED; LIFE IN UNION WITH THE RISEN ONE

1. *If*] The "*if*" not of conjecture but of assumption, as in ii. 20. He takes them all for granted, as really united to Christ by a living faith, sealed by holy Baptism.

then] The thought goes back to all the previous statements of the Christian's glorious position and privilege in Christ. In view of these Divine facts, the poor expedients of a mechanical religious routine are seen to be as needless as they are futile. The secret of moral victory is opened, and it consists in using the powers conveyed to the believer through federal and vital oneness with his Head.

ye...be risen] Lit. and far better, **ye did rise**, or **were raised**. The time-reference is, ideally, to the hour of Christ's Resurrection; biographically, to their own union with Him by faith. Of that faith their baptism, with its immersion and emersion, was symbol, seal, and monument. See above on ii. 12.

In Christ the Crucified they had "died to" the guilt, and so to the despotic claim, of sin. In Christ the Risen they had "risen to" a life of full acceptance, and also to life-power, and life-endowments, derived from His "indissoluble life" (Heb. vii. 16); in fact, to the possession of the indwelling Spirit which He, as Risen, "shed forth" (Acts ii. 33), and which gives to the limb the strength and holiness of the Head, to be used and realized. See above on ii. 12.

with Christ] The holy Union appears in every word.

seek those things *which are above*] As the exile seeks home (Heb. xi. 14), or as a thing gravitating seeks its centre. The precept bears full on the problem last in view, how to meet "the indulgence of the flesh." It is best met by the *looking-away* of the soul, heavenward, Christward, in the recollection of its new and eternal life in Him. The "*things above*" are thus "*sought*" both as the goal of hope and the antidote to temptation.—For the phrase the "things above" (here and ver. 2), cp. Joh. viii. 23: "*I am from the things above.*"

where] The "*things above*" are just so far *localised* as they have to do with the glorified Body of the incarnate and ascended Lord.

Christ sitteth] Better, **Christ is, seated**. (So R.V.)   Vulgate,

118 / Colossians 3

2 Set your affection on *things* above, not on *things* on the
3 earth. For ye are dead, and your life is hid with Christ in

Christus est...sedens.—First, His *presence* "there," in general, is in
view; then, His *session.*
"*Seated*":—cp. Matt. xxvi. 64; Mar. xvi. 19; Luke xxii. 69; Eph.
i. 20; Heb. i. 3, viii. 1, x. 12, xii. 2; Rev. iii. 21. See Psal. cx. 1, with
the quotations Matt. xxii. 44 (and parallels); Zech. vi. 13; Acts ii. 34;
Heb. i. 13 (cp. 1 Cor. xv. 24—27).—The imagery denotes the repose
and empire of the ascended Christ, who has for ever done the work of
sacrificial offering, and now "sits" to dispense the blessings He has
wrought. Two exceptions only appear; Acts vii. 56, where He
"stands" to aid and welcome the martyr; Rev. v. 6, where the mystic
Lamb, new ascended, "stands" close by the throne, not on it, but
about to approach and (xxii. 3) claim it.
on the right hand] I.e., on the throne, at the Father's "right hand."
—The words not only state a fact, but have here a special significance.
To "seek the things above" is to go out in spirit towards a Christ
triumphant and reigning, and therefore all-competent to save and bless.
2. *Set your affection* &c.] Not "*affections*," but "*affection*," *affectus*,
the tendency, bias, of the mind.—More lit., "*think* the things &c."; in
the sense not of articulate thought but rather of character, as we call
a man thoughtful, high-thoughted, and the like. R.V., well, **Set your
mind** &c. Latin Versions, *sapite.* Luther, *Trachtet nach dem, was
droben ist.*—The verb, *phronein*, appears (itself or its cognates) e.g.
Matt. xvi. 23; Rom. viii. 5; Phil. ii. 5, iii. 19 (the exact antithesis to
this passage).
Grace only can fix the "affection" heavenward; but the Christian,
none the less, is to use thought and will in the matter.
things *on the earth*] Lit. and better, **the things**, &c.—Cp. Phil. iii.
19.—The special reference is to earth as the scene of temptation, the
field of conflict with "the flesh." And the Christian is warned never to
meet this conflict in a spirit secretly sympathetic with the foe because
conversant only with the interests and expedients of things present and
visible. The man who was absorbed in "earthly" care, or pleasure,
and the man who understood no heavenly secrets of moral victory, but
used only "earthly" expedients ("*touch not, taste not,* &c."), would
alike be "setting the mind on earthly things."—See further on ver. 5.—
Nothing in these words bids us shut our eyes to the riches of creation,
or regard the charm of human affection as in itself evil. The precept is
to be read in its context; it forbids an "earthly" programme for the
aims and the means of the Christian life.
3. *For*] The heavenward, Christward, "affection" of the Christian
is *reasonable*, when his spiritual relation to Christ is seen.
ye are dead] Lit. and better, **ye died**; in Christ's death for and to
sin. See above on ii. 11, 12, 20.
your life] assumed to be actually theirs, because He who died,
and to whom they were united by faith, rose again. See above on
ii. 12, for the nature and import of this wonderful life, which implies the

God. When Christ, *who is* our life, shall appear, then shall ye also appear with him in glory.

remission of a death-sentence, but also far transcends it. It is in fact, in its full and inmost sense, the life of the glorified Head made present and powerful in His members by the Holy Spirit. Cp. 1 Cor. vi. 17; Gal. ii. 20.

is hid] The Greek tense is the perfect. The life was, *and is*, "*hid*"; continuously, from its first gift. "*You died*," on the other hand, is given in the aorist (in the Greek). The "death" is fact *accomplished*, the resulting "life" is fact *continuing*.

"*Hid*":—with the double suggestion of *safety* and *concealment*. He "with" Whom it is hidden is there "where no thief approacheth," and also where "the world seeth Him no more." The main emphasis is on the latter fact. And the Apostle's practical aim is to direct the Christian away from the visible, mechanical, routine of Pharisaic or Essenic observance to the secrets of holiness which are as invisible to natural sight as is Christ Himself, in Whom they reside.—We do not think, as Lightfoot, that there is any reference just here to *baptismal burial*, in which the baptized person was significantly *hidden* beneath the water. For the baptismal rite instantly went on to an emersion, signifying a life in some sense *manifest*.

with Christ] Again the mystical Union is in view; the vital secret of the whole matter.

in God] the Father. The word GOD is here, as very often (see e.g. Phil. ii. 6), used of the Father with a certain distinctiveness. See above, i. 3, and note there.—What is "with" the glorified Christ is "*in God*," inasmuch as the Son is "in the bosom of the Father" (Joh. i. 18). Cp. Joh. xvii. 21, 23.

4. *When Christ...shall appear*] R.V., somewhat more closely, **shall be manifested**; leaving the Secret Place of His glory to return to human sight, in His Second Advent. The verb is used in the same connexion, 1 Pet. v. 4; 1 Joh. ii. 28, iii. 2 (probably).—In connexion with the visible "manifestation" of the Son at the First Advent it occurs e.g. 1 Tim. iii. 16; 1 Joh. i. 2; and in connexion with the "manifestation" of the Risen One after death, Mar. xvi. 12, 14; Joh. xxi. 14.—The import of the word in all these passages far transcends mere visibility, and gives the thought of a discovery of what He is Who is seen; but it implies a quite literal visibility. "This same Jesus, *in like manner*, shall come" (Acts i. 11).—This is the one place in the Epistle where the Lord's glorious Return is distinctly mentioned (see i. 5, for a pregnant allusion to it). In the Ephesians no explicit reference to it occurs (but see Eph. iv. 30).

who is *our life*] The truth of the previous verse is repeated in an intenser form. The "life" which is "hid *with* Him," in respect of your possession of it, is, in respect of itself, nothing less than HE. So is Christ's exalted life the direct secret of your regenerate life and faculty, that *it* is *Christ*, and nothing secondary. The Holy Spirit is "the Lord, the Life-*Giver*" (Nicene Creed); but *the Life* is the Son of God, as the

5 Mortify therefore your members which are upon the earth;

Redeemer and Head of His saints.—Cp. Joh. vi. 57, xi. 25, xiv. 6; Gal. ii. 20; 1 Joh. v. 11, 12.

"*Our life*":—he has just said, "*your* life is hid, &c."; now he "hastens to include himself among the recipients of the bounty" (Lightfoot).

shall ye also appear] **be manifested.** "*It hath not yet been manifested what we shall be*" (1 Joh. iii. 2). The believer has a supernatural secret of peace and holiness, but it is hidden; and the Divine *quality* of the effects will not be fully "manifested" till the Cause is "manifested." Again, the effects, though in a partial sense "manifested" even now, "in our *mortal flesh*" (2 Cor. iv. 11), are as to their Divine *quantity* still "hidden," till the final glorification of the saints. Then, the oneness of the members with their Head will be seen, in all its living power and wonder, and their perfect holiness will be discovered to be *all* "of Him." So "the sons of God will be *manifested*" (Rom. viii. 19) in respect of the nature and the greatness of their sonship.

The Apostle's practical aim is to bring his converts to use their "hidden" life the more freely and confidently, in view of its promised issues, and to cheer them by the same prospects under the cross of sorrow, temptation, limitation, or whatever else "conceals," in God's present order, their life eternal.

with him] from whom the glorified are never separated. Cp. 1 Thess. iii. 13, iv. 14.

in glory] His glory, the effulgence, visible and spiritual, of His presence; shared by His members. Cf. Rom. viii. 17, 18, 21 ("*the liberty of the glory*, &c."); 1 Joh. iii. 2. And see 1 Cor. xv. 43; Phil. iii. 21.

5—12 UNIVERSAL HOLINESS THE NECESSARY ISSUE OF THE LIFE OF UNION: THE NEGATIVE SIDE

5. *Mortify therefore*] Observe the "*therefore.*" *Because of* the possession of a hidden *life*, and in its power, they were to put sin *to death*. Here is no mere assertion of duty, but an implied assurance of power, the power of *life*, life welcomed and developed. So, in nature, the rising sap of the tree makes the dead leaf fall.

"*Mortify*":—the verb occurs elsewhere, in Biblical Greek, only Rom. iv. 19; Heb. xi. 12; in both cases of Abraham's physical condition in old age. Its plain meaning is to reduce to a state of death, or like death; a state helpless, inoperative. The Christian, in the power of his hidden life in Christ, is thus to deal with his sins; entirely to renounce the thought of compromise or toleration, and to apply to them the mighty counter-agent of his union with his Head.

The verb is in the aorist tense; decisive and critical action is in view. The believer, reminded of his resources and of the will of God, is now, with full purpose, to "*give to death*" (Conybeare) all his sins, and to carry that purpose out with critical decision at each moment of temptation, in the power of his true life.

Colossians 3 / 121

fornication, uncleanness, inordinate affection, evil con-
No assertions of an attained "sinless perfection" are warranted by such a word. The following context is enough to shew that St Paul views his converts as all along morally imperfect. But that side of truth is not in view here; the Christian is called here to an unreserved decision of will and to a full use of Christ's power.

In the closely parallel words, Rom. viii. 13, the verb (another verb in the Greek) is in the *present* tense, indicating the need of continuous *action* after however critical a *decision*.

your members] Your limbs, as if of an invisible, non-material, *body*, viewed in its separate organs. A bold but intelligible transition of thought thus speaks of the organ rather than of its action; giving a more concrete effect to the mental picture. See below, the next note but one.

Lightfoot compares the phrases "*old man, new man.*"—See below however on vv. 9, 10.

upon the earth] Conversant, sympathetic, with "*earth*" as the scene of temptation, and not with heaven, where lies the Source of victory.— Cp. the language of Article XVII:—"Such as feel in themselves the working of the Spirit of Christ, mortifying the works of the flesh, and their earthly members, and drawing up their minds to high and heavenly things."

fornication, &c.] Lightfoot places a colon before this word in the Greek, and goes on to the imperative verb "*put off*" (ver. 8) for the (broken) grammatical government. The startling identification of "*members*" with sins is thus avoided. But the construction is extremely difficult and really unlikely. The R.V. constructs as the A.V.

"*Fornication*":—a sin often in view in the Epistles; evidently an evil wofully rife, but not the less ruthlessly condemned. Cp. 1 Cor. vi. 9, 13, 18; Gal. v. 19; Eph. v. 3; 1 Thess. iv. 3; Heb. xiii. 4. See our note on Eph. v. 3. It is to be decisively "done to death" by the Christian.

uncleanness] A word of wider reference than "*fornication*," and so conveying a still stronger appeal. Act, word, thought, unworthy of the member of the All-Pure Christ—all are to be put to death in the power of His life.

inordinate affection] Lit. and better, **passion** (R. V.). Cp. Rom. i. 26; 1 Thess. iv. 5; the other places where the Greek (*pathos*) occurs in N. T. The word denotes lust from *the passive* side of experience, *uncontrollable* desire, to which the man is a slave. All the more significant is the implied statement that even this form of sin is to be, and can be, "done to death" in Christ.

evil concupiscence] *Concupiscentiam malam,* Latin Versions; and so all the English Versions, except Wyclif, "*yvel coveitise,*" and R. V., **evil desire.**—"*Passion*" and "*desire*" (or, in older English, "*lust*") are combined, 1 Thess. iv. 5, and collocated, Gal. v. 24. "The same vice may be viewed as a [passion] from its passive and a [desire] from its active side... The epithet ("*evil*") is added because ["desire"] is capable of a good sense." (Lightfoot).

122 / Colossians 3

6 cupiscence, and covetousness, which is idolatry: for which *things'* sake the wrath of God cometh on the children of dis-
7 obedience: in the which ye also walked sometime, when ye

covetousness...idolatry] "*Avarice, whiche is servyce of mawmetis*"[1] (Wyclif).—See Eph. v. 3, 5 for a close parallel. Lightfoot here sees a reference to covetousness in its ordinary sense; "the covetous man sets up another object of worship besides God." And he shews clearly that the Greek word never, *of itself*, denotes sensual lust. But cp. this passage with Eph. iv. 19, v. 3, 5; 1 Cor. v. 11; 1 Thess. iv. 6; and it will appear that it at least lends itself to a *connexion with* sensual ideas, just as our word "greed" lends itself to a connexion with avarice. If so, the "*idolatry*" of the matter lies in its sensuous and unwholesome *admiration*, developing into acts of evil.

"*Which is*":—more precisely, **seeing that it is**.

6. *For which* things' *sake*, &c.] See Eph. v. 6 for an almost verbal parallel, only observing that the words "*on the children of disobedience*" should *perhaps* be omitted from the reading here; they are possibly an early insertion from Ephesians.

"*The wrath of God*":—the eternal *personal* antagonism of the Holy One, as such, to sin. It is no impulsive "passion," but it is also no figure of speech, however it may be ignored or explained away.—Cp. Joh. iii. 36; Rom. i. 18, ii. 5, 8, v. 9, ix. 22; 1 Thess. i. 10; Rev. vi. 16, xix. 15, &c.; and see Eph. ii. 3, with our note.

"*Cometh*":—**is coming**; is on its way, till in "the day of wrath" (Rom. ii. 5) it falls.

on the children of disobedience] So Eph. v. 6.—Documentary evidence is in favour of the retention of these words, but some important documents omit them. Lightfoot pronounces them an interpolation from Eph., but R. V. text retains them.

7. *In the which*] "*things*," mentioned just above.—Otherwise we may render, "*among whom*" (R. V. margin); i.e. among "the children of disobedience." If those words are not retained in the text, this latter rendering of course falls.

walked] The same verb is rendered (by A. V.) in the parallel, Eph. ii. 3, "*had our conversation*," that is, our action and intercourse in life. The metaphor "*walk*" in such a sense is common in St Paul. See above on i. 10.—With this searching appeal to memory cp. 1 Cor. vi. 11; Eph. ii. 2, iv. 22, v. 8; Tit. iii. 3; 1 Pet. iv. 3.

sometime] "*Sumtyme*," Wyclif; antique English for "*once on a time*." So "*sometimes*" in the A. V. of Eph. ii. 13.—In Eph. ii. 3 (parallel here) the A. V. renders the same Greek, "*in times past*."

lived] Not merely "*existed*," or "*dwelt*," but found what seemed "*life*." See on ii. 20 above. From the "*life*" issues the "*walk*," as Lightfoot points out.—"He argues from the withdrawal of the cause to the withdrawal of the effect" (Calvin).

in them] Far better, with MSS. &c., **in these things** (R. V.).

---

[1] *i.e.*, idols. Strangely enough, the word is a corruption of *Mahomet*, the name of the great *Iconoclast*.

lived in them.   But now you also put off all *these;* anger, 8
wrath, malice, blasphemy, filthy communication out of your
mouth.   Lie not one to another, seeing that ye have put off 9

8. *But now*]   Under the divinely altered case of their conversion
and union with Christ.
you also]   As well as all other true believers.
put off]   The Greek is *imperative*, and so the English is to be taken;
but the English is verbally ambiguous between imperative and indicative.—In Christ, they were already, ideally and potentially, *divested* of
sin; they were now, as if never before, to realize and act upon that
divestiture.   Cp. Eph. iv. 25; and see Rom. xiii. 12.
all these]   Lit., "*the all (things),*" the whole congeries of sins.—
Here, as perpetually, comes in the principle that the Christian character
is a sinless *character*, to be realized and lived out by its possessor, who
assuredly discovers in the process that he is not a sinless *person*, while
he is gifted in Christ with a Divine liberty from serving sin.
anger, wrath]   The two words occur together Rom. ii. 8; Eph. iv.
31; Rev. xvi. 19, xix. 15.   The word rendered "*anger*" is rather
chronic, that rendered "*wrath*" rather acute—an outburst.   See Trench,
Synonyms, § XXXVI.
malice]   The Greek word sometimes bears the sense of "*evil*," "*ill*,"
in general; e.g. Matt. vi. 34.   But in lists of vices (cp. here Rom. i. 29,
Tit. iii. 3; 1 Pet. ii. 1) it means what we mean by "*malice*."—It is the
vice which lies below anger and wrath, as a root or spring.
blasphemy]   Greek, *blasphêmia;* so Eph. iv. 31, where A. V. renders
evil-speaking (so better, or, with R. V., **railing**).   We now confine
"*blasphemy*" to railing against God and Divine things; but the
Greek has no such limit.   Cp. (in the Greek) e. g. 1 Cor. iv. 13, x.
30; Tit. iii. 2.
filthy communication]   "**shameful speaking**," R. V.; "*abusive
conversation*," Alford; *turpiloquium*, Old Latin Version.   The reference to "abuse" rather than pollution is made likely by the words
in context, *anger*, &c.   But Lightfoot remarks that the reference to
pollution is still latent; the "abuse" must be, as he renders here, "*foul-
mouthed* abuse."   The derivation and usage of the Greek word suggest
this.
9. *Lie not*]   Cp. Eph. iv. 25.   Entire truthfulness is an essential
Christian characteristic, for Christ is "the Truth."   In the light of His
words and deeds it is certain that nothing untruthful, not even the most
"pious" of "frauds," can possibly be holy.—The uniform emphasis on
truthfulness in the precepts of Scripture is the more significant of the
origin of Scripture when we remember the proverbial Oriental laxity
about truth.   See our note on Eph. iv. 25.
one to another]   As Christian to Christian (cp. Eph. iv. 25).   Not that
truth was to be spoken less to heathen or misbeliever; as if *fides non
servanda esset cum ethnicis, cum hæreticis*.   But Christian intercourse was
to be, so to speak, *the nursery-plot* for the right temper in all intercourse.
seeing that ye have put off]   So R. V.   Lightfoot recommends the

10 the old man with his deeds; and have put on the new *man*, which is renewed in knowledge after the image of him that

translation "*putting off*," taking this as part of the exhortation; as if to say, "put off the old man and lie no more." This is fully allowed by the grammar; but we think that the parallel in Eph. iv. 21—24 (see our notes there) is much in favour of the A. V. and R. V. See further below on ver. 10.—In position, possession, idea, they *had* "*taken off*" "the old man." In experience, they *were to* "*take off*" the related sins.

the old man] Elsewhere only Rom. vi. 6; Eph. iv. 22 (where see our notes). In Romans it is a thing which "was crucified with Christ." —It may be explained as "*the old state*," the state of the unregenerate son of Adam, guilty under the sentence of the eternal law, and morally the slave of sin. To "take off" the old Man is to quit that position, stepping, in Christ, into the position of acceptance and of spiritual power and liberty.—"*The old Man*" is thus not identical with "the flesh," which is an abiding element (Gal. v. 16, 17) in the regenerate, though it need never be the ruling element.—The phrases "old Man" and "new Man" have a probable inner reference to the First and Second Adam respectively (Rom. v. 12—19; 1 Cor. xv. 21, 45—49). The "*taking off*" and "*putting on*" here may be explained as meaning, practically, "you broke connexion (of guilt and helplessness) with the First Adam, and formed connexion (of acceptance and of life) with the Second."

with his deeds] See Rom. viii. 13 for the same Greek word; "*the practices, machinations* of the body." And cp. Acts xix. 18.—"The old Man" is, so to speak, the parent of "the deceitfulness of sin" in all its phases; connexion with "the new Man" is the death-blow to it, as the anxious conscience is set at rest, the relation of the believer to God wholly altered, and a spiritual force not his own given to him.

10. *and have put on*] See the last note but one. Cp. Eph. iv. 24; and ver. 12 below, with note.

the new man] Practically, the new position of acceptance and the new spiritual power of the regenerated self; with a reference in the phrase to the believer's connexion with "the Second Man," Christ[1].

By union with Him his members become (be it said with reverence and caution) repetitions of Him the glorious Archetype. To come to be "in Him" is thus to "*put on* (*Him as*) *the New Man*," in sharing His acceptance and His life and power. See further, our note on Eph. iv. 24.

is renewed] Lit. and better, **is being renewed**; a present not aorist participle.—In the parallel place in Eph. "the new man" "*was created*," as a definite fact; here he is continuously "*being renewed*," maintained as it were by a continuous creative act. (Cp. for the verb in a kindred context, 2 Cor. iv. 16.)—Practically, the thought is of the

---

[1] In the Ignatian Epistles (*Ep. ad Eph.* c. xx.) occurs the phrase, "the dispensation of *the New Man, even Christ*." If this was written as early as A.D. 110 it is an important comment here.

created him : where there is neither Greek nor Jew, circum- 11
believer's maintained union with His Lord, and his realization in that union of continued peace and spiritual power. As if the Head, for the member, were evermore "made new," and so always newly reflected and as it were reproduced in the member.—Lightfoot compares, in contrast, Eph. iv. 22; "the old man is *being corrupted*, is *decaying.*"

in knowledge] Lit. and better, **unto knowledge.** The daily "renewal" is such as to result continually in the regenerate man's spiritual vision of Christ, intimacy with Him, insight into His will.—On the word *epignôsis*, see on i. 9.

after the image of him that created him] I.e., so as to be like God, who "created," constituted, the new creation as He did the old. Cp. the close parallel, Gen. i. 26, 27; a passage no doubt in St Paul's mind here.

The reference is to the Father, not the Son, as the Creator; cp. the parallel, Eph. iv. 22, "created *after God*;" and the place in Genesis. He is the eternal Original; "the new man" realizes his ideal in likeness to Him, generated by communion with Him in Christ.

Even here, we think, may be traced reverently an allusion to Christ as "the Second Man." He, truly, is not *"created"* as to His Being and Person, which is necessary and eternal; but as Son of Man, and as Head of His Church, in respect of His Work and Office, Scripture represents Him as the willing Result of the Father's will. In this respect He, as well as His followers in Him (Eph. ii. 10), "lives because of the Father" (Joh. vi. 57). But while this reference lies, as we think, in the depths of the passage, its manifest practical import is that the regenerate member of the blessed Head needs and receives daily "renewal by his Holy Spirit," leading to a fuller knowledge of, and so a truer likeness to, the Father of Jesus Christ.

The suggestion that "the image" is in fact Christ, (so Chrysostom; cp. above i. 15; 2 Cor. iv. 4) is not likely in view of the parallel, Eph. iv. 24, with its simple phrase "according *to God*." See Lightfoot's note.

11. *where*] "*in*" "*the new Man.*" This phrase is a further suggestion of the inner reference to Christ as the New Man which we find in this passage and the Ephesian parallel. Certainly the language of *locality* accords better with such a reference than with a reference *merely* to the regenerate state of the Christian.

there is neither] The Greek is emphatic; **there exists neither.** "Not merely the fact but the possibility" is negatived (Lightfoot). In Christ, such differences *cannot breathe*.

Greek nor Jew] Cp. Rom. x. 12; 1 Cor. xii. 13; Gal. iii. 28 (a close verbal parallel). The word *Hellên* in such antithetical places "denotes all nations not Jews that made the language, customs and learning of the Greeks their own" (Grimm's *N.T. Lexicon*, ed. Thayer). In this sense it is used e.g. Joh. vii. 35, where A.V. renders "*Gentiles*." See too Acts xi. 20 (true reading), xiv. 1, &c.

circumcision nor uncircumcision] Cp. Rom. ii. 25—27, iii. 30; 1 Cor. vii. 19; Gal. v. 6, vi. 15; and see Eph. ii. 11.

126 / Colossians 3

cision nor uncircumcision, barbarian, Scythian, bond *nor*
12 free: but Christ *is* all, and in all. Put on therefore, as the
elect of God, holy and beloved, bowels of mercies, kind-

barbarian, Scythian] The word *barbaros*, in Greek, first denoted a speaker of an unintelligible language, and so a non-Greek, whatever his state of society or culture. It thus included the Romans, and in pre-Augustan Latin writers is even used as a synonym for Latin. But "from the Augustan age the name belonged to all tribes which had no Greek *or* Roman accomplishments" (Liddell and Scott, *Greek Lexicon*).

"*Scythian:*"—an intensification of the previous word. The Scythians, a wandering race, akin probably to the modern Turks, were regarded by both Greeks and Jews as the wildest of wild tribes, (though the opposite view, strangely, had been taken by early Greek thought, idealizing the unknown. Thus Æschylus (cent. 5 B.C.) calls the Scythians "*well-ordered*").—Lightfoot points out that to the Jews the Scythians were specially a name of terror and savagery, for in the reign of Josiah they had poured into Palestine (Herodotus i. 105—6); an invasion not recorded in Scripture, but perhaps indicated in Jer. i. 13—16; Ezek. xxxviii.—ix.

bond nor *free*] Cp. 1 Cor. xii. 13; Gal. iii. 28; Eph. vi. 8 (with notes in this series on ver. 5); and see 1 Cor. vii. 22.—Onesimus and Philemon would be at hand as living illustrations of this brief but wonderful statement.

but Christ is *all and in all*] More exactly, to paraphrase, **but all things, and in all (persons), are—Christ.** Such was the union of every believer with Him, that each was to each an embodiment as it were of His presence and life. In this respect all differences, national, ritual, educational, social, were assimilated in the eyes of faith and love. Facts of race, history, status, were not indeed contradicted, but they were overruled, and transfigured into mere varying phases of a central union in the Lord, Who shone equally through all His members.

This short sentence is at once a radical contradiction to some of the deepest prejudices of classical paganism and of (distorted) Judaism, and a wonderful positive revelation.

12—17 UNIVERSAL HOLINESS: THE POSITIVE SIDE

12. *Put on therefore*] They had already "*taken off the old Man*" and "*put on the new*" (ver. 9, and notes). But the ideal would need to be made real, in obedient faith.

the elect of God] For the same phrase (or nearly), cp. Matt. xxiv. 31; Luke xviii. 7; Rom. viii. 33; Tit. i. 1; and cp. Mar. xiii. 20; Joh. xiii. 18, xv. 16, 19; Rom. ix. 11, xi. 5, 7, 28; 1 Cor. i. 27, 28; Eph. i. 4; 2 Tim. ii. 10.—The word rendered "*elect*" (and its cognates) is generally used in the N.T., where the highest level of Divine purpose, or spiritual privilege, is in view, and with a tendency to emphasize the sovereign and (humanly) uncaused mercy of the "choice." See

ness, humbleness of mind, meekness, longsuffering; forbear- 13
ing one another, and forgiving one another, if any *man* have
a quarrel against any: even as Christ forgave you, so also *do*

our note on Eph. i. 4.—At the same time the truth of a sovereign choice
is constantly found in connexions where (as here) *practical holiness* is in
view. See e.g. Rom. viii. 29. It is mentioned here only to enforce the
most practical "obligations of nobility."

beloved] In the Greek, a *perfect* participle passive (so 1 Thess. i. 4;
2 Thess. ii. 13), indicating the settlement and fixity of the Divine love;
"on whom He *has set His love.*" On the application to a whole community of such terms as those used in this verse, see above on i. 2.

bowels of mercies] Better perhaps **a heart of compassion**; having
regard to the English use of the word "heart" as a symbol for tenderness of feeling. See our notes on Phil. i. 8; Philem. 7.

kindness] Almost, **sweetness**; the character which offers sympathy
and invites confidence. See Trench, *N.T. Synonyms*, Second Series,
§ xiii.

humbleness of mind] One word in the Greek.—See above on ii. 18,
23, for the same word (there rendered in A.V. "*humility*") in a very
different context. It occurs Eph. iv. 2 (A.V., "*lowliness*"); Phil. ii. 3
(A.V., "*lowliness of mind*"); where see notes in this Series.—The
word is not older in Greek than the N.T., and the grace is essentially
Christian, the attitude of a soul which has lost its pride in the discovery
of the mercy of its salvation.

meekness] Grouped similarly with "*humbleness*" Eph. iv. 2; where
see note in this Series. It is the grace of submission under trial.

longsuffering] See note, ch. i. 11.

13. *forbearing one another*] "*in love*," adds Eph. iv. 2. The life
of Christian patience has beneath it the living secret of love, the effect
and reflection of the love of Christ.

forgiving one another] Lit., "*forgiving yourselves*," as in Eph. iv. 32,
where see note in this Series. The A.V. is obviously true to grammatical usage.—It is implied that there would be occasions for forbearance and forgiveness, even in this happy and holy community.

a quarrel] "*a querel*," Wyclif; *querelam*, Latin Versions.—"*A
quarrel*," derived through French from Latin, means properly (as here)
a complaint (so R.V. here), *a charge*. Our modern use of the word
would imply *a wrangle* ("it takes two to make *a quarrel*"). But the
case supposed is where A has not done right by B, and B responds by
forgiving A, in Christ, and thus avoiding a wrangle.—For a practical
illustration of the precept, see e.g. 1 Cor. vi. 7.

against any] We say, "a quarrel *with* any," because we now use the
word "*quarrel*" in the lowered sense of a wrangle.

even as Christ forgave] R.V. "*even as* the Lord *forgave.*" The
reading thus rendered has important but not (as it seems to us) decisive
support from MSS. &c. Its reference meanwhile is probably still to
Christ; but under the special character of the heavenly *Master*. (Cp.
Matt. xviii. 27, quoted by Lightfoot, who reads "*the Lord*" here.)—See

14 ye. And above all these *things put on* charity, which is the
15 bond of perfectness. And let the peace of God rule in your
hearts, to the which also ye are called in one body; and be

the parallel, Eph. iv. 32. There the *Father* is the Divine Forgiver; here probably the Son. The Two are One; and the Son, while the Father's Channel of forgiveness, is also the infinitely free and gracious Giver of it. Cp. Acts v. 31.—Observe the deeply practical use of the assurance of pardon.

14. *above all these* things] Or, "*upon* all these things." Perhaps the words convey both the *supreme importance* of love, and its relation to other graces as their *embracing bond;* see just below. "Love is the outer garment" (rather, the girdle?) "which holds the others in their places" (Lightfoot).

put on] The words are supplied from ver. 12.

charity] Or, **love**. See on ch. i. 4. Love, says Leibnitz, is that which seeks its joy in the good of another.—"Hypocrisy can do Christian actions; charity alone does them christianly" (Quesnel).

which is] The Greek implies that "*love*" must be thus "*put on*" *because* it is, &c.

the bond of perfectness] I.e., the bond, or tie, which makes and secures the "*perfectness*," wholeness, fulness, harmony, of the Christian character, both in the individual and in society. Chrysostom, quoted by Lightfoot, says (on this place), "If love is lacking, all other good is nothing; it dissolves." The man without love is, in effect, the man whose very virtues are selfish; "*unto himself*."

"*Perfectness:*"—see note on ch. i. 28.

15. *the peace of God*] Read, with decisive documentary evidence, **the peace of Christ.** Cp. Joh. xiv. 27, xvi. 33. It is the chastened but glad tranquillity caused by knowledge of Christ, and communion with Him, as our all-sufficient Atonement, Life, Friend, and King.

rule] Lit., **arbitrate** (so R.V. margin). The Lord's peace, received and enjoyed, is *to decide* every internal debate between self and God, self and others; to give its casting-vote always on the side of holy love. "I have peace with God, and in God, through Christ; how can I use such a gift but for the Giver?"—The Greek verb, *brabeuein*, means first to act as an athletic umpire, then generally to arbitrate, then to rule. The two latter meanings blend here.

Wyclif has "*enioie*," and the Rhemish (Romanist) Version "*exult*." Both are from the Vulgate Latin, *exsultet;* this probably is a free *interpretation* of the Greek, which was taken to mean "*to have its way*," and so, "*to break forth into joy*."

in your hearts] Such settlement of debates *there* would quite preclude all harsh conflicts *in the community*.

to the which] **Into which (peace).**

ye are called] Cp. Eph. iv. 4, where the "*call*" of grace appears in a similar connexion.—On the meaning of "*call*," "*calling*," in the Epistles (a meaning nearly represented by the popular use of the word "*conversion*" in religion now) see note in this Series on Eph. i. 18.

ye thankful. Let the word of Christ dwell in you richly in all 16
wisdom; teaching and admonishing one another in psalms
and hymns and spiritual songs, singing with grace in your

in one body] I.e., so as to form one body, in which now you
are. Cp. again Eph. iv. 4. Each true convert was, as such, brought
into Divine peace, so as to be a living unit in a divinely peaceful
society.
Here for the last time in the Epistle is named the mystical Body,
vivified and ruled by its glorious Head. See i. 18, 24, ii. 19.
thankful] See below, ver. 17.
16. *the word of Christ*] The precise phrase occurs here only. It is
(surely, though Lightfoot advocates the explanation, "Christ's word to
the Christian; His influence speaking in the heart") the message of
His Gospel, the terms of the revelation of His personal Glory, redeeming work, and holy will. This "*word*" might be conveyed in
the Old Scriptures (see e.g. Rom. xv. 4, xvi. 26; Gal. iii. 8; 1 Pet. ii.
6), or by the mouth or pen of Christian Apostles and Prophets.—Cp.
e.g. Acts iv. 29, vi. 2, viii. 14, xiii. 26, xv. 7, 35, xvii. 13, xix. 10, xx.
32; 1 Cor. i. 18, xiv. 36; 2 Cor. v. 19; Eph. i. 13; 1 Thess. iv. 15;
2 Thess. iii. 1; 2 Tim. ii. 9; Tit. i. 9; Heb. vi. 1; Jas. i. 18; 1 Pet.
i. 23; Rev. i. 9, vi. 9.—Thus both O. T. citations and such Christian
watchwords as 1 Tim. i. 15; 2 Tim. ii. 11, would be "*the word of
Christ*"; and as each portion of the New Scriptures (2 Pet. iii. 16)
appeared and was received its words too would be "*the word of
Christ.*"—The definiteness of the Gospel is powerfully emphasized by
its designation as *a word, a message.*
dwell in you] as what has become a permanent part of your thought.
richly] See on i. 27 for St Paul's love of the imagery of wealth.—
The heavenly "word" was to be abundant as a store (Psal. cxix. 11)
in their memories, and also as an element in their thought and
utterance.
in all wisdom] They were not merely to know "the word" verbally,
but to handle and apply it with spiritual fitness and rightness. The
supreme example appears in our Lord's use of "the word" of the
O. T.; Matt. iv.—Such "*wisdom*," infinitely higher than that of the
mere critical enquirer, would be learnt in communion with the Lord of
the Word. Cp. Eph. i. 17.
teaching and admonishing one another] The Greek is out of grammatical connexion with the previous clauses, but fully intelligible. See
Lightfoot's excellent note.—"*One another*":—lit. "*yourselves.*" See
note on ver. 13; and on Eph. v. 19.
"*Teaching...admonishing*":—in the parallel, Eph. v. 19 (where see
our notes throughout), we have merely "*speaking.*"—The spiritual importance of Christian hymnody comes out impressively here. It is no
mere luxury of devotion, certainly no mere musical pleasure; it is an
ordained vehicle of instruction and warning.
psalms...hymns...spiritual songs] Verbatim as Eph. v. 19. To
summarize our comment there; it is impossible to draw absolute limits

17 hearts to the Lord. And whatsoever ye do in word or deed, *do* all in the name of the Lord Jesus, giving thanks to God and the Father by him.

18 Wives, submit yourselves unto your own husbands, as it

between these kinds of sacred music; but on the whole the *psalm* may be exemplified by (in the O.T.) the songs of the Psalter, and (in the N.T.) those of Luke i., ii., their Christian parallel; the *hymn* by the chant of the disciples, Acts iv.; and the *song* or ode (*ôdê*) by such rhythmic "words" as those of 2 Tim. i. 11. This last citation is notably full of both "*teaching*" and "*admonition.*"

"*Spiritual songs*":—not necessarily inspired, as Scripture, but pregnant with spiritual truth. Yet it is at least possible, from the recent mention of "the word of Christ," that "songs" due to inspired authorship are here referred to, at least specially.—Luther, master and lover of hymns, writes in his Version here, out of the fulness of his heart, *mit geistlichen* lieblichen *Liedern.*

with grace] Lit., "*in the grace*"; conditioned by "*the grace given unto you.*"—"*Grace*" here is, in effect, the presence of God in the believer, with its holy, loving power.

17. *whatsoever ye do*] See below ver. 23 for the same phrase; and for similar precepts of holy absoluteness cp. Prov. iii. 6; 1 Cor. x. 31. The Christian life is nothing less than the whole life of the Christian, lived "unto the Lord" (Rom. xiv. 6—8); everything in it is related to Him.

in the name of the Lord Jesus] As it were *quoting* Him (to yourselves, and if need be to other men) as the Master ("*Lord*") who sets the task and owns and uses the servant. On another reference of the same phrase see our note on Eph. v. 20.

giving thanks] "*always for all things,*" adds Eph. v. 20. The two parallels complement each other; the one Epistle more specially bids the Christian do God's will, the other more specially bids Him love God's will, and give thanks for it, in everything.

and the Father] "*And*" should probably be omitted.

by Him] The Mediator of our thanks, as of the Father's gifts. Cp. Rom. i. 8, xvi. 27; Heb. xiii. 15; 1 Pet. ii. 5, iv. 11.

"O God," says Quesnel on this verse, "who is a Christian, if all our words and actions are to be a sacrifice of praise, offered to God through Jesus Christ as our Priest, Pontiff, Mediator; with Him as God's true Victim; in Him as God's Temple; on Him as God's Altar; after Him as our Law and Model; under Him as our Master and King; in His spirit, purposes, motives, disposition, aim, as He is our Head?"

18—IV. 1   UNIVERSAL HOLINESS: RELATIVE DUTIES

18. *Wives*] Cp. 1 Pet. iii. 1—6 and the close parallel, with its large expansion, Eph. v. 22, &c.

The Christian Home, the masterpiece of living Christianity, is now

is fit in the Lord. Husbands, love *your* wives, and be not 19
bitter against them. Children, obey *your* parents in all 20
presented as the special field for the practice of the holy principles just stated.

submit yourselves] with the noble loyalty of "the weaker vessel" to the husband who, in the order of nature (i.e. of God its Orderer), is the leader in the marriage union. No submission as of a vassal is meant; the man is (1 Pet. iii. 7) to "*give honour to the wife.*" Her relative attitude is to be that of every Christian to every other (Eph. v. 21; 1 Pet. v. 5), the attitude of unselfish service, only emphasized by the special fact of man's ordained leadership.

own] The word is probably to be omitted; a natural and obvious gloss upon the text.—Cp. 1 Cor. vii. 2 for the apostolic prohibition of polygamy.

fit in the Lord] The order of nature is thus affirmed by grace. Wifely loyalty is not only a human but a Christian law; it has relation to union with Christ. See at large Eph. v. 22—24.

"*Is fit*":—lit., "*was fit.*" Lightfoot compares our past tense in "*I ought*," and says that in such phrases is perhaps implied an essential *a priori* obligation.

19. *Husbands*] Cp. Eph. v. 25—33; 1 Pet. iii. 7.

love] A word deepened and hallowed indefinitely by the Gospel, in reference to matrimonial truth and tenderness. See our note on Eph. v. 25.

be not bitter] with the wretched irritability of a supposed absolute superiority and authority. "The husband's primacy is not for dominion but for guidance, with sweetness, wisdom and peace" (Quesnel).—To be "*bitter,*" in the sense of angry, is a phrase of O. T. Greek. See the LXX. in e.g. Jerem. xliv. (Heb. xxxvii.) 15 (where A. V. reads "*they were wroth*"); Hab. i. 6.—Cp. Eph. iv. 31.

20. *Children*] Cp. Eph. vi. 1—3.

obey] The same word as that below, ver. 22. The wife "submits herself" as to a guiding *friend*; the child, and the servant, recognize in parent and master a lawful *commander*.

Disobedience to parents, as a definite act of rebellion against God (Exod. xx. 12, xxi. 17; Lev. xix. 3, xx. 9; Deut. v. 16), is always noted in Scripture as a grave crime, and a symptom of general moral mischief. Cp. Deut. xxi. 18—21; Prov. xx. 20, xxx. 17; Matt. xv. 4—6; Rom. i. 30; 2 Tim. iii. 2.—It is in the school of the well-ordered Christian home that the true idea of the Christian's position, filial in its freedom, yet (1 Cor. ix. 21) "*law-abiding* unto Christ," should be first illustrated as well as taught.

parents] Mothers as well as fathers. Scripture uniformly upholds the authority of the mother. See reff. in last note, and Prov. i. 8, vi. 20.

in all things] with the sole limitation of the supreme claims of the Heavenly Father, which may conceivably collide with those of the earthly parents. Cp. Matt. x. 37. But let the child be slow indeed to apply this principle in practice. The case can scarcely arise save

132 / Colossians 3

21 *things:* for this is well pleasing unto the Lord. Fathers, provoke not your children *to anger*, lest they be discouraged.
22 Servants, obey in all *things your* masters according to the flesh; not with eyeservice, as menpleasers; but in singleness

where the parent directly and positively requires the child to renounce the Lord.

well pleasing unto the Lord] Jesus Christ. Quesnel beautifully says, "Why does He seem here specially to delight in filial obedience? Because it was His own universal virtue, the soul and law of all His actions."

21. *Fathers*] We may (as in Eph. vi. 4, where see note) equally well render **Parents.** Cp. Heb. xi. 23, in the Greek. Still, the father is the natural *representative* of the dual parental authority.

provoke not...to wrath] **Chafe, irritate.** The Greek word is as old as Homer (e.g. *Iliad*, I. 32, IV. 5), who almost always uses it of *provocation to combat*. Unwise, unloving, parental despotism, exacting, needlessly chiding, interposing for the sake of interposition, is a fatally sure challenge to the child's will. The Christian father should handle that will as kindly as firmly.

be discouraged] Lose hope, the hope of pleasing, the animating expectation of doing right and so winning the "well done" of love. The eternal Father "upbraideth not" (Jas i. 5; cp. Isai. lvii. 16).— Luther has here, *auf dass sie nicht scheu werden*.

22. *Servants*] **Bondservants, slaves.** Cp. Eph. vi. 5—8; and see I Cor. vii. 21, 22; I Tim. vi. 1, 2; Tit. ii. 9, 10; Philemon; I Pet. ii. 18—25; and cp. Luke xvii. 7—10.—On the relation of the Gospel to slavery, see below, *Introd.* to the Ep. to Philemon, ch. iv.

in all things] See above, on ver. 20.

according to the flesh] With the implied thought that the master was not master of his bondman's *spirit*, and that master and bondman alike were bondmen, spiritually, of Christ. So Eph. vi. 5, where this clause is somewhat enlarged. The "*neither bond nor free*" of v. 11 above leaves thus undisturbed the actual duties of social status.

eyeservice] Eph. vi. 6. The word occurs there and here only, and was perhaps coined by St Paul. It means the "service" which works only when inspected, and does not come from the unseen source of love and goodwill.

menpleasers] Seeking merely the personal comfort of approval or indulgence, in a purely selfish and therefore insincere "*pleasing*." Such obsequiousness might conceal deep contempt or malice all the while. See note on Eph. vi. 6.

singleness] Lit., **simplicity**; the desire to do right for its own sake, or rather for the sake of the heavenly (and also the earthly) Master; as against the selfish aim of the "men-pleaser." See 1 Tim. vi. 2 for a practical comment.—The phrase is verbatim as in Eph. vi. 5, where see our note. And see the last words of Eph. vi. 6; "*doing the will of God from the soul.*"

fearing God] Read, **fearing the Lord** Christ, the true Master, with

Colossians 3 / 133

of heart, fearing God: and whatsoever ye do, do *it* heartily, 23
as to the Lord, and not unto men; knowing that of the 24
Lord ye shall receive the reward of the inheritance: for ye
serve the Lord Christ. But he that doeth wrong shall re- 25

the fear of reverent loyalty. The word *"fear"* is used in Scripture of
holy and perfectly happy reverence too often to need quotation.

23. *whatsoever ye do*] even in the daily round of servile tasks. For
the phrase and its significance, see above, ver. 17 and note.

do it *heartily*] Lit., **work from the soul.** Cp. Eph. vi. 6.

as to the Lord] Whose will expressed itself for them in each act of
common duty. What a transfiguration of the life for the man, or woman,
whom law and custom regarded as merely a purchasable "living chattel"!
See *Introd.* to the Ep. to Philemon, p. 155.

not unto men] as the ultimate reasons and constraints.

24. *knowing*] as a certainty of the Gospel. So Eph. vi. 8. For
the Christian's prospect of *"reward"* cp. Matt. v. 12, vi. 1, 4, xvi. 27;
Luke vi. 35, xiv. 14; Rom. ii. 6—10; 2 Cor. v. 10; Heb. x. 35; Rev.
xxii. 12; &c. The obedience of love is infallibly remembered by Him
to whom it is rendered. "Well done, good and faithful servant" (Matt.
xxv. 21, 23), is His certain ultimate response to every true act of the will
given up to Him. This, as presented in Scripture, is entirely harmonious
with the sure doctrine of our justification for Christ's Merit only,
embraced by faith only (Art. xi.). It is the recognition of love by love,
of grace by the Giver.

receive] The Greek may be rendered, **receive as your due.** The
reward, from one point of view mere grace and gift, is from another,
because God has promised it, a debt.

the reward] The Greek implies an *exact requital.* See Lightfoot's
note. Even "the cup of cold water" (Matt. x. 42) has its remembrance
and loving recompense.

of the inheritance] That is, the reward *consists* in the inheritance; is involved in the bright prospect of it.—For a somewhat similar phrase cp. i.
12 (and notes). But the reference here is, surely, to the eternal future. So
1 Pet. i. 4, and Eph. i. 14. That future is but the issue of the present,
in which "Christ is in us, the hope of glory" (i. 27). But the issue is
so "far better" (Phil. i. 21) than its prelude and embryo that it is
relatively a new thing in prospect.—Lightfoot remarks that, by a
beautiful paradox, the *slave* is here also an *heir*, which by human law he
could not be. He is God's heir (Gal. iv. 7) by Divine law. Elsewhere,
in other connexions, "slave" and "heir" are contrasted: e.g. Gal. iv. 1.

for] Probably the word is to be omitted. It is a good *note* to the
sentence, so to speak, pointing the meaning: "ye shall receive your
reward from the Master; *for* Christ is the Master, and He never fails in
requital."

ye serve the Lord Christ] We may render, **Christ is the Master
whose bondmen ye are.** Cp. Eph. vi. 6.—The Greek may be rendered,
"*serve*, &c.," imperatively. But the context favours the indicative.

25. *But he that doeth wrong*] The spiritual emancipation of the

ceive *for* the wrong which he hath done : and there is no
4 respect of persons. Masters, give unto *your* servants that
which is just and equal; knowing that ye also have a Master
in heaven.

2 Continue in prayer, and watch in the same with thanks-

slave writes the law of duty on his heart.—The case of Onesimus was
surely in the Apostle's mind throughout this passage.

shall receive] from the Divine Master and Judge; the next words, with
their parallel in Ephesians, fix the reference. The Gospel, the great
charter of liberty for man, always refuses him licence, even where he is
the victim of oppression. See *Introd.* to the Ep. to Philemon, p. 158.

no respect of persons] "with the Master who is in heaven" (Eph. vi. 9).
—See Exod. xxiii. 3, 6, for a striking example of Scriptural equity : "*thou
shalt not countenance a poor man in his cause*"; "*thou shalt not wrest
the judgment of thy poor in his cause.*" Here and in Eph. vi. 9 we
have identically the same principle, the impartiality of God, applied
alike to the conscience of the slave and to the conscience of his owner.

CH. IV. 1   THE SUBJECT CONCLUDED

1. *Masters*] Cp. Eph. vi. 9.
give unto] **Provide for.** The Greek verb suggests deliberate care.
that which is...equal] In the Greek, **equality, equity.** The word
in the classics often means "equality" in the political sense, as against
arbitrary privilege; and the Gospel, by publishing for ever the spiritual
equality of all men before God, secures all that is vital in that matter.
But the meaning "*impartiality,*" "*equity,*" is more in place here; the
master is not commanded to surrender his status, but to respect the
interests of the slave as faithfully as his own, and to banish caprice and
favouritism. This, consistently carried out, was a long and sure step
towards the end of slavery; for nothing could be a more direct contradiction to the root-idea of ancient slavery. See pp. 156, etc. below.
"Your slaves should find you fathers rather than masters" (Jerome).

knowing...heaven] Nearly verbatim as Eph. vi. 9. The Lord's
sovereignty is the true guarantee of human liberty.

2—6   PRAYER: INTERCOURSE WITH NON-CHRISTIANS

2. *Continue in prayer*] **Persevere at prayer.** Cp. Eph. vi. 18,
where the like precept is prefaced by the elaborated thought of the
spiritual combat and armour. Cp. for the phrase Rom. xii. 12.—Here
as there he returns from the details of life to the great spiritual requisites
to any true life for God.

"*Continue*":—it is implied that prayer is no mere spiritual luxury or
interlude; it is sacred business, with its difficulties and its labour. Cp.
Luke xxi. 36; Phil. iv. 6; 1 Thess. v. 17.

"*Prayer*":—"the Christian's vital breath." The word includes all
the elements of adoring converse with God—confession, petition,
thanksgiving, ascription.

Colossians 4 / 135

giving; withal praying also for us, that God would open 3
unto us a door of utterance, to speak the mystery of Christ,
for which I am also in bonds: that I may make it manifest, 4

watch] Cp. the Lord's own "*watch and pray*"; Matt. xxvi. 41;
Mar. xiv. 38. And on spiritual watchfulness generally, as against the
coma of the world, cp. Matt. xxiv. 42, 43; Mar. xiii. 35—37; Luke xii.
37; Acts xx. 31; 1 Cor. xvi. 13; 1 Thess. v. 6; 1 Pet. v. 8; Rev. iii.
2, 3, xvi. 15.

in the same] The watching was to be conditioned and maintained in
the exercise of prayer. The believer was to be ready both for the
tempter and for the Judge in the strength of spiritual contact with God.

with thanksgiving] which, though a normal element in true prayer,
tends to be forgotten, especially under trial, and so needs special
mention. Cp. ch. i. 12, ii. 7, iii. 15, 17.

3. *praying also for us*] Cp. Rom. xv. 30; Eph. vi. 19; 1 Thess. v.
25; 2 Thess. iii. 1; Heb. xiii. 18. He wisely covets for his apostolic
work, and the work of his friends, the prayers of the obscurest watchful
believer.

open...a door of utterance] Lit., **a door of the word** of the Gospel,
i.e., an opportunity for the missionary. For the phrase cp. 1 Cor. xvi. 9;
2 Cor. ii. 12; where, as here, the "*open door*" is not the emboldened
mouth (which is chiefly in his thought Eph. vi. 19, 20) but the favourable
circumstances. Cp. for a partial parallel Acts xiv. 27, and perhaps
Rev. iii. 8.

to speak] Such was the use to which the "open door" of occasion
would be put.

the mystery of Christ] Cp. Eph. iii. 4 for the same phrase. The
word mystery is frequent with St Paul; he uses it in some 21 places,
of which 11 lie in this Epistle and Ephesians. On the word, see above
on i. 26.—"*Of Christ:*"—with whose Person, Work, and Life, the great
Secret was vitally bound up. See on i. 27.

for which] **On account of which.** "St Paul might have been still at
large if he had been content to preach a Judaic Gospel" (Lightfoot).
Cp. Acts xxi. 13, xxviii. 20.

I am...in bonds] Lit., **I have been bound.** Cp. Eph. vi. 19 and our
notes. And see Eph. iii. 1, iv. 1; Phil. i. 7, 13, 14, 16; Philem. 10,
13.—It is easy to read, and to forget, this passing allusion. But what
must have been the hourly trial to a sensitive spirit, of this attachment
day and night to a (probably) pagan sentinel, perhaps wholly devoid of
generous instincts!

4. *That I may make it manifest*] Cp. Eph. vi. 20. The request for
prayer for opportunity glides into that for prayer for grace to use it.

"*Make manifest*":—the word is the same as that in e.g. 2 Cor. iv.
10, 11. It is used only here by St Paul in just this connexion, and here
probably means more than merely exposition. The message, set in
the light of the messenger's life in God, was to be a "*revelation.*"

I ought] under the holy obligation of my commission. Cp. 1 Cor. ix.
16; and see Acts xx. 24; Rom. i. 14, 15.

5 as I ought to speak. Walk in wisdom toward them that
6 are without, redeeming the time. Let your speech *be* alway with grace, seasoned with salt, that *you* may know how ye ought to answer every man.

5. *Walk*] See above, on i. 10.

in wisdom] In the "sanctified good sense" of those who would avoid all needless repulsion of word or manner, and seize all good occasion. Such practical wisdom was quite another thing than the would-be philosophy which he repudiates in e.g. 1 Cor. i., ii. It was "the meekness of wisdom" (Jas. iii. 13, 17) which would commend the disciple's witness in a life as practical in its goodness as it was divine in its secret. Cp. Eph. v. 15.

toward] **With regard to**; not (as some explain) in the sense of conciliation, as if "advancing *to meet* them"; though such action is of course implied in its place.

them that are without] Outside the Christian circle, "the household of faith." Cp. 1 Cor. v. 12, 13; 1 Thess. iv. 12 (a close parallel); 1 Tim. iii. 7.—They are "the Gentiles" of e.g. 1 Pet. ii. 12. The parallel phrase occurs in the Rabbis—*hachîtsônîm*; see Lightfoot's note.

redeeming the time] **Buying out** (from other ownership) **the opportunity**; securing each successive occasion of witness and persuasive example *at the expense of* steady watchfulness. Cp. Eph. v. 16 (and our notes) for the same phrase with a more general reference. The disciple, while ready to confess his Lord anywhere and at any time, is yet to use Christian "wisdom," and not to despise laws of opportunity. The "*out of season*" of 2 Tim. iv. 2 means, "irrespective of *your own* convenience." St Paul himself, in the Acts, is a perfect instance of the union of holy courage with the truest tact and good sense.

6. *your speech*] **Talking, discourse.** The precept here may well be applied to the Christian's *whole* use of the tongue (see Eph. iv. 29). But the context gives it a special reference, surely, to his *discourse about the Gospel with those "without."*

alway] Observe the characteristic absoluteness of the Christian precept.

with grace] Lit., **in grace**. See above, on iii. 16. Lightfoot explains, "*with acceptance, pleasingness*"; and quotes from the Greek of Psal. xliv. (Heb. and Eng. xlv.) 2; Ecclus. xxi. 16. But would not this be a unique, and so unlikely, use of the word in St Paul?

seasoned with salt] which they were (Mar. ix. 50) to "have in themselves." The reference of the metaphor is fixed by the practical parallel, Eph. iv. 29; "*corrupt, decayed, discourse.*" The "*salt*" is the power of Christ's grace, banishing all impurity of motive, and all uncleanness of allusion, and at the same time giving the pleasant "savour" of sound and nourishing "food for thought."—The classics, Latin and (less commonly) Greek, use the "salt" of speech as a metaphor; but almost always in the sense of wit, pleasantry, often of the very kind censured Eph. v. 4. Seneca speaks of "poisoned salt,"

All my state shall Tychicus declare unto you, *who is* a be- 7
loved brother, and a faithful minister and fellowservant in
the Lord: whom I have sent unto you for the same purpose, 8

venenati sales, meaning malicious jests.—"*Seasoned &c.*" here is constructed in the Greek with "*speech.*"
that you *may know*] As those will who, in the grace of God, remember this sound rule of discourse.
to answer every man] "who asketh you a reason of the hope that is in you" (1 Pet. iii. 15), in whatever spirit. The thought is, surely, not so much of cleverly adjusted repartee, as of the clear, kindly candour and good sense which would so state the truth of Christ, in the "answer," as to meet any and every questioner with conciliation.

7—9 Personal Information

7. *All my state*] Rather more lit., **My circumstances generally.** The same phrase occurs Phil. i. 12.—Latin Versions, *Quæ circa me sunt omnia.*
Tychicus] Cp. Eph. vi. 21; and our note there. Tychicus is named also Acts xx. 4; 2 Tim. iv. 12; Tit. iii. 12. He appears to have belonged to the province of Asia, and probably to Ephesus. He was, evidently, loved and honoured by the Apostle; was beside him, occasionally at least, in his first imprisonment; and was faithful to him to the end. His name, though not common, occurs in inscriptions and on coins belonging to Asia Minor.—Wyclif, curiously, has "*titicus.*"
See the art. *Tychicus* in Smith's *Dict. of the Bible;* Ellicott on Eph. vi. 21; Lightfoot here, and p. 11 of his *Philippians.*
a beloved brother] Lit., and better, **the** &c. So in Ephesians. The article indicates a certain speciality; almost as if it were "*that* beloved brother, &c."
faithful minister] Greek, *diaconos*. So in Ephesians. On the word, see note above, on i. 7; and on Eph. vi. 21. The word here (and in Eph.) points probably to Tychicus' personal helping attendance on the Apostle.
and fellowservant] A designation not given in Ephesians.
On the word see note above on i. 7, where Epaphras is similarly denoted. It is interesting to find these two Asiatic saints alike described by their discriminating father in God as eminently known for active unselfish service.—Lightfoot gives the fact that the term *fellowservant* was a customary address, in the early Church, from a bishop to *a deacon* (*diaconos*); probably because of its use here and i. 7; an interesting instance of the birth and growth of formula.
in the Lord] His life, and work, was conditioned and animated by his union with Christ and His Church.
8. *I have sent*] Greek, "*I sent.*" But the English is true to our idiom. He means that the letter and Tychicus are sent together; the aorist, the "epistolary past" of Greek, must be rendered as a perfect in English to convey this thought. So Eph. vi. 22, where see our note.

138 / Colossians 4

that he might know your estate, and comfort your hearts;
9 with Onesimus, a faithful and beloved brother, who is *one* of
you. They shall make known unto you all *things* which *are*
10 *done* here. Aristarchus my fellowprisoner saluteth you, and

for the same purpose] **For this very purpose**, R.V. Word for word as in Eph. vi. 22. The "*purpose*" is that just stated (ver. 8), and now more fully explained.

that he might know] **That ye might know**, R.V. This is the more probable reading, though the text has considerable support, particularly in early Versions. Lightfoot urges for the change (besides manuscripts) that it is unlikely that St Paul should so emphasize ("*for this very purpose*") Tychicus' *mission of information*, and then suddenly give as its first object *a work of enquiry*. Further, that transcribers were more likely to assimilate the person and number of the verb to the "*he might comfort*" just below, than elaborately to assimilate a "*he might know*" here to the "*ye might know*" in Ephesians.

comfort] See on ii. 2.

9. *Onesimus*] On his name and story see below, on Philem. 10, and *Introd.* to the Ep. to Philemon, ch. iii.

a faithful and beloved brother] Lit., and better, **the**, &c. See above on ver. 7. This rescued slave is raised, in Christ, to a brother's place beside Tychicus, the Colossians, and Paul himself, and is at once welcomed into the family of God.—St Paul implicitly assumes Philemon's pardon and welcome for Onesimus.

is one *of you*] Or, **belongs to you**, a fellow-Colossian. A beautiful euphemism for Onesimus' *legal* connexion with Colossæ; and it was, for Christians, as true as it was beautiful.

all things *which* are done *here*] Lit., more generally, **all the things here**; circumstances and proceedings alike.

10—14 SALUTATIONS

10. *Aristarchus my fellow-prisoner*] **My fellow-captive** (Latin Versions, *concaptivus*), fellow-prisoner-*of-war*. So Epaphras is called, Philemon 23 (where see note). And so Andronicus and Junias, Rom. xvi. 7. The word indicates either that Aristarchus was, or had been, in prison with St Paul in the course of his missionary *warfare*, or that he was now in such close attendance on him that St Paul lovingly calls it an imprisonment.

The name Aristarchus occurs here, in Philemon, and Acts xix. 29, xx. 4, xxvii. 2; and it is morally certain that we have one man in all these places. He was a Thessalonian; he accompanied St Paul on his third journey, and was, with Gaius, seized at Ephesus, when the riot broke out. (Just possibly, the word *fellow-captive* may be a free allusion to that terrible hour.) He was with St Paul later when he returned from Greece to Asia, and either accompanied or followed him on to Syria, for he sails with him from Syria for Rome. We know no more of him; tradition makes him bishop of Apamea, in Asia Minor, east of Colossæ.

Marcus, sister's son to Barnabas, (touching whom ye received commandments: if he come unto you, receive him;)

Marcus] The name occurs also Acts xii. 12, 25, xv. 37, 39; 2 Tim. iv. 11; Philem. 24; 1 Pet. v. 13. We may assume the identity of the man in all the places, and that he is the "John" of Acts xiii. 5, 13. We gather from these mentions that Marcus was also called Johannes; the latter, probably, as his Hebrew home-name, the former as his alternative name for Gentile intercourse. So Saul was Paul, and Jesus (ver. 11) was Justus; and so it is often now with Jews in Europe. (It is noticeable that the Jewish name drops away as the narrative proceeds; "*John Mark*," or "*John*," is only "*Mark*" in Acts xv. and in the Epistles.) His father is not mentioned; his mother was a Mary (Miriam), who lived at Jerusalem, whose house was a rendezvous of the disciples A.D. 44, to which Peter, released from prison, went as to a familiar place. He was cousin (see next note) to Barnabas. Peter calls him "*my son*"; spiritually, of course, assuming the identity of person in all the mentions of Marcus. Perhaps Peter, in the house of Mary, met her son and drew him to the Lord, thus "begetting him again." With Paul and Barnabas, as their "helper," he set out on their mission-journey (A.D. 45), but left them at Perga for Jerusalem, for a reason not known, but not approved of by Paul. Some seven years later he accompanied Barnabas on a second mission to Cyprus, after the "sharp contention" of the two Apostles. But that difference was not permanent (see 1 Cor. ix. 6); and now, nine or ten years later again, we find him with St Paul at Rome, and perhaps about to return (see this verse), with his blessing, to Asia. Later again, probably (but see Appendix B), he is with his spiritual father, Peter, at Babylon (probably the literal Chaldean Babylon, not the mystical, Rome). And then, again later, probably, he is with or near Timothy in Asia; and Paul, a second time imprisoned, sends for him, as "useful for him for personal service." Here end our certain notices. In Scripture, he *may* be the "certain young man" of Mar. xiv. 51, 52. Tradition, from early cent. 2 onwards, makes him the writer of the Second Gospel, and to have compiled it as in some sense Peter's exponent. (Cp. Eusebius, *History*, III. 39; and see Salmon, *Introd. to N. T.* p. 110, etc.) Later tradition (first recorded cent. 4) makes him founder and first bishop of the Alexandrian church.

sister's son] Rather, **cousin.** Latin versions, *consobrinus*; Wyclif, "*cosyn*." The Greek, *anepsios*, bears the meaning "*sister's son*" in later Greek, but its derivation and earlier usage fix it here to mean a cousin-german, the child of the other's own aunt or uncle.—Etymologically, it is remotely akin to our "*nephew*"; but that word also has varied its reference. In the A.V. of 1 Tim. v. 4 it means "*descendants*," such as grandchildren; representing a different Greek word.—This kinship explains no doubt, in part, the wish of the loving Barnabas to retain Marcus as his helper (Acts xv.).

ye received commandments] No doubt through some previous emissary from Rome to Asia.

140 / Colossians 4

11 and Jesus, which is called Justus, who are of the circumcision. These only *are my* fellowworkers unto the kingdom

if he come] An intended visit of Marcus to Asia is implied. Perhaps he was on his way to the residence there which later brought him into connexion with Peter in Chaldea. See note on Marcus, just above.

receive him] It is implied that some misgiving about Marcus lingered among the followers of St Paul. The "commandments" had announced Marcus' full restoration to St Paul's confidence, and so to that of his converts; now they were to act upon them.

11. *And Jesus*] The Grecized form of *Jehoshua* (later, *Jêshua*), "*Jehovah's Help*"; a very common Jewish proper name. In the N.T., besides the countless places where it is the name of our Blessed Lord, and this place, it occurs Acts vii. 45; Heb. iv. 8; (of Joshua); and (according to well-supported readings) Luke iii. 29, where A.V. has "*Jose*"; and (perhaps) Matt. xxvii. 16; "*Jesus* Barabbas."

Legend gives Jesus Justus a bishopric, that of Eleutheropolis, in Judea.

called Justus] A Latin name, like Marcus and Paulus; see note on ver. 10.

Lightfoot (see his note in full) shews that this name, "*Righteous*," was in common use among Jews and proselytes, as "denoting obedience to the law." We find it Acts i. 23, xviii. 7. The third bishop of Jerusalem, according to Eusebius (*History*, III. 35) was "a Jew, named Justus"; and the eleventh (*ibid.* IV. 5) bore the same name. The name occurs, slightly modified (*Yousti, Youstâ*), in the Rabbinical writings. The feminine, Justa, is the name of the Syrophenician in the *Clementine Homilies*, a Judaizing book of cent. 3, where she appears as a proselytess.

"*Called*":—implies that Jesus Justus was better known by his Latin than by his Hebrew name.

who] Aristarchus, Marcus, Jesus.

are of the circumcision] For the phrase cp. Acts x. 45, xi. 2; Rom. iv. 12; Gal. ii. 12; Tit. i. 10. It appears to mean converts to Christianity of Jewish birth (or proselytism). In Acts xi., Gal., Tit., cited above, "the men of circumcision," shew a more or less partizan-like spirit towards the freedom of the Gospel. But this does not prove that the phrase bore necessarily a party colour, only that exclusives, Judaizers, would naturally appear, if anywhere, among the Hebrew Christians.

These only] Probably he means, these only of all "the men of the circumcision" at Rome, while the large majority were acting as in Phil. i. 15, 16. Alford takes the whole passage to be *practically* one statement, in loose grammatical connexion, as if it ran "Of the men of the circumcision these alone are &c."—We must not press the word "*only*" too far; he probably speaks here of leaders, not of the mass.—Cp. Phil. ii. 20; 2 Tim. iv. 16.

my *fellowworkers*] Cp. for the word in similar connexion, Rom. xvi. 3, 9, 21; 2 Cor. viii. 23; Phil. ii. 25, iv. 3; 1 Thess. iii. 2 (perhaps);

of God, which have been a comfort unto me. Epaphras, 12 who is *one* of you, a servant of Christ, saluteth you, always labouring fervently for you in prayers, that ye may stand perfect and complete in all the will of God. For I bear 13

Philem. 1, 24. He loves the thought of partnership in his work for his Lord, see e.g. Phil. i. 7.—The word "*my*" is not in the Greek, but it is evidently implied.

unto the kingdom of God] See above i. 13, and note; and our notes on Eph. v. 5. The phrase here means, in effect, "so as to promote the reign of God, in Christ, over man and in him, here and hereafter."

which have been] The Greek might almost be paraphrased, "*proving*," or "*as they have proved.*" He means that their cooperation largely consisted in their proving "*a comfort*," instead of acting in opposition.— "*Have been*":—more exactly, "*were*," or "*did prove.*" But the English perfect well represents the Greek aorist here. See note on ver. 8.

a comfort] The Greek noun, *parêgoria*, occurs here only in the Greek Bible; the cognate verb occurs Job xvi. 2, in the Greek version of Symmachus. The English word, in its common use, exactly renders it. The Latin Versions have *solatium;* Wyclif, "*solace.*"—His heart, often wounded by Judaistic opposition, was specially *consoled* by the loving loyalty of these Jewish Christian friends.

12. *Epaphras*] Cp. i. 7, and note.

who is one *of you*] Cp. ver. 9, and note.

a servant of Christ] A designation true of all Christians; see Eph. vi. 6. Here it seems to denote a man in whom the holy "bondservice" was markedly illustrated; perhaps specially in his pastoral or missionary character. Cp. 2 Tim. ii. 24.

"*Of Christ*":—read, **of Christ Jesus**.

labouring] **Wrestling;** "as Jacob of old with the Angel."—See notes on i. 29, ii. 2; and cp. Rom. xv. 30.—Epaphras prayed as one who *grappled with* trials to faith and perseverance in the work of prayer.—The word "*fervently*" is inserted in the A.V. (as in older English Versions) to express the intensity of a wrestle.—The Latin Versions, somewhat weakly, have *semper sollicitus pro vobis;* Wyclif, better (though rendering from them), "*euer bisie for you.*"

in prayers] Lit., "*in the prayers*," almost as if, "*in his prayers.*" Epaphras was Paul's true scholar in the school of intercession. See i. 9.

stand] **Stand fast** better represents the best-supported reading here.

perfect] See note on the word, i. 28. And cp. Phil. iii. 15, and note.

complete] I.e., "*filled full.*" So Old Latin, *adimpleti;* Vulgate, *pleni;* all English Versions before A.V., "*full.*" R.V., **fully assured**; adopting another and better supported reading, which gives the verb used also in e.g. Rom. iv. 21, xiv. 5; and cognate to the noun used ch. ii. 2, where see note. The usage of this verb (see Lightfoot's note) leaves the rendering "*filled*" still possible; but the parallels

him record, that he hath a great zeal for you, and them that 14 are in Laodicea, and them in Hierapolis. Luke, the beloved 15 physician, and Demas, greet you. Salute the brethren which

in St Paul are in favour of R.V.—Epaphras prayed, in effect, that their Christian consistency might be *mature* ("*perfect*") and *consciously decided*.

in all the will] More lit., "*in every will*"; **in every part of the will**. The thought is the attentive obedience which holds sacred *each detail* of the Master's orders. Cp. Eph. v. 15—17; and see above ch. i. 10.

13. *zeal*] **Labour**, R.V. (so Latin Versions; Wyclif, "*traveil*"), adopting a somewhat better supported reading, of which that represented in A.V. is probably a transcriber's *explanation*.

Laodicea] See on ii. 1; and *Introd.* p. 13.

Hierapolis] The third mission-station in the valley of the Lycus, looking across the river, southward, a distance of about six miles, to Laodicea. See *Introd.*, ch. i.

14. *Luke*] *Loucas*, **Lucas**; *Lucanus* abbreviated. It is interesting to find the Second and Third Evangelists (see ver. 8) in one small group around St Paul here. Cp. Philem. 24; 2 Tim. iv. 11.—Lucas had accompanied St Paul to Rome; so the "*we*," "*us*," &c., of Acts xxvii., xxviii., implies. He is not named in Philippians, which is probably to be dated earlier than Colossians (see *Philippians* in this Series, pp. 14, 15, and above, p. 22); he may have left Rome and returned between St Paul's arrival and the writing of this Epistle. He appears again in 2 Tim. iv. 11 as the one personal attendant of the Apostle in his last imprisonment.

Tradition, vaguely supported at the best, says that he was born at Antioch in Syria; that he was one of the Seventy; that he was the anonymous disciple of the Walk to Emmaus; or, on the contrary, that he was a convert of St Paul's; that after his master's death he preached in Dalmatia, Gaul, Italy, and Macedonia; and that he died a martyr, in Achaia, or Bithynia, near the end of cent. 1. Lightfoot points out that he appears here as *not* "of the circumcision," and therefore as a Gentile; and that this is "fatal" to the tradition that he was one of the Seventy. He surely indicates this himself in the exordium of his Gospel (i. 2), implying that he was *not* an "eyewitness of the word."—See generally Smith's *Dict. of the Bible*, art. *Luke*, and Dr F. W. Farrar's edition of St Luke in this Series, *Introduction*, ch. ii.

the beloved] The adjective suggests a *loveable* man, tender and true; a character profoundly welcome to the life-worn heart of the Apostle. He uses it elsewhere of individuals, Rom. xvi. 5, 8, 9, 12; Eph. vi. 21; above, i. 7, iv. 7, 9; 2 Tim. i. 2; Philem. 1, 2, 16. Cp. 2 Pet. iii. 15; 3 Joh. 1, 2, 5, 11.

physician] "Indications of medical knowledge have been traced both in the third Gospel and in the Acts" (cp. Farrar, cited above, p. 21, note). "It has been observed also that St Luke's first appearance in company with St Paul (Acts xvi. 10) nearly synchronizes with

are in Laodicea, and Nymphas, and the church which is in his house. And when *this* epistle is read amongst you, 16

an attack of the Apostle's constitutional malady (Gal. iv. 13, 14), so that he may have joined him partly in a professional capacity. There is no ground for questioning the ancient belief (*Irenæus* iii. 14, 1 sq.) that the physician is also the Evangelist...St Paul's motive in specifying him as the physician may...have been...to emphasize his own obligations to his medical knowledge. The tradition that St Luke was a painter is quite late." (Lightfoot.)

It may be observed that, whatever were the laws of "*the Gift of Healing*," they threw no discredit, in St Paul's view, on the skill and knowledge of the trained physician.

"To [St Luke]—to his allegiance, his ability, and his accurate preservation of facts—we are alone indebted for the greater part of what we know of the Apostle of the Gentiles" (Farrar).

Demas] Mentioned also Philem. 24; 2 Tim. iv. 10. In the latter place he is contrasted with the faithful Luke: "*Demas hath forsaken me, having loved this present world*"; i.e., probably, preferring escape and life to the perils of association with Paul in his last crisis. The colourless mention of him here, just after "*the beloved*" Luke, suggests that already Demas was not all a Christian should be.—Probably he "was a Thessalonian (2 Tim. iv. 10) and...[probably] his name was Demetrius" (Lightfoot. The Bishop refers for more detail to his, alas, never-accomplished Introduction to Thessalonians).

15—17   LAODICEA; ARCHIPPUS

15. *Salute...Laodicea*] The places were only twelve miles apart.

Nymphas] A Laodicean; his name in full was, probably, Nymphodorus. See Lightfoot's full note here, on name-contractions in *-as*.—In some Greek MSS. this name is accented as if it were *Nympha*, a feminine name, and "*his house*" just below is read "*her house*." But this is very improbable, as it would assume that the name was written in a *Doric* form, *Nymphâ* not *Nymphê*.—The Latin Versions, reading thus, have *Nympham*; and Wyclif, "*the womman nymfam.*"

the church which is in his house] R.V., **their house**; following a better supported reading. The plural refers, probably, to Nymphas and his family.

"*The church...in their house*":—for the word "*Church*" used, as here, in its most limited sense, a Christian congregation of neighbours, see Rom. xvi. 5; 1 Cor. xvi. 19; Philem. 2. (Cp. Rom. xvi. 14, 15.)—The Nymphas family at Laodicea were perhaps the wealthy converts there, owning a large house; themselves numerous; and they offered their great room as a meeting place for worship and "the breaking of bread" to other converts. Very possibly this was *the one* meeting-place in Laodicea; and the greeting in this verse, if so, is to the Laodiceans first individually then in congregation.—The Latin Versions have, *domestica ejus ecclesia*.

Bingham (*Antiquities*, viii. 1) collects allusions to Christian places of

144 / Colossians 4

cause that it be read also in the church of the Laodiceans;
17 and that ye likewise read the *epistle* from Laodicea. And
say to Archippus, Take heed to the ministry which thou
18 hast received in the Lord, that thou fulfil it. The salutation

worship in the first century. He shews that special *chambers* were set apart, but does not shew that whole *buildings* were, in those first days, consecrated to devotion. By the third century at latest this became common. See our note on Rom. xvi. 5.

16. this *epistle*] Lit., **the epistle**; as Rom. xvi. 22; 2 Thess. iii. 14. "*The letter now before you.*"

is read] I.e., **shall have been read.**

in the church of the Laodiceans] Hierapolis is not mentioned in this charge. Was Laodicea already beginning to grow "*lukewarm*" (Rev. iii. 15) as the sister-church was not?

"A similar [and still more solemn] charge is given in 1 Thess. v. 27. The precaution here is probably suggested by the distastefulness of the Apostle's warnings" (Lightfoot).

the epistle *from Laodicea*] I.e., which will reach you *viâ* Laodicea. On the question whether this was our "Epistle to the Ephesians" see *Introd.*, ch. v.

17. *say to Archippus*] Probably the son of Philemon (cp. Philem. 2, and notes, and Lightfoot, *Colossians* &c., pp. 374, 5). He was apparently an ordained minister in the mission-church, either at Colossæ or (less probably, surely; see on Philem. 2) at Laodicea. St Paul, perhaps, had misgivings about his zeal and care, and, without saying as much, aims here at his conscience *through his flock*. Or, quite possibly, Archippus had been appointed to take the place of Epaphras when Epaphras left for Rome; and this warning bears only on the thought that his work was just beginning. See further below, p. 152.—In those simple days such an appeal through the people to the pastor was easy; "lordship over God's heritage" (1 Pet. v. 3) was no part of the Apostles' programme of the pastorate.

the ministry] *Diaconia;* Latin Versions, *ministerium*. The word in itself has no necessary reference to an *ordained* "ministry." But the context here makes such a reference at least highly probable; Archippus evidently stood out as a "*worker*" in a sense quite special and deeply sacred. On the other hand, the reference is probably not to the "diaconate" (Phil. i. 2; 1 Tim. iii. 8, &c.) specially. In Laodicea, as in Philippi, there might well be more than one "deacon." And the deacon's office, while sacred and important, was scarcely such as to occasion this solemnity of appeal. Archippus, we believe, was (at least for the time) the chief "pastor and teacher" (Eph. iv. 12) of Colossæ.

which thou hast received] Lit. and better, **didst receive.** Cp. Acts xiv. 23; Tit. i. 5. And for St Paul's own "reception of ministry," and his ideal of it, see Acts xx. 24.

in the Lord] Pregnant words. It was only as a man in union with Christ that he had "*received*," and could "*fulfil*," his ministry.

fulfil it] Lit., **fill it full;** so that his "*works should be found filled*

by the hand of me Paul. Remember my bonds. Grace *be* with you. Amen.

¶ Written from Rome to the Colossians by Tychicus and Onesimus.

before God" (Rev. iii. 2). No duty of his ministry was to be ignored; he was to "take heed to *himself, his doctrine*, and his flock" (Acts xx. 28; 1 Tim. iv. 16).—"A minister of Christ is often in highest honour with men for the performance of one half of his work, while God is regarding him with displeasure for the neglect of the other half" (R. Cecil, quoted by Abp Trench, on Rev. iii. 2).

18. FAREWELL

18. *The salutation by the hand of me Paul*] Here he takes the pen from the amanuensis (see Rom. xvi. 22), and writes the final words in autograph.—In 2 Thess. iii. 17 ("*so* I write") this is evidently done to warrant the authenticity of the letter. And see another reason, Philem. 19. But obviously it might be done habitually at the close of Epistles, for reasons only of care and affection; they would always value "his own hand."—The "script" of St Paul seems to have been large and laboured; see Gal. vi. 11; where render "in *what large letters* I have written." (He seems to have written *that* Epistle all in autograph.)

Remember my bonds] The chain would drag and rattle as he took the pen. See note on ver. 3 above.

Their "*remembrance*" would be shewn in love, in intercession, and above all in fidelity to the Gospel for which their Apostle rejoiced to suffer.

Grace be *with you*] This short benediction occurs elsewhere only at the close of 1 Tim., 2 Tim. As Lightfoot suggests, the more definite and developed phraseology, "*The grace of our Lord Jesus Christ, &c.*," might in these later days of St Paul's ministry "pass without saying."

On the meaning of "*grace*," see note on i. 2 above.

Amen] The evidence for omission here is considerable. See our note on Eph. vi. 24.

THE SUBSCRIPTION

Written &c.] Lit., **To the Colossians it was written from Rome, by means of Tychicus and Onesimus.** So in the *Textus Receptus*. Of other forms some omit "*To the Colossians*"; some add, at the end, "*and Timotheus*." In our oldest MSS. the form is the same as that of the Title (see note there): TO (THE) COLOSSIANS, or COLASSIANS.

The Subscriptions (to St Paul's Epistles), in their longer form (as in the A.V.) are ascribed to Euthalius, a bishop of the fifth century, and thus to a date later than the earliest extant MSS. (See Scrivener, *Introd. to the Criticism of the N.T.*, ed. 1883, p. 62.)

The Subscription here is obviously true to fact, as are those appended to Rom., Eph., Phil., Philem., 2 Tim. Other Subscriptions are either (1 Cor., Gal., 1 Tim.) contradictory to the contents of the respective Epistles, or (Thess., Tit.) difficult to reconcile with them.

IN philanthropy as in science there are three stages—the prelude, the epoch, and the sequel. The prelude is a period of aspiration, and half-blind guesses. The epoch brings the expression of the truth to its highest point. In the sequel, the principle, once fixed in words, is extended and developed in practice. It would be no difficult task to apply the analogy to the influence of Christianity on slavery. As far as the Epistle to Philemon is concerned, the epoch has come.

Bp ALEXANDER, in *The Speaker's Commentary*.

WE are all the Lord's Onesimi.

LUTHER

THE EPISTLE TO PHILEMON

INTRODUCTION

Chapter 1

AUTHENTICITY OF THE EPISTLE

THE external evidence is ample, from the time of Tertullian onward. From him we gather (*Contra Marcion.*, v. 21) that even Marcion's *Apostolicon*[1] contained *Philemon:* " The shortness of this Epistle has favoured its escape from the tampering hands (*falsarias manus*) of Marcion ;" that is to say (so Jerome, Preface to *Philemon*, explains), Marcion had more or less altered every other Epistle which he had admitted, but not this. Origen (*Homily* xix. *on Jeremiah*) quotes Philem. 14 almost verbatim, as what "Paul said, in the Epistle to Philemon, to Philemon about Onesimus." He quotes ver. 7 in his Commentary on St Matthew, tractate 34: "As Paul says to Philemon ;" and again, ver. 9: "By Paul it is said to Philemon, *But now as Paul the aged* (*senex*)." In the Ignatian Epistles there are some apparent allusions to the Epistle. The writer several times (*To the Ephesians*, ii. ; *To the Magnesians*, xii.; *To Polycarp*, i., vi.) uses the Greek phrase rendered in the A.V. of Philem. 20, " *Let me have joy of thee.*"

In the fourth century the authenticity was sometimes denied, and more often the Epistle was attacked[2] as unworthy to be reckoned Scripture. This is inferred from defences of the Epistle made incidentally by e.g. Chrysostom and Jerome, in

---

[1] See above, p. 38, *note*.
[2] Lightfoot speaks of the "fierce" opposition to the Epistle. Is not this word too strong?

the Prefaces to their Expositions. Jerome says that "some will have it that it is not Paul's, others that it has nothing in it for our edification;" "some will not receive it among Paul's Epistles, and say that Paul did not always speak as the organ of Christ's voice in him." Chrysostom says that they are "worthy of countless accusations" who reject this Epistle, as "concerned about so small a matter, and on behalf of an individual only."[1] "The spirit of the age," says Lightfoot, "had no sympathy with either the subject or the handling...Its maxim seemed to be, *De minimis non curat evangelium*," trifles are beneath the notice of the Gospel. Evidently the objections noticed by Chrysostom and Jerome have not only no moral but no critical value.

Baur, with an unhappy consistency, rejecting *Ephesians* and *Colossians*, rejected *Philemon* also, though with an almost apology, admitting that "this little letter" is penetrated "with the noblest Christian spirit," and that his criticism may seem over-sceptical. On his curiously trivial objections (e.g. the *frequent* use of the word rendered "*bowels*" in the A.V., a word admittedly Pauline) Alford[2] remarks: "I am persuaded that if his section on the Epistle to Philemon had been published separately and without the author's name, the world might well have supposed it written by some defender of the Epistle, as a caricature on Baur's general line of argument."

Chapter 2

TESTIMONIES TO THE EPISTLE

ST CHRYSOSTOM, in his *Hypothesis*, or Account of the Contents, introductory to his expository Sermons on *Philemon*, speaks of its value with eloquent simplicity. Not only, he says, ought Epistles to have been written about such small and homely matters, but we could long that some biographer had recorded for us the minutest details of the lives of the Apostles; what they

---

[1] See the quotations, Lightfoot, p. 383, *notes*.
[2] *Greek Testament*, iii. 113.

Introduction / 149

ate, what their daily doings were, what their manner and their utterance. As to this Epistle, think of its many profitable lessons. We learn to neglect nothing, when a Paul can take such pains about a runaway thieving slave. We learn not to think the slave-kind below the reach of good, when this same slave and thief became so virtuous (ἐνάρετος) that Paul would fain have him for his companion and attendant. We learn that slaves ought not to be taken from their masters, when we see Paul refuse to keep Onesimus at his side. If a slave is of high character (θαυμαστός) he ought to remain as he is, to be an influence for good in the household. Say not that servile duties must hinder his devotion to higher things; Paul himself says, *If thou mayest be made free, use it rather:* that is, stay as you are, and glorify God[1]. Do not tempt the heathen to blaspheme, saying that Christianity (Χριστιανισμός) tends to the subversion of human relations. One more lesson from the Epistle; we ought not to be ashamed of our slaves when they are good, if this greatest of men could say such noble things about a slave. Now, will any one venture to call this Epistle superfluous?

Luther writes of the Epistle to Philemon with characteristic human tenderness and Christian insight: "This Epistle sheweth a right noble lovely example (*ein meisterlich lieblich Exempel*) of Christian love. Here we see how St Paul layeth himself out (*sich annimpt*) for poor Onesimus, and with all his means pleadeth his cause with his master; and so setteth himself as if he were Onesimus, and had himself done wrong to Philemon. Yet this he doth not with force nor constraint, as if he had full right. Nay, he putteth himself out of his rights; whereby he constraineth Philemon (to perceive) that he also must strip himself of his rights. Even as Christ did for us with God the Father, thus also doth St Paul for Onesimus with Philemon. For Christ also hath put Himself out of His rights, and with love and humbleness hath prevailed with His Father that He should lay aside His wrath and His rights, and receive us to grace, for Christ's sake, who so earnestly intercedeth for us,

[1] We give without comment this explanation of a difficult text.

and layeth Himself out so tenderly for us. For we are all His Onesimi, if we believe it (*so wirs gleuben*)".[1]

Erasmus, in a note on ver. 20, says: "This Epistle, short as it is, shews us how eminently humane[2] Paul was...What could even a Tully have said, in such a matter, more charming (*festivius*) than what we have here? Some indeed, in name Christians, in spirit entirely hostile to Christ, count nothing learned, nothing elegant, which is not also pagan (*ethnicum*). They think the bloom of style quite lost where any mention of Christ comes in, with any relish of His teaching; whereas the first requisite in eloquence is to suit style to subject. I can but wonder the more that any man should have doubted the authenticity of this Epistle; nothing could be more perfectly Pauline in method and manner of treatment."

Bengel thus begins his brief commentary: "This familiar letter, wonderfully elegant, about a purely private matter, is inserted in the New Testament for the benefit of Christians as a specimen of consummate wisdom in the treatment of things of this life on higher principles. Frankius" (Franke, the saintly professor of Halle, 1653—1727) "says: 'The Epistle to Philemon, taken alone, far surpasses (*longissimè superat*) all the wisdom of the world'"[3].

Renan[4], in words whose falsetto still leaves their praise significant, calls the Epistle, "A true little chef-d'œuvre of the art of letter-writing."

There is a letter of the younger Pliny's (a generation later

---

[1] Quoted in part by Lightfoot, p. 383. We have used his translation of his extracts almost verbatim, and completed the quotation. It forms Luther's *Vorrede auff die Epistel S. Pauli an Philemon*, in his German Bible (ed. Wittemberg, 1540). No one who knows Luther's theology will unduly press one sentence of the above passage as if he meant to say that the Eternal Father, the Giver of the Son, was reluctant to pardon. It is his pictorial way of putting the work of atonement and intercession in view of the claims of eternal holiness. He has a supreme example in our Lord's parables of the Friend at Midnight and the Judge and Widow.

[2] So I paraphrase *Paulum hominem singulari quadam præditum humanitate*.

[3] *Gnomon N. Testamenti, in loco*.

[4] Quoted by Lightfoot, p. 384.

Introduction / 151

than St Paul), the 21st in the ninth book of his Letters, written to his friend Sabinian, asking him to forgive an offending freedman[1]. Its subject is akin to that of our Epistle, and the two have often been compared. It reads as follows:

"Your freedman, who so greatly displeased you, as you told me, has come to me, fallen at my feet, and clung to them as if they were your own; he wept much, begged much, was much silent too, and in brief guaranteed to me his penitence. I think him really reformed, for he feels that he has sinned. You are angry, as I know; justly angry, as I also know; but clemency wins its highest praise when the reasons for anger are most just. You have loved the man, and I hope you will yet love him again; in the interval (*interim*) you are only asked to let yourself be brought to forgive. You will be quite free to be angry again if he deserves it; and this will have the more excuse if now you yield. Allow something for his youth, something for his tears, something for your own indulgence (of him); do not put him to torture, or you may torture yourself too. For tortured you are when you, kindliest of men, are angry. I fear I may seem rather to insist than entreat, if I join my prayers to his. But I will join them, the more fully and without reserve as I chid him sharply and severely, adding a stern warning that I could never beg him off again. This for *him*, for I had to frighten him; but I take another tone with *you!* Perhaps I shall entreat again, and win again; so the case is one in which I may properly entreat, and you may properly bestow. Farewell."

It is a graceful, kindly letter, written by a man whose character is the ideal of his age and class; the cultured and thoughtful Roman gentleman of the mildest period of the Empire. Yet the writer seems somewhat conscious of his own epistolary felicity, and his argument for the offender is much more condescending than sympathetic. His heart has not the depth of Paul's, nor are his motives those of the Gospel, which taught Paul to clasp Onesimus in his arms, and to commend him to Philemon's, as a friend in God for immortality. From the merely literary

---

[1] See below, p. 156. Sabinian might conceivably get the *libertus* condemned to slavery again.

152 / Introduction

view-point, a perfect freedom of style, along with a delicate tact of manner, easily gives the letter to Philemon the palm over that to Sabinian[1].

Chapter 3

THE CHIEF PERSONS OF THE EPISTLE

THE chief persons mentioned in the Epistle we know only from it and from *Colossians*. The chief (certain or probable) details of their lives and circumstances are given in our notes on the text.

PHILEMON appears as a well-to-do Colossian convert; the proof of his competency of means is not his possession of a slave, for he might have owned only one or two, but his power, well and widely used, to befriend his needing fellow-Christians. He thus appears as an illustration of the fact that primeval Christianity, while calling all Christians to a genuine surrender to Christ of both the self and the property, never condemned the right of property as between man and man, and left the individual perfectly free to ask whether or no his surrender of all to the Lord involved the surrender of his permanent stewardship for the Lord. APPHIA, probably Philemon's wife, is called "a deaconess" of the Colossian Church by M. Renan[2], and by other writers, but without proof. In a letter dealing entirely with a domestic matter the mention of her name has no necessary or official significance. The mention of the name of ARCHIPPUS here with Apphia's makes it extremely likely that he was the son at home with his parents, whether or no his pastoral duties (Col. iv. 17) extended beyond Colossæ to the neighbouring Church or Churches. That he was in some sort of sacred office appears from Col. iv. 17; perhaps the solemnity of the message there was occasioned not, as usually suggested, by misgivings in St Paul's mind, but by some development of Archippus' duties consequent on Epaphras' absence in Italy[3].

---

[1] We find from a later letter (ix. 24) that Sabinian forgave the freedman. Pliny asks him to be ready in future to forgive *without an intercessor*.

[2] *Saint Paul*, p. 360.

[3] Ramsay (*The Church in the R. Empire*, p. 469) recites the legend

Introduction / 153

ONESIMUS, the runaway slave of this Christian household, stands almost visibly before us, as St Paul's allusions trace the sketch of his degradation, his spiritual regeneration, his grateful love, and his transfiguration into the resolute doer of right at a possible heavy cost. Dr F. W. Farrar, in his powerful historical story, *Darkness and Dawn*, has imagined a possible history of Onesimus which assists our realization of the time and conditions. The youth appears there as a Thyatiran, freeborn, but sold to pay family debts; accompanies Philemon, "a gentleman of Colossæ," to Ephesus, on a visit which issues in the conversion of Philemon and his household through St Paul's preaching; returns to find "dull and sleepy Colossæ" unbearable after brilliant Ephesus; steals money of his master's that he may run away, first to Ephesus, and then to Rome; there is taken into the household of the Christian Pudens, and thence in time is transferred to Nero's; finds his way through many adventures to the gladiators' school, and to the arena; witnesses the massacre of the slaves of Pedanius; accompanies Octavia, Nero's rejected wife, a secret Christian, to her exile in the island of Pandataria; thence, after her death, finds his way, an awakened penitent, to St Paul; whom ultimately, after emancipation, he attends through his last labours, and to his death.

Historically, we know nothing, outside these Epistles, of the later life of Onesimus. That Philemon granted St Paul's requests, we may be sure; that he formally set free his slave, now his brother in Christ, we may be almost as sure. In *Colossians* (iv. 9), St Paul speaks of Onesimus in terms which would be impossible if he had felt any serious doubt of the reception Philemon would accord to the penitent. But beyond this point we lose all traces. In the Ignatian Epistles an Onesimus appears as bishop of Ephesus; but the date of these letters falls at earliest after A.D. 105, and the name was common; it is

of "The Miracle of Khonai," in which St Michael protects a holy fountain from desecration by bidding the rocks cleave asunder and receive the waters which the pagans had dammed up to flood it. In this legend (probably of cent. 9, in its present form) the first guardian of the fountain is one *Archippos*, "born of pious parents at Hierapolis."

not very likely that we have our Onesimus there. He is otherwise variously said to have been bishop of Berea, in Macedonia, to have preached in Spain, to have been martyred at Rome, or at Puteoli. Lightfoot finds no hadow of historical evidence for any of these accounts.

Chapter 4

SLAVERY, AND THE ATTITUDE OF CHRISTIANITY TOWARDS IT

SLAVERY was universal among ancient nations, and is prominent in the picture of both Roman and Greek civilization. In the Greek cities of the fourth and fifth centuries before our Era the slave population was often relatively vast; at Athens, about 300 B.C., it is said that the slaves numbered 400,000, and the free citizens 21,000; but perhaps this means the total population of slaves as against the free adult males only. Even thus however the slaves would number four to one. In the later days of the Roman Republic, and under the Empire, the slaves of Roman masters were immensely numerous. It was not uncommon for one owner to possess some thousands; two hundred was a somewhat usual number; and to keep less than ten was hardly possible for a man who would pass muster in society.

Speaking generally, the slave of the Greek was in a better position than the slave of the Roman. Within limits, the law gave a certain protection to his person, and he could not be put to death without a legal sentence. If not a domestic proper, he was more commonly employed in handicrafts (in which he earned for the owner who fed and lodged him) than was the Roman slave, who was more commonly the mere tool of luxury, often of its most degraded kinds. The relation of Onesimus to Philemon, we may suppose, in quasi-Greek Colossæ, was practically governed by Greek law and usage, though this perhaps might be over-ridden for the worse, where the master was cruel, by the imperial law[1].

[1] But see further, Appendix M.

Introduction / 155

But the mitigations of Greek slavery did not go very far. To a great extent the slave was entirely in his owner's hands; he could always be severely punished corporally[1]; his word was never taken in court but under torture. In general he was regarded by the law as the personal property of his owner, saleable at any time in the market; just as a horse is now its owner's "thing," though the law may interfere with his treatment of it in extreme cases. "The rights of possession with regard to slaves differed in no respect from any other property"[2].

And what the law enforced, philosophy supported. In the *Politics* of Aristotle, in the few opening chapters, in a discussion of the Family as the unit of society, several passages bearing on slavery occur. The great thinker regards the slave as the physical implement of the master's mind; as being to his owner what the ox is to the man too poor to keep a slave (ch. ii.); as distinguished from the master by a natural (φύσει) difference, not merely a legal; as a living tool, a living piece of property (chattel). Between master and slave there is no proper reciprocity; the master may be a hundred things besides the slave's master, the slave is absolutely nothing but the master's slave; all his actions and relations move within that fact; he is wholly his (ὅλως ἐκείνου). Defined exactly, he is a human being who naturally (φύσει) is another's, not his own (ch. iv.); whose function (δύναμις) is to be such, while yet he shares his master's reason so far as to perceive it, without precisely *having* it (ch. v.). Such natural slavery, as distinguished from that of captivity by war, is good for both parties, just as the body and the limb are both benefited by their relation; the slave is as it were a portion (μέρος) of the master, as it were a living, while separated, portion of his body (ch. vi.).

Such a theory strikes accidentally, so to speak, on some noble aspects of human relation, and wonderfully illustrates the relation of the redeemed and believing to their redeeming Lord;

[1] Onesimus was probably a *Phrygian* slave; and there was a proverb, *Phryx plagis emendatur*, "*You school a Phrygian with the whip.*"
[2] See at large Smith's *Dict. of Greek and Roman Antiquities*, s. v. *Servus* (*Greek*); and Becker's *Charicles*, Excursus on "*The Slaves.*"

but its main bearing is all in the fatal direction of seeing in the slave a creature *who has no rights;* in short, a thing, not a person. The cool, pregnant sentences of Aristotle must have satisfied intellectually many a hard-hearted slave-master in the Greek society of St Paul's time[1].

When we turn from the Greek slave of that time to his Roman fellow (and Onesimus, at Rome, would run all the risks of a Roman runaway), we come on a still darker picture. The Emperor Claudius (A.D. 41—A.D. 54) did something for him[2], in ways which however shew how bad the general condition was. He set free certain sick slaves whom their masters had *exposed to die*, and decreed that if such slaves were killed, in lieu of death by exposure, it should be murder. Yet even Claudius, and at the same time, directed that a freedman, if giving his ex-master (*patronus*) cause of complaint, should be enslaved again. For disobedience, in short for anything which in the private court of the *dominica potestas* was a crime in his master's eyes, the slave might be privately executed, with any and every cruelty. In the reign of Augustus, the noon of Roman culture, one Vedius Pollio, a friend of the Emperor's, was used to throw offending slaves into his fish-pond, to feed his huge electric eels (*murænæ*). He was one day entertaining Augustus at table, when the cupbearer broke a crystal goblet, and was forthwith sentenced to the eels. The poor fellow threw himself at the Prince's feet, begging, not to be forgiven, but to be killed in some other way; and Augustus, shocked and angered, ordered the man's emancipation (*mitti jussit*), and had Pollio's crystals all broken before him, and his horrible pool filled up; but he did not discard his friend. "'If,' says Horace (*Satires*, I. iii. 80), 'a

---

[1] There is another and brighter side to the slave-question in Greek literature. Euripides takes an evident pleasure in giving to slaves, in his Tragedies, characteristics of truth and honour, and makes his persons moralize much on the equal nobility of virtue in the slave and in the freeman. See F. A. Paley, *Euripides* (*Bibliotheca Classica*), I. pp. xiii. xiv. Yet even Plato recommends a law for his ideal Commonwealth, by which a slave, if he kills a freeman, must be given up to the kinsmen and *must* be slain by them. The killer of *his own* slave is merely to go through a ceremonial purification.

[2] Suetonius, *Claudius*, c. 25.

Introduction / 157

man is thought mad who crucifies his slave for having filched something from...the table, *how much more mad* must he be who cuts his friend for a trifling offence!'"[1] In brief, the slave in Roman law is a thing, not a person. He has no rights, not even of marriage. To seek his good is in no respect the duty of his master, any more than it is now the duty of an owner to improve his fields *for their own sake.*

The vast numbers of the slaves occasioned a tremendous sternness of repressive legislation[2]. By a law of the reign of Augustus, if a slave killed his master, not only he but every slave under the same roof was to be put to death. In the year 61, the year of St Paul's arrival at Rome, perhaps after his arrival, this enactment was awfully illustrated. A senator, Pedanius Secundus, Prefect of the City, had been murdered by one of his slaves ; and the law called for the death of *four hundred* persons. The Roman populace, wonderful to relate, was roused to horror, and attempted a rescue. The Senate, gravely debating the case, resolved that the execution must proceed ; it was a matter of public safety. Then the roads were lined with troops, and the doom was carried out to the end[3].

"A runaway slave could not lawfully be received or harboured. The master was entitled to pursue him wherever he pleased, and it was the duty of all authorities to give him aid...A class of persons called *fugitivarii* made it their business to recover runaway slaves[4]."

It has been urged in defence of the principle of slavery that the Patriarchal and Mosaic institutions protected it, and that the Apostles do not denounce it. Mr Goldwin Smith has ably discussed this problem in his Essay, cited just above, *Does*

---

[1] Goldwin Smith, *Does the Bible sanction American Slavery?* (1863), p. 30. We quote largely below from this masterly discussion. The story about Vedius Pollio is told by Seneca, *De Irâ*, iii. 40, and by Dion Cassius, liv. 23.

[2] They were not assigned a distinctive dress, for fear they should realize their numbers. They usually wore the common dress of the poor, a dark serge tunic, and slippers.

[3] Tacitus, *Annals*, xiv. 42.

[4] Smith's *Dict. of Gr. and Rom. Antiquities*, s. v. *Servus* (*Roman*). See in general also Becker's *Gallus*, Excursus on "*The Slaves.*"

158 / Introduction

the Bible sanction American Slavery? He points out that in the patriarchal stage of society a certain absolutism, lodged in the father-chief, was natural and necessary, but also by its nature limited and mitigated; and that the whole drift of the legislation of the Pentateuch is towards the protection not of slavery, but of the slave, who there has manifold rights, is never for a moment regarded as other than a person, and at the Paschal Meal, as well as in all the other functions of religion, takes his place beside his master and the rest of the household. As regards the attitude of the Apostles, Mr Goldwin Smith writes as follows (pp. 54 etc.):

"The New Testament is not concerned with any political or social institutions; for political and social institutions belong to particular nations, and particular phases of society...Whatever is done (by Christianity) will be done for the whole of mankind and for all time. If it be necessary for the eternal purpose of the Gospel, St Paul will submit to all the injustice of heathen governments...If it be necessary for the same purpose, the slave of a heathen master will patiently remain a slave.

"Nothing indeed marks the Divine character of the Gospel more than its perfect freedom from the spirit of political revolution. The Founder of Christianity and His Apostles were surrounded by everything which could tempt human reformers to enter on revolutionary courses...Everything, to all human apprehension, counselled an appeal to the strong hand; and strong hands and brave hearts were ready to obey the call...Nevertheless our Lord and His Apostles said not a word against the powers or institutions of that evil world. Their attitude towards them all was that of deep spiritual hostility and entire political submission...Had this submission...not been preached by them, and enforced by their example, the new religion must, humanly speaking, have been strangled in its birth. The religious movement would infallibly have become a political movement....And then the Roman would have...crushed it with his power. To support it against the Roman legions with legions of angels was not a part of the plan of God...[1]

[1] See some admirable remarks in the same direction in the late

Introduction / 159

"The passages in the New Testament relating to the established institutions of the time, inculcate on the disciples resignation to their earthly lot on spiritual grounds...(But) they do not inculcate social or political apathy; they do not pass...upon the Christian world a sentence of social or political despair...

"The relation of the Gospel to slavery is well stated in a passage quoted by Channing from Wayland's *Elements of Moral Science*:—'The very course which the Gospel takes on this subject seems to have been the only one which could have been taken in order to effect the universal abolition of slavery. The Gospel was designed...for all races and for all times. It looked not at the abolition of this form of evil for that age alone, but for its universal abolition. Hence the object of its Author was to gain it a lodgment in every part of the world, so that by its universal diffusion among all classes of society it might... peacefully modify and subdue the evil passions of men, and thus without violence work a revolution in the whole mass of mankind. In this manner alone could its object, a universal moral revolution, be accomplished. For if it had forbidden *the evil* instead of subverting *the principle*, if it had proclaimed the unlawfulness of slavery, and taught slaves to *resist* the oppression of their masters, it would instantly have arrayed the two parties in deadly hostility throughout the civilized world ;...and the very name of the Christian religion would have been forgotten amidst universal bloodshed. The fact, under these circumstances, that the Gospel does not forbid slavery affords no reason to suppose that it does not mean to prohibit it ; much less...that Jesus Christ intended to authorize it.'

"Not only did...the Apostles spread principles and ideas which were sure to work the destruction of slavery, and of the other political and social wrongs of which that corrupt and unjust world was full; but they embodied them in an Institution, founded by their Lord, of which it may be said that though so little revolutionary in appearance that the most jealous tyranny might have received it into its bosom without misgiving, it ex-

Prof. H. Rogers' suggestive Lectures (1874) on *The Superhuman Origin of the Bible inferred from Itself* (Lect. iii.). (Editor.)

ceeded in revolutionary efficacy any political force which has ever been in action among men. At the Supper of the Lord the conqueror was required...to partake in the holy Meal with the conquered, the master with the slave, and this in memory of a Founder who had died the death of a slave upon the Cross, and who at the institution of the Rite had performed the servile office of washing His disciples' feet...Nor has the Lord's Supper failed to accomplish its object in this respect where it has been administered according to the intention of its Founder...

"No sooner did the new religion gain power...than the slave law and the slave system of the Empire began to be undermined by its influence...The right of life and death over the slave was transferred from his owner to the magistrate. The right of correction was placed under humane limitations, which the magistrate was directed to maintain. All the restrictions on the emancipation of slaves were swept away. The first Christian Emperor recognized enfranchisement as a religious act, and established the practice of performing it in the Church, before the Bishop, and in the presence of the congregation. The liberties of the freedman were at the same time cleared of all odious and injurious restrictions. This remained the policy of the Christian Empire. The Code of Justinian [cent. 6] is highly favourable to enfranchisement, and that on religious grounds...

"But the Roman world was doomed; and...partly because the character of the upper classes had been...incurably corrupted by the possession of a multitude of slaves. The feudal age succeeded;...and a new phase of slavery appeared. Immediately Christianity recommenced its work of alleviation and enfranchisement. The codes of laws framed for the new lords of Europe under the influence of the clergy shew the same desire as those of the Christian Emperors to...assure personal rights to the slave. The laws of the Lombards...protected the serf against an unjust or too rigorous master; they set free the husband of a female slave who had been seduced by her owner; they assured the protection of the churches to slaves who had taken refuge there, and regulated the penalties to be inflicted for their faults. In England the clergy secured for the slave rest on the Sunday, and liberty either to rest, or work for himself, on a number of holy-days. They exhorted their flocks to leave the savings and earnings of the prædial slave untouched. They constantly freed the slaves who came into their own possession. They exhorted the laity to do the same, and what living covetousness refused they often wrung from death-bed penitence...

"If then we look to the records of Christianity in the Bible, we find no sanction for American slavery there. If we look to the history of Christendom, we find the propagators and champions of the faith assailing slavery under different forms and in different ages, without concert, yet with a unanimity which would surely be strange if Christianity and slavery were not the natural enemies of each other."

Mr Goldwin Smith alludes thus[1] to our Epistle: "In a religious community so bound together in life and death as that of the early Christians, the relation between master and slave, though it was not formally dissolved, must have been completely transfigured, and virtually exchanged for a relation between brethren in Christ. The clearest proof of this is found in that very Epistle...which those who defend slavery on Scriptural grounds regard as their sheet-anchor in the argument. St Paul sends back the fugitive slave Onesimus to his master Philemon. Therefore, we are told, slavery and fugitive slave laws have received the sanction of St Paul...It is very true that St Paul sends back a fugitive slave to his master. But does he send him back *as a slave?* The best answer to the argument drawn from the Epistle to Philemon is the simple repetition of the words of that Epistle [vv. 10—19]...Onesimus is not sent back as a slave, but as one above a servant, a brother beloved... Such a feeling as the writer of the Epistle supposes to exist in the hearts of Christians as to their relations with each other, though it would not prevent a Christian slave from remaining in the service of his master, would certainly prevent a Christian master from continuing to hold his fellow Christian as a slave."

[1] *Does the Bible, &c.*, p. 64.

162 / Introduction

It may not be out of place to quote here two passages which will bring out another side of the matter:

"Our Lord's miracles upon slaves must not be forgotten. He did not hesitate to set out for the house of the Centurion at Capernaum, at the request of the messengers, in order to heal a paralysed slave. His last act as a free man before His death was to heal the wounded ear of the slave Malchus. He Himself 'took the form of a slave,' both in ministering to others in His life, and also in the manner of His death. Thus He glorified the relation; and His Apostles were not ashamed to magnify it by styling themselves 'the slaves or bondmen of Jesus Christ'"...

"If the abolition of slavery is to turn all servants into hirelings, and make cash payment the only tie between employers and employed, the change will not be an unmixed benefit...If there is to be no bond between servants and masters and mistresses except the contract that determines the time of labour and the rate of payment, then all that ennobles the relation will be lost. Better have the slavery of Onesimus than that. On both sides there ought to be some acknowledgement of *a bond*, that should not be degraded into bondage, but should make the servant of to-day what the slave of the Old Testament was, *only not a son*, and capable of filial relationship, if the need should arise. 'If the Son shall make you free, ye shall be free indeed,' not to depart but to abide in the house for ever, as sons and heirs of God through Christ."[1]

To much the same purpose is the following extract, from the Preface to *Philemon* in the Berlenburg (or Berleburg) Bible (about 1727); a German translation of the Bible, with Commentary, emanating from a mystic school of Pietism:

"This Epistle is much the shortest of the Epistles of Paul which are contained in Scripture, but it is very nobly (*herrlich*) and lovingly written...It is really sad that beginners in the Christian life will not take it with a better grace when they have

[1] C. H. Waller, D.D., *Handbook to the Epistles of St Paul*, pp. 178—180.

to be servants. Too commonly among the Anabaptists[1] people want not to submit to the straits (*Elend*) of human life, but to be free. But this is mere self-love; as if we were already really capable of freedom. God helps us to freedom, in Christ, but He does not meanwhile take away from us the burthens of this life, which we must endure in the patience of Christ. The newly converted, even in the early Church, if servants, wanted no longer to do their duty by their Christian masters. The thought is (*man denckt*), 'I am as pious as my master!' But the self-spirit (*Ichheit*) must die. The Apostles were constrained to raise their admonition against such a state of things. Christianity is essentially submissive (*Das Christenthum ist was unterthäniges*). So we ought not to burst loose, but to shew that we have a broken spirit."

In closing, we quote a few lines from the recently (1889) recovered *Apology*, or Defence of Christianity (the earliest extant writing of its kind), written by the philosopher Aristides, and addressed to Hadrian, or possibly to Antoninus Pius, about A.D. 130. The author speaks as in some sense an independent observer:

"Now the Christians, O King, by going about and seeking have found the truth...They know and believe in God, the Maker of heaven and earth, in whom are all things and from whom are all things...They do not commit adultery or fornication, they do not bear false witness, they do not deny a deposit, nor covet what is not theirs; they honour father and mother; they do good to those who are their neighbours, and when they are judges they judge uprightly;...and those who grieve them they comfort, and make them their friends; and they do good to their enemies; and their wives, O King, are pure as virgins, and their daughters modest; and their men abstain from all unlawful wedlock and from all impurity, in the hope of the recompense that is to come in another world; but as for their servants or handmaids, or their children, if they have any, they persuade them to become Christians for the love

---

[1] The reference is to revival movements of the time, which, with many admirable results, had their aberrations.

they have towards them; and when they have become so they call them without distinction brethren."[1]

Chapter 5

ARGUMENT OF THE EPISTLE

1—3. PAUL, a prisoner for Jesus Christ's sake and by His will, with the Christian brother Timotheus, greets Philemon, that true fellow-worker for Christ [at Colossæ,] and the dear [Christian sister, Philemon's wife,] Apphia, and [Philemon's son] Archippus, true comrade in Christ's missionary warfare. May all blessing be upon them from the Father and from the Lord Jesus Christ!

4—7. He thanks his God for Philemon by name, whenever his converts are present in his prayers, hearing, as he has heard [from Epaphras] of his faith reposed on the Lord Jesus and the love he so practically shews towards all his Christian neighbours; praying that the charitable bounty prompted by his faith may tell all around him, giving [the recipients and witnesses of it] a fuller view of all the graces Christians possess, to the glory of Christ. For indeed Paul has received great joy and encouragement on account of Philemon's life of love [reported to him,] as he thinks how the hearts of the Christians have found rest [from the strain of poverty and care] by the aid of this his true brother.

8—21. So [writing to one who understands *love*,] Paul, though he might claim an apostolic right to speak more freely and authoritatively to Philemon about duty, yet in view of their personal Christian affection rather comes as his suppliant; just in the character of Paul, the aged, and now not only old but helpless, in imprisonment for Christ. He is Philemon's suppliant for a son of his (Paul's), a son whom he has begotten [to a new life in Christ] in his Roman prison. It is Onesimus ("*Helpful*"), [Philemon's domestic slave]; once anything but *profitable* to Philemon, [for he had pilfered from him, and absconded,] but profitable

---

[1] *Texts and Studies; the Apology of Aristides* (Cambridge, 1891), p. 49. The translation here given is that of Mr J. Rendel Harris, from the Syriac Version of the Apology. See also an admirable little volume, *The newly recovered Apology of Aristides*, by Helen B. Harris (Mrs Rendel Harris).

Introduction / 165

now to Philemon, aye and to Paul too, [to whom Onesimus has been devotedly serviceable.] He sends him back to his master [with this letter;] *him*, or let him rather be called a piece of Paul's own heart! He could half have wished to keep Onesimus at his side, to be his loving attendant (as the substitute of loving Philemon) in this imprisonment endured for the Gospel's sake. But he would not act so without Philemon's decision, [which of course he could not get, at such a distance;] otherwise the kindness on Philemon's part would at least have seemed to be a thing of compulsion, not of freewill. And perhaps it was on purpose for such a return to Philemon, in an indissoluble union, for time and for eternity, that Onesimus had been sent away from him for a little while; [to be given back now by the Lord] no more as a mere slave, but as a brother, a dear brother, dearest to Paul, dearer than dearest to Philemon, to whom he is now joined both by earthly and by spiritual ties. If Philemon, then, holds Paul for an associate [in faith and life], he must receive Onesimus just as he would receive Paul. If Onesimus had stolen, or was in debt, before his flight, let the amount be charged to Paul; here is his autograph note for the repayment. Meanwhile, he will not dwell on the thought that Philemon owes to Paul [not only the new-making of Onesimus but] himself besides, [as his son in the faith of Christ.] Ah, let Philemon give Paul joy, and rest his heart, by action worthy of a man in Christ. He has written thus with full confidence of his assent, and more than assent, to the request.

22. Meanwhile, will Philemon prepare lodgings for him [at Colossæ?] He expects to be restored to his beloved converts, in answer to their prayers.

23—24. He sends greetings to Philemon from [his old friend] Epaphras, who shares his prison; and from Marcus, Aristarchus, Demas, Lucas, who are working with Paul for Christ.

25. May the presence and power of Christ be with the inner life of Philemon and his family.

GRACE makes the slave a freeman. 'Tis a change
That turns to ridicule the turgid speech
And stately tones of moralists, who boast,
As if, like him of fabulous renown,
They had indeed ability to smooth
The shag of savage nature, and were each
An Orpheus, and omnipotent in song:
But transformation of apostate man
From fool to wise, from earthly to Divine,
Is work for Him that made him. He alone,
And He, by means in philosophic eyes
Trivial and worthy of disdain, achieves
The wonder; humanizing what is brute
In the lost kind, extracting from the lips
Of asps their venom, overpowering strength
By weakness, and hostility by love.
                                        COWPER.

COMMENTARY ON PHILEMON

P^{AUL}, a prisoner of Jesus Christ, and Timothy *our* brother, 1
unto Philemon *our* dearly beloved, and fellowlabourer,

TITLE

The oldest known form is the briefest, TO PHILEMON. That in the A.V. is from the Textus Receptus. Other forms are, PAUL'S (or THE HOLY APOSTLE PAUL'S) EPISTLE TO PHILEMON. One title runs, THESE SURE THINGS WRITES PAUL TO FAITHFUL PHILEMON.[1]
See note on the title of Colossians.

1—3   GREETING

1. *Paul*] See on·Col. i. 1.

a prisoner] To the Colossians he had said "*an Apostle.*" Here he speaks more personally. Cp. for the phrase, or its like, Eph. iii. 1, iv. 1; 2 Tim. i. 8; below, ver. 9.

of Jesus Christ] If he suffers, it is all in relation to his Master, his Possessor. See our note on Eph. iii. 1.—Outwardly he is Nero's prisoner, inwardly, Jesus Christ's.

Timothy our *brother*] See notes on Col. i. 1. This association of Timothy (Timotheus) with himself, in the personal as well as in the public Epistle, is a touch of delicate courtesy.

Philemon] All we know of him is given in this short letter. We may fairly assume that he was a native and inhabitant of Colossæ, where his son (see below, and on Col. iv. 17) lived and laboured; that he was brought to Christ by St Paul (ver. 19); that he was in comfortable circumstances (see on vv. 2, 10); and that his character was kind and just, for St Paul would suit his appeals to his correspondent; and that his Christian life was devoted and influential (vv. 5—7). In fact the Epistle indicates a noble specimen of the primitive Christian.—See further, *Introd.* to the Ep. to Philemon, ch. iii.

The name Philemon happens to occur in the beautiful legend of Philemon and Baucis, the *Phrygian* peasant-pair, who, in an inhospitable neighbourhood, "entertained unawares" Jupiter and Mercury

---

[1] The omission of one syllable in this Greek title (so as to read βαιά instead of βέβαια) makes it run as a hexameter line, and gives the sense
"*Paul on* a slender *theme thus writes to the faithful Philemon.*"
If we are right in this guess, perhaps this title was devised by a *depreciator* (pp. 147, 148) of the Epistle, and afterwards altered, at the expense of metre, by some wiser man.

168 / Philemon

2 and to *our* beloved Apphia, and Archippus our fellowsoldier,
3 and to the church in thy house : Grace to you, and peace,
from God our Father and the Lord Jesus Christ.

(Ovid, *Metam.*, viii. 626—724), "gods in the likeness of men" (see Acts xiv. 11).

Philemon, in legend, becomes bishop of Colossæ (but of Gaza according to another story), and is martyred there under Nero. Theodoret (cent. 5) says that his house was still shewn at Colossæ.—See further Lightfoot, p. 372.

fellowlabourer] See on Col. iv. 11. Philemon, converted through Paul's agency, had (perhaps first at Ephesus, then on his return to Colossæ) worked actively in the Gospel, whether ordained or no.

2. our *beloved Apphia*] Read, probably, **our** (lit., **the**) **sister Apphia**. The Vulgate combines the two readings, *Appiæ sorori carissimæ*.—We may be sure that Apphia was Philemon's wife. Her name was a frequent Phrygian name (written otherwise *Aphphia*; other forms found are *Apphê, Aphphê*), and had no connexion with the Latin *Appia*. See Lightfoot's abundant evidence, pp. 372—4.—We know Apphia from this passage only. Legend says that she was martyred with Philemon at Colossæ.—See further above, p. 152.

Archippus] Probably Philemon's son and (Col. iv. 17) a missionary-pastor of Colossæ and its neighbourhood. Of him too we know nothing outside these allusions; his martyrdom, when he suffered with his parents, is a legend only.—Lightfoot (p. 375) inclines to think that his pastorate lay at Laodicea, reasoning from the passage Col. iv. 15—17. But would he not have lived at Laodicea, if so? And if so, would he have been saluted thus, in this letter referring wholly to the home, in closest connexion with his (assumed) parents, and just before a mention of "*the church in their house*"? On the other hand, Archippus may have had to do with the mission at Laodicea, perhaps as superintending pastor, while resident at Colossæ. Possibly he had lately undertaken such an extension of charge, and this might be referred to Col. iv. 17. But (see note there) we incline to think that that verse refers to Archippus and to a recent appointment to ministry at *Colossæ.*—See further above, p. 152.

See note on the Subscription to the Epistle, for a (late) mention of Archippus as "*the deacon*" of the Colossian Church.

our fellowsoldier] In Christ's great missionary campaign. Cp. Phil. ii. 25, and our note. For the imagery, cp. 2 Cor. x. 3—5; 1 Tim. i. 18; 2 Tim. ii. 3, 4.—Wyclif, "*archip oure euene kny3t.*"

the church in thy house] Cp. Col. iv. 15, and note. Philemon's house was the Christian *rendezvous* of Colossæ, and his great room the worship-place.

3. *Grace be unto you*, &c.] Verbatim as in the received text of Col. i. 2; where see notes. In this private Letter, written about a practical matter, as much as in the public and didactic Letter, all is hallowed with the blessed Name.

Philemon / 169

I thank my God, making mention of thee always in my 4
prayers, hearing of thy love and faith, which thou hast 5
toward the Lord Jesus, and toward all saints; that the 6

4—7 THANKSGIVING AND PRAYER

4. *I thank my God*] For the phrase precisely cp. Rom. i. 8;
1 Cor. i. 4; Phil. i. 3 (where see our note). All the Epistles of
St Paul, save only *Galatians*, contain a thanksgiving in their first
greetings.
"*My God:*"—so Rom., 1 Cor., Phil., just quoted, and Phil. iv. 19.
Profound personal appropriation and realization speaks in the phrase.
making mention of thee] So Rom. i. 9; Eph. i. 16, where see note;
1 Thess. i. 2; and cp. Phil. i. 3. How often the names written in his
Epistles must have been uttered in his prayers!
always] Alford, Lightfoot, and R.V., connect this word with "*I
give thanks*"; the Greek order of the sentence allowing it. Ellicott
divides as A.V. The question, happily unimportant, is very much one
of rhythm and balance, and we think this inclines to A.V. If so, he
means that Philemon is habitually mentioned whenever his converts are
present in his thanksgivings.
in] Lit., "*on*"; on occasion of, at the times of.
5. *hearing*] doubtless from Epaphras, perhaps with Onesimus' con-
firmation from *his* point of view. The Greek implies *a process* of
hearing; the subject was *continually* present in conversation.
love] See below vv. 7, 9. The whole letter is from love to love.
faith] Some commentators (see Ellicott's note, where the view is
discussed and rejected) explain this as "*fidelity*" (as probably Gal. v. 22
and certainly Tit. ii. 10). But that meaning is rare in St Paul, and
needs strong evidence for adoption in any given case. The ruling
meaning, "*trust, reliance,*" is quite in place here.
toward...toward] The "received" Greek text, retained here by
Lightfoot, has two different prepositions, which we may render **toward**
and **unto** respectively; "*toward*" the Object of faith, "*unto*" the
objects of love.
toward the Lord...saints] R.V. (and so Alford) reads the whole
passage; "*thy love, and the faith which thou hast toward* &c.," making
"*the faith*" only, not "*thy love*," refer to *both* the Lord and the saints;
(the man's reliance on Christ *coming out in* a "work of faith," called
briefly "*faith*"—see ver. 6—towards the saints). But Lightfoot, we
think rightly, distributes the references of love and faith, cross-wise, to
the saints and the Lord respectively. Cp. for support Col. i. 3, 4, a
passage written so nearly at the same time. No doubt the arrangement of the Greek, on this view, is peculiar. But in this domestic letter
several natural liberties of language occur.
"*All saints*":—read, **all the saints**, with whom Philemon had to do.
—On the word "*saints*" see note on Col. i. 2.
6. *that*] This word refers back to the "*prayers*" of ver. 4; ver. 5
being a parenthesis of thought. As in his other thanksgivings, so

communication of thy faith may become effectual by the acknowledging of every good *thing* which is in you in Christ
7 Jesus. For we have great joy and consolation in thy love,

in this, he passes at once into prayer that the good he rejoices in *may grow*.

the communication] R. V., "*fellowship.*" The Greek word occurs Rom. xv. 26; 2 Cor. ix. 13; Heb. xiii. 16 (and the verb, Rom. xii. 13; Gal. vi. 6; Phil. iv. 15); in the sense of charitable distribution, bounty. So it seems to be here. Philemon, comparatively wealthy, was the generous giver to his poorer fellow-believers.

of thy faith] I.e., which thy faith prompts, and in that sense makes. Philemon's faith was as it were the inward "distributor to the necessities of the saints," while his hand was the outward. The phrase, so explained, is unusual, but other explanations are much further fetched.

may become effectual] **Operative** (Ellicott), or **effective** (Lightfoot). He prays that Philemon's life of practical love may "*tell*" around him. —Wyclif, "*may be made opene.*" This is from the Latin, which (see Lightfoot) depends on a slight variant (one letter only) in the Greek.

by the acknowledging] Lit. and better, **in the (true) knowledge.** As the recipients and witnesses of his goodness saw more and more clearly the motive and spirit of it, they would have a truer insight (*epignôsis*) into the power of the Gospel; and "*in*" that insight would consist the deepest "effect" of Philemon's goodness.—On the word here rendered (R. V.) "*knowledge,*" see on Col. i. 9.

every good thing] Every grace; the gift of love in all its practical manifestations.

in you] Probably read, **in us**; us Christians as such. So Ellicott, Alford, Lightfoot, and margin R. V.

in Christ Jesus] Read, **unto Christ** (perhaps omitting **Jesus**).— "*Unto*" Him:—i.e., to His glory, the true aim of the true life of grace. The servant is so to live that not only shall he be seen to be beneficent, but his beneficence shall be seen to be due to Another, whose he is.—Perhaps these words go with "*the knowledge*" just above; as if to say, "your good *shall be recognized* to His glory." But this collocation is not necessary.

7. *we have*] Better, **I had**; i.e., when the news reached me.

joy] Another reading, ill-supported, has "*grace*"; which would bear here the sense of thankfulness. One Greek letter only makes the difference.

consolation] R. V., **comfort**, which is better. The Greek word commonly denotes rather strengthening, enc*our*agement, than the tenderer "consolation"; and the word "comfort" (*con*fortatio) fairly represents it (see on Col. ii. 2). The news of Philemon's love had *animated* the Apostle.

in thy love] Lit. and better, **on (account of) thy love**; this life of "faith which worked by love" (Gal. v. 6).

the bowels] Better perhaps, **the hearts.** So R. V. See our note on Phil. i. 8. In the Greek classics the word here used means "the *nobler*

because the bowels of the saints are refreshed by thee, brother. Wherefore, though I might be much bold in 8 Christ to enjoin thee that which is convenient, *yet* for love's 9 sake I rather beseech *thee*, being such a one as Paul the

vitals," as distinguished from the intestines; and though the LXX. do not follow this usage, it fairly justifies us in adopting in English the "nobler" word, by which we so often denote "*the feelings*."
are refreshed] Lit. and better, **have been refreshed** or **rested**. See the same verb, and tense, 2 Cor. vii. 13. The cognate noun occurs, e.g. Matt. xi. 28.—The tired hearts of the poor or otherwise harassed Christians had found, in Philemon, a haven of *rest*.—See ver. 20 for the same phrase again.
by thee] Lit., **through thee, by means of thee**. He was *the agent* for his Lord.
brother] The word of holy family-affection is beautifully kept for the last.—See on Col. i. 2.

8—21   A PERSONAL REQUEST: ONESIMUS

8. *Wherefore*] Because I am writing to one whose life is the fruit of *a loving* heart.
though I might be much bold] Lit., "*having much boldness*"; but the insertion of "*though*" rightly explains the thought.—"*Boldness*":— the Greek word, by derivation, means **outspokenness**, and its usage almost always illustrates this. See on ii. 15 above, and our note on Eph. iii. 12.—He has the right to "*say anything*" to Philemon.
in Christ] Whom he represents as apostle, and who also unites him and Philemon in an intimacy which makes outspokenness doubly right.
enjoin] A very strong word. The cognate noun occurs Tit. ii. 15; "rebuke with all *authority*."—"Love must often take the place of authority" (Quesnel).
convenient] **Befitting**; the French *convenable*. So Eph. v. 4, where the same Greek (which occurs also Col. iii. 18; see note) is represented. In older English this was a familiar meaning of "*convenient*"; thus Latimer speaks of "voluntary works, which...be of themselves marvellous...*convenient* to be done." See the *Bible Word Book*.
9. *for love's sake*] Lit., "*because of the love*"; i.e., perhaps, "because of *our* love." Ellicott, Alford, and Lightfoot take the reference to be to (Christian) love in general. But the Greek commentators (cent. 11) Theophylact and Œcumenius (quoted by Ellicott) explain the phrase as referring to *the* love of the two friends; and this is surely in point in this message of personal affection.
beseech] The verb is one which often means "*exhort*," in a sense less tender than "*beseech*." But see e.g. Phil. iv. 2 for a case where, as here, it evidently conveys a *loving* appeal.
being such a one as] Does this mean, "*because* I am such," or "*although* I am such"? The answer depends mainly on the explanation of the next following words.

10 aged, and now also a prisoner of Jesus Christ. I beseech thee for my son Onesimus, whom I have begotten in my

Paul the aged] *Paulus senex*, Latin Versions; "and so apparently all versions" (Ellicott). So R.V. text. Its margin has "*Paul an ambassador*"; and this rendering is advocated by Lightfoot in a long and instructive note. He points out that not only are *presbûtês* ("*an elder*," which all MSS. have here) and *presbeutês* ("*an envoy*") nearly identical in form, but that the latter word was often spelt by the Greeks like the former. And he points to Eph. v. 12 (see our note there), where "*the ambassador in chains*" expressly describes himself—a passage written perhaps on the same day as this. So explaining, the phrase would be a quiet reminder, in the act of entreaty, that the suppliant was no ordinary one; he was the Lord's envoy, dignified by suffering for the Lord.

But, with reverence to the great Commentator, is not the other explanation after all more in character in this Epistle, which carries a tender pathos in it everywhere? A fresh reminder of his *dignity*, after the passing and as it were rejected allusion to it in ver. 8, seems to us to be out of harmony; while nothing could be more fitting here than a word about age and affliction. The question whether St Paul was "an old man," as we commonly reckon age, is not important; so Lightfoot himself points out. At all periods, men have called themselves old when they felt so; Lightfoot instances Sir Walter Scott at fifty-five. (St Paul was probably quite sixty at this time.) And it is immaterial whether or no Philemon was his junior. If he were Paul's coeval, it would matter little. The appeal lies in the fact of the writer's "failing powers," worn in the Lord's service; and this would touch an equal as readily as a junior. To our mind too the phrase, "*being such a one as*," conveys, though it is hard to analyse the impression, the thought of a pathetic *self-depreciation*.

On the whole we recommend the rendering of the A.V. and (text) R.V. But by all means see Lightfoot's note.

also a prisoner of Jesus Christ] See on ver. 1.—"*Also*":—the weakness of age was *aggravated* by the helplessness of bonds.

10. *I beseech thee*] See on the same word just above.

my son...whom I have begotten] Lit., "*whom I begot*." But English demands the perfect where the event is quite recent.

"*Son*": "*begotten*":—cp. 1 Cor. iv. 15: "I begot you, *through the Gospel*." The teacher who, by the grace of God, brings into contact the penitent soul and Him who is our Life, and by faith in whom we become "the children of God" (Gal. iii. 26), is, in a sense almost more than figurative, the convert's spiritual father. The spiritual relationship between the two is deep and tender indeed. The converted runaway had taken his place with Timothy (1 Tim. i. 2; 2 Tim. i. 2) and Titus (Tit. i. 4) in St Paul's *family circle*.

See Gal. iv. 19 for the boldest and tenderest of all his *parental* appeals.

Onesimus] The name stands last in the sentence, in the Greek; a perfect touch of heart-rhetoric.

Philemon / 173

bonds: which in time past was to thee unprofitable, but 11
now profitable to thee and to me: whom I have sent again: 12
thou therefore receive him, that is, mine own bowels: whom 13

"The name was very commonly borne by slaves" (Lightfoot, p. 376).
It means "*Helpful*," "*Profitable*"; and such words were frequent as
slave-names. Lightfoot (p. 376, note) quotes among others *Chrestus*
("*Good*"), *Symphorus* ("*Profitable*"), and *Carpus* ("*Fruit*"). Female
slaves often bore names descriptive of appearance; *Arescousa* ("*Pleasing*"), *Terpousa* ("*Winning*"), &c.
On Onesimus and his status see *Introd.* to this Epistle, ch. iii., iv.

11. *in time past*] In the Greek, simply, **once**.
unprofitable] A gentle "play" on "*Helpful's*" name; an allusion, and no more (for no more was needed), to his delinquencies. To Onesimus himself Paul had no doubt spoken, with urgent faithfulness, of his *sin* against his master. What the sin had been we can only guess, beyond the evident fact that he had run away. Vv. 18, 19, suggest that he had robbed Philemon before his flight, though the language does not imply more than petty crime of that kind.
Perhaps Philemon would recall the "unprofitable bondservant" of the Lord's parable, a parable recorded for us by "the beloved physician" now at Paul's side (Luke xvii. 10).
and to me] "An after-thought...According to common Greek usage the first person would naturally precede the second" (Lightfoot). The words are a loving testimony to Onesimus' devotion.

12. *whom I have sent again*] Lit., "*I did send*"; the "epistolary aorist," as in Col. iv. 8, where see note.—How much lies behind these simple words; what unselfish jealousy for duty on St Paul's part, and what courage of conscience and faith on that of Onesimus! By law, his offended master might treat him exactly as he pleased, for life or death. See *Introd.*, ch. iv., and Appendix M.
"No prospect of usefulness should induce ministers to allow their converts to neglect relative obligations, or to fail of obedience to their superiors. One great evidence of true repentance consists in returning to the practice of those duties which had been neglected" (Scott).
receive] **Welcome**; the same word as that in Rom. xiv. 1, 3, xv. 7; and below, ver. 17.
But there is strong evidence for the omission of this word, and (somewhat less strong) for the omission of "*thou therefore*." This would leave, **him, that is** &c., as the true reading. If so, this clause should be linked to that before it;—**Whom I have sent back—him, that is,** &c.—a bold but pathetic stroke of expression. Such a connexion seems better than that adopted by Lightfoot, who begins a new sentence with "*him,*" and seeks the verb in ver. 17.
mine own bowels] **Mine own heart**; see on ver. 7. The Greek might, by usage, refer to Onesimus as St Paul's *son*; as if to say, "bone of my bone." But, as Lightfoot points out, this would be unlike St Paul's use of the word everywhere else; with him, it always indicates *the emotions.*—*Cor, corculum* ("*sweetheart*"), are somewhat similarly used in Latin, as words of personal fondness.

174 / Philemon

I would have retained with me, that in thy stead he might
14 have ministered unto me in the bonds of the gospel: but
without thy mind would I do nothing; that thy benefit
15 should not be as *it were* of necessity, but willingly. For
perhaps he therefore departed for a season, that thou

13. *I would*] Lit., "*I was wishing*"; the imperfect indicates a half-purpose, stopped by other considerations. Lightfoot compares for similar imperfects Rom. ix. 3; Gal. iv. 20.
me] Lit., **myself.**
in thy stead] **On thy behalf**; as thy representative, substitute, agent. He assumes the loving Philemon's personal devotion.
ministered] as personal attendant; the habitual reference of the verb. Cp. e.g. Matt. iv. 11, viii. 15; Luke xvii. 8, xxii. 26; Joh. xii. 2; 2 Tim. i. 18.
of the gospel] "For the hope of Israel," and of the world, "he was bound with this chain" (Acts xxviii. 20). Cp. Phil. i. 13.
On the word "*Gospel*" see note on Col. i. 5.
14. *mind*] Properly, "*opinion*," **decision.** Latin Versions, *consilium.*
would I do nothing] Lit., "*nothing I willed to do.*" The A.V. represents the idiom rightly.
that thy benefit] The primary reason, doubtless, was that it was Onesimus' *duty* to return, and Paul's to give him up. But this delicate subsidiary motive was not less real.
"*Thy benefit*":—lit., "*thy good,*" **thy kindness.** The reference seems to be to Philemon's general kindness to his friend, of which the permission to Onesimus to stay would have been an instance. So Ellicott.
not as it were *of necessity, but willingly*] It might seem that he almost suggests to Philemon to *send Onesimus back to him*. But this is not likely in itself, in view of the long and costly journey involved; and besides, he looks forward to visit Colossæ himself before long (ver. 22). What he means is that he sends back Onesimus, because to retain him would be to get a benefit from Philemon willing *or not*, and Philemon's "good" had always been willingly given.
"*As it were*" softens the "*of necessity*"; Philemon might not be unwilling, but there would be *the look of* his being so.
15. *For*] He gives a new reason for Onesimus' return. Perhaps it was *on purpose for* such a more than restoration that he was permitted to desert Philemon. So to send him back is to carry out God's plan.
perhaps] He claims no insight into the Divine purpose, where it is not revealed to him.
departed] Lit., **was parted.** From one point of view, that of providential permission, the *run*away was *sent* away. Chrysostom (quoted by Lightfoot) beautifully compares Gen. xlv. 5, where Joseph says to his brethren, "*God did send* me before you."
for a season] Lit., "*for an hour.*" So 2 Cor. vii. 8; Gal. ii. 5.
receive him] The Greek verb is often used of *receiving payment*; e.g.

shouldest receive him for ever; not now as a servant, but 16
above a servant, a brother beloved, specially to me, but
how much more unto thee, both in the flesh, and in the
Lord? If thou count me therefore a partner, receive him 17
as myself. If he hath wronged thee, or oweth *thee* ought, 18

Matt. vi. 2, 5, 16. We might almost paraphrase, "*get him paid back*"; as if he had been "*lent to the Lord.*"

for ever] Lit., "*eternal,*" aiônion. The adjective tends to mark *duration as long* as the nature of the subject allows. And by usage it has a close connexion with things spiritual. "*For ever*" here thus imports both natural and spiritual permanence of restoration; "for ever" on earth, and then hereafter; a final return to Philemon's home, with a prospect of heaven in Philemon's company.

16. *not now as a servant*] **No more as bondservant.** Not that he would cease to be such, necessarily, in law; St Paul does not say "*set him free.*" But in Christ he was free, and of kin.

a brother beloved] Cp. 1 Tim. vi. 2 for the same thought from the slave's point of view. These simple words are an absolute and fatal antithesis to the principle, and so ultimately to the existence, of slavery.

"Christianity alone can work these holy transformations, changing a temporal servitude into an eternal brotherhood" (Quesnel).—See further, *Introd.*, ch. iv., particularly pp. 163, 164.

specially to me] Lit., **most of all to me.** Philemon's beloved "*brother*" was Paul's most beloved "*son.*"

but how much more} A verbal inconsistency, conveying a thought of noble warmth and delicacy. He had said "*most to me*"; but after all it is "*more than most*" to Philemon.

in the flesh] A remarkable phrase, as if slavery were a sort of kinship. This thought appears, as a fact, in combination (and contrast) with the harshest theories of ancient slavery. Thus Aristotle (*Polit.*, i. ii.; see *Introd.* to this Epistle, ch. iv.) writes, "the slave is *a portion of* his master; as it were a living, though separated, portion of *his body.*" And again: "he shares his master's reason, so far as to perceive it." The Gospel would of course assimilate and enforce with all its power *that* aspect of the connexion.

in the Lord?] In whom there is "neither bond nor free," and in whom now master and slave were "one man" (Gal. iii. 26—28).

17. *count*] Lit., "*have,*" **hold.** The word is similarly used Luke xiv. 18; Phil. ii. 29.

a partner] **An associate, a fellow**; in faith and interests. The Apostle is altogether the man, the friend.—Cp. 2 Cor. viii. 23.—Wyclif, "*as thou haste me a felowe.*"

receive] On the word, see note on ver. 12.

as myself] **As me**; and so as your "*fellow,*" in Christ. "After calling the slave...his brother, his son, his heart, what can this apostolic soul do further but call him his other self?" (Quesnel).

18. *If he hath wronged thee*] Lit., **But if he wronged thee**, before, or when, he fled. See on ver. 11. Horace (*Sat.*, I. i. 78) says how

176 / Philemon

19 put that on mine account; I Paul have written *it* with mine own hand, I will repay *it*: albeit I do not say to thee how
20 thou owest unto me even thine own self besides. Yea, brother, let me have joy of thee in the Lord: refresh my
21 bowels in the Lord. Having confidence in thy obedience

the anxious master "fears lest his slaves should pillage him and fly" (*ne te compilent fugientes*).

oweth] The slave might be trusted by his master with money for purchases; or he might work at a trade, or do casual service for others, his master claiming the proceeds. Thus he might be his owner's debtor. See Smith's *Dict. of Greek and Roman Antiquities*, art. *Servus*.

put that on mine account] Latin Versions, *hoc mihi imputa;* Wyclif, "*asette thou this thing to me*."—Such collections as the Philippians sent (Phil. iv. 10—18) enabled him to offer this generous guarantee.

19. *I Paul have written it*] Lit., "*did write it;*" an "epistolary aorist" (Col. iv. 8); "the tense commonly used in signatures" (Lightfoot).— Here, surely, he takes the pen (cp. Col. iv. 18) and writes his indebtedness in autograph, with a formal mention of his own name; then, he gives the pen back to the amanuensis.

"A signature to a deed in ancient or mediæval times would commonly take the form..."*I* so-and-so" (Lightfoot).

I will] The "*I*" is emphatic in the Greek.

albeit I do not say] Lit., and better, **that I say not, not to say.**

thou owest unto me...besides] As if to say, "I am restoring to you Onesimus, *made new*; this far more than clears any loss he cost you when he fled; thus you are *indebted*, even in money's worth, to me; and *besides*—you owe me yourself."

thine own self] The converted man "comes *to himself*" (Luke xv. 17) as never before. "It is a new creation" (2 Cor. v. 17); as it were a new self. Under God, this is due to the human bringer of the converting word; and so to him, under God, the convert feels instinctively a moral indebtedness; he owes him help and service in the new life.

20. *Yea*] So (in the Greek) Matt. xv. 27; Phil. iv. 3.

brother] Again the word of love and honour, as in ver. 7.

let me have joy of thee] We may render, less warmly, "*Let me reap benefit of thee.*" So the Geneva Version; "*Let me obteyne this fruit of thee.*" But the Greek usage of the verb before us here, *in the optative*, in which it often conveys a "*God bless you,*" favours the text. He does not merely ask to be served, but to be made very happy.—Tyndale renders, "*Let me enioie thee.*"

Latin Versions, *Ita, frater, ego te fruar;* which Wyclif, mistaking, renders, "*so brother I schal use thee.*"

in the Lord] All is "*in Him,*" for His living members.

refresh my bowels] **Refresh**, or **rest, my heart.** See on ver. 7 above.

in the Lord] Read undoubtedly, **in Christ.**

Philemon / 177

I wrote unto thee, knowing that thou wilt also do more than I say. But withal prepare me also a lodging: for I 22 trust that through your prayers I shall be given unto you. There salute thee Epaphras, my fellowprisoner in Christ 23

21. *thy obedience*] The obedience of love, as to a father and benefactor. Cp. Phil. ii. 12. Not love of authority, but a tender gravity in a case so near his heart, speaks here.

I wrote] Better, in English epistolary idiom, **I have written**.

also do more than I say] He means, surely, that Philemon will emancipate his slave-brother. But he does not say so in set terms. "The word emancipation seems to be trembling on his lips, and yet he does not once utter it" (Lightfoot, p. 389).—See further *Introd.*, ch. iv.

22   HE HOPES TO VISIT COLOSSÆ

22. *But withal*] Here is a different matter, yet not quite apart from the main theme. "There is a gentle compulsion in this mention of a personal visit to Colossæ. The Apostle would be able to see for himself that Philemon had not disappointed his expectations" (Lightfoot). And more; would not the joy of the prospect make "obedience" on Philemon's part doubly willing?

prepare] The verb is in the singular.

a lodging] The Greek may mean either "*lodging*" or **hospitality**. General Greek usage is in favour of the latter. The "*hospitality*" would no doubt be gladly provided in Philemon's own house; but St Paul, with his unfailing courtesy, does not *ask* this.

I trust] **I hope**. He makes no prophecy, where none is authorized. Even when (as Rom. xv. 24, 28) he speaks positively of his plans, it is with an evident reservation of "if the Lord will." The prospect of Rom. xv. had by this time been much modified.

through your prayers] which "move the hand of God," being all the while part of His chain of means. For St Paul's estimate of the power of intercessory prayer see e.g. Rom. xv. 30—32 (a close parallel); 2 Cor. i. 11; Phil. i. 19.—Neither for him nor for the Colossians did the deep peace of self-resignation mean Stoic apathy, nor, surely, even the "indifference" of the Mystics.

I shall be given unto you] With a noble *naïveté* he recognizes his own dearness in the eyes of his converts; he does not affect to think that his return would not be "*a gift*" to them.

Lightfoot cites Acts iii. 14, xxv. 11, for the use of the Greek verb in connexion with *a person*.

23—25   SALUTATIONS

23. *There salute thee*] Cp. Col. iv. 10.
Epaphras] Cp. Col. i. 7, and note.
my fellowprisoner] Cp. Col. iv. 10, and note. This passage is in favour of explaining the term there also to mean "a visitor who is so much with me as to be, as it were, in prison too."

24 Jesus ; Marcus, Aristarchus, Demas, Lucas, my fellow-
25 labourers. The grace of our Lord Jesus Christ *be* with
your spirit. Amen.

¶ Written from Rome to Philemon, by Onesimus a servant.

24. *Marcus, Aristarchus, Demas, Lucas*] Cp. Col. iv. 10, 14, and notes.

This group of names (with the names of Archippus, ver. 2 above, and Onesimus, ver. 10) links this Epistle to that to Colossæ, in time and place of writing, and in destination.—See Paley's acute remarks (*Horæ Paulinæ*, ch. xiv.) on the subtle tokens of independence in the two lists and so of literary genuineness. See also Salmon, *Introd. to N.T.*, pp. 467, 468.

my fellowlabourers] A favourite word with St Paul; see above, ver. 1.

Demas stands here among the faithful. But see on Col. iv. 14.

25. *The grace of our Lord Jesus Christ*] So Rom. xvi. 20, 24; 1 Cor. xvi. 23; 2 Cor. xiii. 13; Gal. vi. 18 (where the whole formula is verbatim as here); Phil. iv. 23; 1 Thess. v. 28; 2 Thess. iii. 18; Rev. xxii. 21. Cp. 2 Tim. ii. 1.

"*The grace*" is in short the Lord Jesus Christ Himself, in His saving presence and power; Himself at once Gift and Giver. So the Epistle closes, as it began, "*in Him*."

with your spirit] Not "*spirits*"; as if Philemon and his house had, in Christ, "one spirit," one inner life.—See further, Appendix N.—The same phrase occurs Gal. vi. 18 and (in the true reading) Phil. iv. 23; where see our note.

Amen] The word is probably to be retained here. So R.V. text. It is properly a Hebrew adverb, meaning "*surely;*" repeatedly used as here in the O. T. See e.g. Deut. xxvii. 15, &c. ; Jer. xi. 5 (marg. A.V.).

The Subscription

Written from Rome, &c.] Lit., **To Philemon it was written from Rome by means of** (i.e., of course, "*it was sent by hand of*") **(the) domestic Onesimus.** Obviously, the statement is true to fact. On the antiquity of this and similar Subscriptions see note on that appended to Colossians.

A few MSS. (of cent. 8 at earliest) have, (The) Epistle of the Holy Apostle Paul to Philemon and Apphia, owners of Onesimus, and to Archippus the (*sic*) deacon of the Church in Colossæ, was written from Rome by means of (the) domestic Onesimus.

APPENDICES

	PAGE		PAGE
A. Prof. Ramsay on St Paul's Route (Acts xviii., xix.), and on the Chasm at Colossæ ...	179	G. Developments of Doctrine in *Colossians* (Col. i. 16)	186
B. The Epistles to the Colossians &c., and the First Epistle of St Peter (P. 24)	180	H. "*Thrones and Dominions*" (Col. i. 16)	186
		I. Hooker on the Church (Col. i. 18)	188
C. Dr Salmon on Gnosticism and the Colossian Epistle (P. 33)	182	K. Peter Lombard on Baptism (Col. ii. 12)	189
D. The Literature of "Tendency" (P. 40)	182	L. The Disputed Reading of Col. ii. 18................................	190
E. Essenism and Christianity (P. 35)..................................	183	M. Master and Slave at Colossæ (P. 154)	191
F. Christ and Creation (Col. i. 16).	184	N. Dr Maclaren on the last words of *Philemon* (Philem. 25) ...	192

A. PROF. W. M. RAMSAY ON ST PAUL'S ROUTE (Acts xviii. 23, xix. 1), AND ON THE CHASM AT COLOSSÆ (Pp. 18, 19, 21.)

IN an important book just published (Spring, 1893), *The Church in the Roman Empire*, Prof. W. M. Ramsay, of Aberdeen, whose authority is special on the geography and archæology of Asia Minor, has discussed these two problems.

On the first, his conclusion is adverse to Bp Lightfoot. He holds (pp. 91, &c.) that Acts xviii. 23, taken with xix. 1, is most naturally explained by supposing St Paul to travel from *the southern* "Galatian country," the region which included Derbe, Lystra, and Iconium, not from the region commonly called Galatia, in the centre of the peninsula[1]; and so to take not "an enormous circuit through Cappadocia and North Galatia" to Ephesus, his goal, but the direct route, which would pass through Derbe, Lystra, &c., and would lead him by Apamea, Colossæ, and Laodicea on the Lycus, to Ephesus. This theory is elaborately, and we think convincingly, supported in chh. v., vi., of the book. The question of Col. ii. 1 is discussed pp. 93, 94, as "the one difficulty in this journey from which the North Galatian theory is free." He writes as follows:

[1] Both districts were included in the Roman *Provincia Galatia*. See Ramsay's Map of Asia Minor.

"In the first place, the journey, so far as it traversed new country, was evidently rapid and unbroken; for there is no allusion to preaching in new places, but only to the confirming of old converts, until Ephesus was reached. It is therefore quite possible that St Paul might have spent a night either at Colossæ or at Laodiceia, and yet that he might several years afterwards write to the Christians there as persons who had never seen his face. Moreover, though trade and vehicles regularly took the road through Apameia and Laodiceia, foot-passengers might possibly prefer the shorter hill road by the plain of Metropolis and the Tchyvritzi Kleisoura...This path would take them by way of Eumeneia and the Cayster valley, and would save a day's journey."

The interesting question whether there once existed a natural tunnel over the Lycus "in Colossæ," is discussed by Prof. Ramsay, pp. 472—476. His conclusion is that Herodotus is our only unmistakable ancient authority for the existence of such a tunnel just there, and that Strabo, who also speaks of an underground course of the Lycus, appears to correct rather than support him. For Strabo says that the Lycus runs underground for *the greater part of its course*. Now as a fact the "springs" of the Lycus, at the head of the Colossian glen, appear by recent exploration to be not true springs, but the outflow of the river after a long underground course from the upland lake Anava[1]; and this would explain Strabo's statement, while that of Herodotus may be regarded as an inaccurate account of the general phenomena of the limestone channels of the district. As to the deep gorge, or "cutting," found by Hamilton at the site of Colossæ (see our p. 19), Ramsay remarks (p. 476) that "the gorge, as a whole, has been an open gap for thousands of years; on that all are agreed who have seen it...We must admit the possibility that incrustation...may have at a former period completely overarched it for a little way. But such a bridge would not justify Herodotus, who describes a *duden*" [a disappearance of the river] "more than half a mile long."

B. THE EPISTLES TO THE COLOSSIANS AND EPHESIANS AND THE FIRST EPISTLE OF ST PETER (P. 24, *note*)

WEISS (*Einleitung in das N.T.*, pp. 271, 272) discusses the question of a kinship between *Ephesians* (and *Colossians*) and the First Epistle of St Peter, which announces itself as a Circular to the Churches of Asia Minor. He points out the following among other parallels of thought, topic, and expression between *Ephesians* and the Petrine Epistle:

---

[1] Those who know the Jura country will recall the similar immense "source" where the Orbe rushes from the five miles of cavernous tunnel through which it has descended from the Lac de Joux. The Aire, in Yorkshire, shews the same phenomenon on a smaller scale.

(a) Eph. i. 4 ("chosen in Him before," &c.): cp. 1 Pet. i. 2.
(b) ,, i. 19 ("the inheritance"): ,, ,, i. 3—5.
(c) ,, i. 20—21 [cp. Col. ii. 15] ("the connexion of the [Death,] Resurrection, and Ascension with the subjection of all heavenly powers") ,, ,, iii. 22.
(d) ,, ii. 3 (the contrast of the past and present position and condition of the Jewish [?] converts) ,, ,, i. 14—15.
(e) ,, ii. 18 ("access" to God through Christ) ,, ,, iii. 18.
(f) ,, ii. 20 ("the Corner-stone") ,, ,, ii. 6.
(g) ,, iii. 5 (Angels watching the course of man's redemption) ,, ,, i. 11.
(h) ,, iv. 11 (all gifts to be used for "service") ,, ,, iv. 10.
(i) ,, ,, ,, ("shepherds" a designation of Christian ministers) ,, ,, v. 2.
,, v. 21—vi. 9 [cp. Col. iii. 18—iv. 1] (family duties in the Christian aspect, especially on the principle of submission) ,, ,, ii. 18— iii. 7, v. 5.
,, v. 10 (resistance to "the *diabolos*") ,, ,, v. 8.

We may compare too the curious verbal similarity, in the Greek, between Col. ii. 5 and 1 Pet. v. 9.

Such correspondences indicate a probable communication between the writers, or at least that one knew the other's writings; and a general likeness in the needs and characteristics of the Churches addressed. Weiss inclines to date the First Epistle of St Peter earlier than *Colossians* and *Ephesians*. But the internal evidence seems to us insufficient for such a conclusion. Surely the tone of 1 *Peter* betokens *the imminence of a great persecution* far more than that of the Ephesian group of Pauline Epistles; and this speaks for a later date. No one can read St Peter attentively without feeling that in his First Epistle he shews all along the powerful influence upon him of his "beloved brother Paul" (2 Pet. iii. 15), as regards the form and expression of his message. But such a connexion and influence cannot decide the historically delicate question of precise relative date of the two writings.

Prof. Ramsay (*The Church*, &c., ch. xiii.) prefers a late date for 1 *Peter*, placing it after the fall of Jerusalem. He thinks that St Peter's death may have taken place long after St Paul's. But these contentions, on the evidence given, seem to us at best not proven.

C. DR SALMON ON GNOSTICISM AND THE COLOSSIAN EPISTLE (P. 33)

"THE third objection [to the genuineness of *Colossians*] is the Gnostic complexion of the false teaching combated,...which, we are told, could not have characterized any heresy existing in the time of St Paul. But how is it known that it could not? What are the authorities which fix for us the rise of Gnosticism with such precision that we are entitled to reject a document bearing all the marks of authenticity if it exhibits too early traces of Gnostic controversies? The simple fact is that we have no certain knowledge whatever about the beginnings of Gnosticism. We know that it was in full blow in the middle of the second century...But if we desire to describe the first appearance of Gnostic tendencies, we have, outside the New Testament books, no materials; and if we assign a date from our own sense of the fitness of things, we are bound to do so with all possible modesty...With respect to the history of [the] undeveloped stage of Gnosticism, I hold the Epistle to the Colossians to be one of our best sources of information; and those who reject it because it does not agree with their notions of what the state of speculation in the first century ought to be, are guilty of the unscientific fault of forming a theory on an insufficient induction of facts, and then rejecting a fact which they had not taken into account, because it does not agree with their theory."

"I am sure no forger could devise anything which has such a ring of truth as the Epistle to the Colossians."

G. SALMON, D.D., *A Historical Introduction to the Books of the New Testament*, pp. 469, 472, 475.

D. THE LITERATURE OF "TENDENCY" (P. 40.)

Tendenzschriften, "*Tendency-literature*," is a term familiar in modern historical theology. It denotes the writings which betray an artificial and diplomatic intention; narratives for instance written less to record events than to justify movements or theories, and letters not really dictated by circumstances of the hour, but fabricated to explain or to defend. Such has been held by some modern critics to be the true character of the Acts of the Apostles; a narrative written long after date, to heal and obliterate a supposed energetic opposition of "Petrines" and "Paulines." Such has been the account given of the Epistle to the Ephesians, and even of that to the Colossians[1]; letters fabricated as by St Paul, but in reality polemical attacks upon forms

---

[1] See above, p. 38.

of teaching later than his time. An answer to such attacks upon canonical books may be given in part by a comparison of them with books undoubtedly of the "*Tendency*" order. Such a book, a favourable example of its class, has lately (1892) been given to the world, after a long oblivion in the recesses of a tomb in Egypt. It is *The Gospel of Peter*[1]. This narrative of our Lord's Passion and Resurrection bears probable traces of a *Docetic* "tendency"; i.e. it appears to be written with a purpose of adaptation to the theory that "Jesus" was only temporarily "possessed" by "Christ," who forsook the Man at the Cross, so that "Christ" suffered only in appearance (δοκεῖν). It is instructive to see how such "tendency" was, as by a literary law, associated, in those early days, with imaginative weakness. The spirit of uncontrolled yet weak romance comes in at once. *The Cross* is made *to speak;* the Risen One issues from the Tomb *with a stature which touches the sky*. To the literary student this suggests the reflection that the early Christian generations were wholly unskilled in the subtle art of successful historical imagination. To forsake facts, and their record, in favour of compositions bearing an artificial purpose; to personate, with an intention, the writer of another age; was inevitably, at that stage of literary development, to fall into manifest historical absurdity.

Bishop Alexander, of Derry, in a sermon (1890) before the University of Cambridge (since incorporated in his *Primary Convictions*, New York and London, 1893), has admirably expounded the literary phenomena of St Luke xxiv., and has pointed out the *literary* reasons for accepting it as a record of fact. The "management of the supernatural" in narrative is one of the great problems of literature; Sir Walter Scott, in the Introduction to *The Abbot*, has condemned his own attempts to solve that problem in *The Monastery*. But "the supernatural" moves freely in the transparent narrative of St Luke. Is it unfair to say that St Luke was either a literary artist who more than rivalled *Hamlet* and *The Monastery, or* a photographer of facts? It is assuredly true that such a manner is good proof that he was not a "tendency-writer" of the second century.

E. ESSENISM AND CHRISTIANITY (P. 35.)

It has been maintained, sometimes by unfriendly sometimes by friendly critical students of Christianity, that Essenism and the Doctrine of Christ were closely connected, and that our Blessed Lord Himself, and John the Baptist, and James the Lord's Brother, were in some sense Essenes. The *prima facie* case is plausible. John the Baptist was an inhabitant of the desert, roughly clothed, an ascetic in diet, and a baptizer. James is said to have abstained from wine, and from flesh-meat, and from the use of oil and of the razor. Our Lord laid

[1] The work referred to does not bear the name; its first pages are still lost. But there is practical certainty that the identification is correct. For an excellent popular account of it see Mr J. Rendel Harris's book, *The newly-recovered Gospel of Peter*.

the utmost stress upon the vanity of the Pharisaic ritualism, and in some mysterious words in the Sermon on the Mount (Matt. xix. 12) seemed to countenance a possible law of celibacy. His infant Church held goods in common (Acts iv. 34, 35), and despised wealth. But these and some other traits of actual or possible likeness are shewn by Lightfoot (*Colossians*, pp. 158—179) to be entirely negatived by much greater unlikenesses. John the Baptist is a desert solitary, not a member of a desert community, and he nowhere preaches an ascetic life, or a life in community. The account of the asceticism of James is late in date, and probably coloured by imagination; and the Acts and Epistles which suggest that the Judaizing Christians claimed in some sense, rightly or not, his support, shew him as a man whose natural sympathies would be with the Pharisees rather than with the Essenes. Our Lord, unlike the Essenes, rebuked a distorted observance of the Sabbath; mingled freely in human social life; powerfully vindicated the sacredness of marriage and fatherhood; fully observed the Mosaic ceremonial, including the Passover; asserted the resurrection of the body; and, last not least, claimed for Himself the Messiahship, whereas no trace of the Messianic hope appears in our accounts of Essene doctrine. And whereas the Essene "despaired of society, and aimed only at the salvation of the individual," our Lord, in the Divine largeness of His teaching, at once put the utmost stress on the regeneration and holiness of the individual, and laid the foundations of a regenerated society in His doctrine of the relation of His followers, in Him their Head, to the whole circle of human life.

F. CHRIST AND CREATION (Col. i. 16.)

"THE heresy of the Colossian teachers took its rise...in their cosmical speculations. It was therefore natural that the Apostle in replying should lay stress on the function of the Word in the creation and government of the world. This is the aspect of His work most prominent in the first of the two distinctly Christological passages. The Apostle there predicates of the Word [the Son] not only prior but absolute existence. All things were created by Him, are sustained in Him, are tending towards Him. Thus He is the beginning, middle, and end of creation. This He is because He is the very *Image* of the Invisible God, because in Him dwells the Plenitude of Deity.

"This creative and administrative work of Christ the Word [the Son] in the natural order of things is always emphasized in the writings of the Apostles when they touch on the doctrine of His Person...With ourselves this idea has retired very much into the background...And the loss is serious...How much more hearty would be the sympathy of theologians with the revelations of science and the developments of history, if they habitually connected them with the operations of the same Divine Word who is the centre of all their religious aspirations, it is needless to say.

"It will be said indeed that this conception leaves...creation...as much a mystery as before. This may be allowed. But is there any reason to think that with our present limited capacities the veil which shrouds it ever will be removed? The metaphysical speculations of twenty-five centuries have done nothing to raise it. The physical investigations of our own age from their very nature can do nothing; for, busied with the evolution of phenomena, they lie wholly outside this question, and do not even touch the fringe of the difficulty. But meanwhile revelation has interposed, and thrown out the idea which, if it leaves many questions unsolved, gives a breadth and unity to our conceptions, at once satisfying our religious needs and linking our scientific instincts with our theological beliefs."

LIGHTFOOT, *Colossians*, pp. 182, 183.

" From dearth to plenty, and from death to life,
Is Nature's progress, when she lectures man
In heavenly truth; evincing, as she makes
The grand transition, that there lives and works
A soul in all things, and that soul is God.

* * * * * * *

The Lord of all, Himself through all diffused,
Sustains, and is the life of all that lives.
Nature is but a name for an effect
Whose Cause is God. He feeds the secret fire
By which the mighty process is maintain'd...
[All things] are under One. One Spirit, *His
Who wore the platted thorns with bleeding brows*,
Rules universal Nature. Not a flower
But shews some touch, in freckle, streak, or stain,
Of His unrival'd pencil. He inspires
Their balmy odours, and imparts their hues,
And bathes their eyes with nectar, and includes
In grains as countless as the seaside sands,
The forms with which He sprinkles all the earth.
Happy who walks with Him! whom what he finds
Of flavour or of scent in fruit or flower,
Or what he views of·beautiful or grand,...
Prompts with remembrance of a present God."

COWPER, *The Task*, Book VI.

The views outlined by Bishop Lightfoot, in the passage quoted above, are pregnant of spiritual and mental assistance. At the same time with them, as with other great aspects of Divine Truth, a reverent caution is needed in the development and limitation. The doctrine of the Creating Word, the Eternal Son, "in" Whom finite existence has its Corner-stone, may actually degenerate into a view both of Christ and Creation nearer akin to some forms of Greek speculation than to Christianity, if not continually balanced and guarded by a recollection of other great contents of Revelation. Dr J. H. Rigg, in

Modern Anglican Theology (3rd Edition, 1880), has drawn attention to the affinity which some recent influential forms of Christian thought bear to Neo-Platonism rather than to the New Testament. In particular, any view of the relation of Christ to "Nature" and to man which leads to the conclusion that all human existences are so "in Christ" that the individual man is vitally united to Him antecedent to regeneration, and irrespective of the propitiation of the Cross, tends to non-Christian affinities. It is a fact never to be lost sight of that any theology which on the whole gives to the mysteries of guilt and propitiation a less *prominent* place than that given to them in Holy Scripture, tends to a very wide divergence from the scriptural type. Here, as in all things, the safety of thought lies on the one hand in neglecting no great element of revealed truth, on the other in coordinating the elements *on the scale, and in the manner*, of Divine Revelation.

G. DEVELOPMENTS OF DOCTRINE IN COLOSSIANS
(Col. i. 16)

IN the precise form presented in *Colossians* the revelation of the Creative Work of the Son is new in St Paul's Epistles. But intimations of it are to be found in the earlier Epistles, and such as to make this final development as natural as it is impressive. In 1 Cor. viii. 6 we have the "one Lord Jesus Christ, *through whom are all things, and we through Him;*" which is in effect the germ of the statements of Col. i. And in Rom. viii. 19—23 we have a passage pregnant with the thought that the created Universe has a mysterious relation to "the sons of God," such that their glorification will be also its emancipation from the laws of decay; or at least that the glorification and the emancipation are deeply related to each other. Nothing is wanted to make the kinship of that passage and Col. i. evident at a glance, but an explicit mention of Christ as the HEAD of both worlds. As it is, His mysterious but most real connexion with the making and the maintaining of the Universe is seen lying as it were just below the surface of the passage in *Romans*.

H. "THRONES AND DOMINIONS" (Col. i. 16)

WE transcribe here a note from our edition of *Ephesians* in this Series; on the words of Eph. i. 21:

"Two thoughts are conveyed; first, subordinately, the existence of orders and authorities in the angelic (as well as human) world; then, primarily, the imperial and absolute Headship of the Son over them all. The additional thought is given us by Col. i. 16, that He was also, in His preexistent glory, their Creator; but this is not in definite view here, where He appears altogether as the exalted Son of Man after Death. In Rom. viii., Col. ii., and Eph. vi.... we have cognate phrases where *evil* powers are meant....But the context here is distinctly favourable to a *good* reference. That the Redeemer should be "exalted above" powers *of evil* is a thought scarcely adequate in a connexion so full of the imagery of glory as this. That He should be "exalted above" the holy angels is fully in point. 1 Pet. iii. 22 is our best parallel; and cp. Rev. v. 11, 12. See also Matt. xiii. 41; "The Son of Man shall send forth *His* angels."

"We gather from the Epistle to the Colossians that the Churches of Asia Proper were at this time in danger from a quasi-Jewish doctrine of Angel-worship, akin to the heresies afterwards known as Gnosticism. Such a fact gives special point to the phrases here. On the other hand it does not warrant the inference that St Paul repudiates all the ideas of such an angelology. The idea of order and authority in the angelic world he surely endorses, though quite in passing.

"Theories of angelic orders, more or less elaborate, are found in the *Testaments of the Twelve Patriarchs*, (cent. 1—2); Origen (cent. 3); St Ephrem Syrus (cent. 4). By far the most famous ancient treatise on the subject is the book *On the Celestial Hierarchy*, under the name (certainly assumed) of Dionysius the Areopagite; a book first mentioned cent. 6, from which time onwards it had a commanding influence in Christendom. (See Article *Dionysius* in Smith's *Dict. Christ. Biography*). "Dionysius" ranked the orders (in descending scale) in three *Trines*; Seraphim, Cherubim, Thrones; Dominations, Virtues, Powers (Authorities); Principalities, Archangels, Angels. The titles are thus a combination of the terms Seraphim, Cherubim, Archangels, Angels, with those used by St Paul here and in Col. i.

"Readers of *Paradise Lost*, familiar with the majestic line,

'Thrones, Dominations, Princedoms, Virtues, Pow'rs,'

are not always aware of its learned accuracy of allusion. The Dionysian system powerfully attracted the sublime mind of Dante. In the *Paradiso*, Canto XXXVIII., is a grand and characteristic passage, in which Beatrice expounds the theory to Dante, as he stands, in the Ninth Heaven, in actual view of the Hierarchies encircling the Divine Essence:

> 'All, as they circle in their orders, look
> Aloft; and, downward, with such sway prevail
> That all with mutual impulse tend to God.
> These once a mortal view beheld. Desire
> In Dionysius so intensely wrought
> That he, as I have done, ranged them, and named
> Their orders, marshal'd in his thought.'
>
> Cary's *Dante*."

I. HOOKER ON THE CHURCH   (Col. i. 18.)

"THAT Church of Christ which we properly term His body mystical, can be but one; neither can that one be sensibly discerned by any man, inasmuch as the parts thereof are some in heaven already with Christ, and the rest that are on earth (albeit their natural persons be visible) we do not discern under this property whereby they are truly and infallibly of that body. Only our minds by intellectual conceit are able to apprehend that such a real body there is, a body collective, because it containeth a huge multitude; a body mystical, because the mystery of their conjunction is removed altogether from sense. Whatsoever we read in Scripture concerning the endless love and the saving mercy which God sheweth towards His Church, the only proper subject thereof is this Church. Concerning this flock it is that our Lord and Saviour hath promised: 'I give unto them eternal life, and they shall never perish, neither shall any pluck them out of my hands.' They who are of this society have such marks and notes of distinction from all others as are not object unto our sense; only unto God, who seeth their hearts and understandeth all their secret thoughts and cogitations, unto Him they are clear and manifest. All men knew Nathanael to be an Israelite. But our Saviour, piercing deeper, giveth further testimony of him than men could have done with such certainty as He did, 'Behold indeed an Israelite in whom there is no guile.' If we profess, as Peter did, that we love the Lord, and profess it in the hearing of men...charitable men are likely to think we do so, as long as they see no proof to the contrary. But that our love is sound and sincere...who can pronounce, saving only the Searcher of all men's hearts, who alone intuitively doth know in this kind who are His? And as those everlasting promises of love, mercy, and blessedness, belong to the mystical Church, even so on the other side when we read of any duty which the Church of God is bound unto, the Church whom this doth concern is a sensible known company. And this visible Church in like sort is but one....Which company being divided into two moieties, the one before, the other since the coming of Christ, that part which since the coming of Christ partly hath embraced and partly shall hereafter embrace the Christian religion, we term as by a more proper name the Church of Christ....The unity of which visible body and Church of Christ consisteth of that uniformity which all several persons thereunto belonging have, by reason of that one Lord, whose servants they all profess themselves; that one faith, which they all acknowledge; that one baptism, wherewith they are all initiated.... Entered we are not into the visible before our admittance by the door of baptism....Christians by external profession they are all, whose mark of recognisance hath in it those things (one Lord, one faith, one baptism) which we have mentioned, yea, although they be impious idolaters, wicked heretics, persons excommunicable, yea and cast out for notorious improbity....Is it then possible that the selfsame men should belong both to the synagogue of Satan and to the Church of Jesus Christ? Unto that Church which is His mystical body, not possible; because that body consisteth of none but only...true servants and saints of God. Howbeit of the visible body and Church of Jesus Christ, those may be, and oftentimes are, in respect of the main parts of their outward profession....For lack of diligent observing the difference, first between the Church of God mystical and visible, then between the visible sound and corrupted, sometimes more, sometimes less; the oversights are neither few nor light that have been committed."

Of the Laws of Ecclesiastical Polity, III. 1.

K. PETER LOMBARD ON BAPTISM (Col. ii. 12.)

PETER LOMBARD (*ob*. A.D. 1160), known among medieval theologians as "*the Master of the Sentences*" (*Magister Sententiarum*), or simply, "*the Master*," writes as follows in his Treatise on Theology called *Sententiæ* (*Lib*. iv., *Distinctio* iv., §§ 3—7):

"It is asked, how is that text to be received, *As many of you as have been baptized in Christ have put on Christ*....In two manners are we said to put on Christ; by the taking of the Sacrament, or by the reception of the Thing (*Res*). So Augustine: 'Men put on Christ sometimes so far as the reception of the Sacrament, sometimes so far as the sanctification of the life; and the first may be common to the good and the evil; the latter is peculiar to the good and pious.' So all who are baptized in Christ's name put on Christ either in the sense of (*secundum*) the reception of the Sacrament, or in that of sanctification of the life.

"Others there are...who receive the Thing and not the Sacrament... Not only does martyrdom (*passio*) do the work of baptism but also faith and contrition, where necessity excludes the Sacrament...

"Whether is greater, faith or water? Without doubt I answer, faith. Now if the lesser can sanctify, cannot the greater, even faith? of which Christ said, 'He that believeth in me, even if he were dead, he shall live'...[Augustine says,] 'If any man having faith and love desires to be baptized, and cannot so be, because necessity intervenes, the kindness of the Almighty supplies what was lacking to the Sacrament...The duty which could not be done is not reckoned against him by God, who hath not tied (*alligavit*) His power to the Sacraments...'

"The question is often asked, regarding those who, already sanctified by the Spirit, come with faith and love to baptism, what benefit baptism confers upon them? For it seems to give them nothing, since through faith and contrition their sins are already forgiven and they are justified. To which it may be truly replied that they are indeed... justified, i.e. purged from the stain (*macula*) of sin, and absolved from the debt of the eternal punishment, but that they are still held by the

190 / Appendices

bond of the temporal satisfaction by which penitents are bound in the Church. Now when they receive Baptism they are both cleansed of any sins they have contracted since conversion, and are absolved from the external satisfaction; and assisting grace and all virtues are increased in them; so that the man may then truly be called new... Baptism confers much benefit even on the man already justified by faith; for, coming to it, he is now carried, like the branch by the dove, into the ark. He was within the ark already in the judgment of God; he is now within it in that of the Church also...

"Marvel not that the Thing sometimes goes before the Sacrament, since sometimes it follows even long after; as in those who come insincerely (*ficte*). Baptism will begin to profit them (only) when they afterwards repent."

These remarks of a great representative of Scholastic Theology are interesting in themselves, and are instructive also as a caution, from the history of doctrine, against overstrained inferences from the mere wording of, e.g. Col. ii. 12, as if it were unfaithful to history to interpret such language in the light of facts and experience. The great risk of such overstrained exposition is that it tends to exalt the Sacrament at the expense of adequate views of the Grace, and so to invert the scale and relation of Scripture.

L. THE VARIOUS READINGS OF COL. II. 18

MUST we read (*a*) "*The things which he hath not seen,*" or (*b*) "*The things which he hath seen?*"

The documentary evidence may be briefly stated thus:

i. For the omission of "*not*":

Uncial MSS.:—ℵ ABD, the first three of which are, with C, the oldest copies we possess. ℵB were probably written cent. 4, A cent. 5. D probably belongs to cent. 6.

Cursive MSS.:—those numbered 17, 28, 67 in the list of cursive copies of St Paul's Epistles. These belong to centt. 10 and 12. MS. 67 omits "*not*" *by correction only;* the correction is perhaps as late as cent. 15.

Versions:—the Old Latin (perhaps cent. 2) in three of its texts out of the five which contain the Epistle; the Coptic Version called the Memphitic (perhaps cent. 2); and two others.

Fathers:—Tertullian (cent. 2, 3); Origen (cent. 3), but somewhat doubtfully[1]; the commentator Hilary (cent. 4), quoted as Ambrosiaster, as his work is included with the works of Ambrose. Jerome and Augustine (cent. 4, 5) both notice both readings.

---

[1] He cites the text three times. Two of these occur where his Greek is known only through a Latin Version, and one of these two gives "*not*." In the third, we have the Greek. Μή is inserted by the (last) critical Editor, De la Rue.

ii. For the retention of *"not"*:
Uncial MSS.:—C K L P, the first of cent. 5, the others of cent. 9. Besides, the reading οὐ (not μή) is given by a corrector of ℵ, who dates perhaps cent. 7, and by correctors of D, who date perhaps cent. 8.
Cursive MSS.:—*all* with the three exceptions given above; i.e. more than 290 known copies, ranging from cent. 9 to cent. 15 or 16.
Versions:—the Syriac Versions (the earliest is probably of cent. 2); one text of the Old Latin; the Vulgate (Jerome's revision of the Latin); the Gothic, Æthiopic, and others.
Fathers:—Origen (in one place; see further above); Chrysostom; Jerome (with deliberate preference); Augustine (likewise); Theodore of Mopsuestia; Theodoret, "and others" (Lightfoot).
The late Dean Burgon (*The Revision Revised*, p. 356, *note*), thus summarizes the evidence, and remarks upon it:
"We have to set off the whole mass of the copies—against some 6 or 7: Irenæus (i. 847), Theodorus Mops. (*in loc.*), Chrys. (xi. 372), Theodoret (iii. 489, 490), John Damascene (ii. 211)—against no Fathers at all (for Origen once has μή [iv. 655][1]; once has it not [iii. 63]; and once is doubtful [i. 583]). Jerome and Augustine both take notice of the diversity of reading, but only to reject it.—The Syriac versions, the Vulgate, Gothic, Georgian, Sclavonic, Æthiopic, Arabic, and Armenian—(we owe the information, as usual, to Dr Malan)—are to be set against the suspicious Coptic. All these then are with the Traditional Text: which cannot seriously be suspected of error."
It must be added that Lightfoot (*in loco*), and Westcott and Hort (*N.T. in Greek*, ii. 127), suspect the Greek text of Col. ii. 18 of corruption, and suggest or adopt ingenious emendations. The rendering of the clause in question thus altered would be, "*treading the void in airy suspension,*" or, "*treading an airy void.*" We venture to think the reasons for suspicion inadequate.

M. MASTER AND SLAVE AT COLOSSÆ (P. 154.)

WE have conjectured the possibility that Onesimus' legal position might not be quite so bad as that of the slave of a Roman master. But the difference was probably a vanishing one in fact. Dr E. C. Clark, Regius Professor of Laws in the University of Cambridge, kindly informs the Editor that "little is known of the administration of ordinary justice in the Provinces. But almost all except serious cases seem to have been left to the native local authorities. I should think that *no treatment* of a slave by his master could come under the cognizance of a Roman governor; and I see no reason to suppose that the local authorities would be more likely to interfere than the Roman magistrates in similar cases at Rome. Power of life and death would be, I imagine, the rule. The introduction of the theory of a

[1] See just above on this point, in our statement of the evidence for "*not*". (Editor.)

Law of Nature may have led to a few ameliorations in the slave's condition mediately, *i.e.* through the individual action of humane Emperors. But these modifications of the old barbarity have been overrated. I doubt whether any prohibition of the arbitrary killing of a slave was *regularly* made before the time of Hadrian. Philemon would have power, most likely, to treat Onesimus *exactly as he pleased*."

N. Dr MACLAREN ON THE LAST WORDS OF THE EPISTLE TO PHILEMON (Philem. 25.)

In his excellent Expository Commentary on our two Epistles (3rd Edition, 1889) Dr Alexander Maclaren writes as follows:
"The parting benediction ends the letter. At the beginning of the Epistle, Paul invoked grace upon the household 'from God our Father and the Lord Jesus Christ.' Now he conceives of it as Christ's gift. In Him all the stooping, bestowing love of God is gathered, that from Him it may be poured upon the world. That grace is not diffused, like stellar light, through some nebulous heaven, but concentrated in the Sun of Righteousness, who is the light of men. That fire is piled on a hearth, that from it warmth may ray out to all that are in the house....

"The grace of Christ is the best bond of family life. Here it is prayed for on behalf of all the group, the husband, wife, child, and the friends in their home-Church. Like grains of sweet incense sprinkled on an altar-flame, and making fragrant that which was already holy, that grace sprinkled on the household fire will give it an odour of a sweet smell, grateful to men and acceptable to God.

"That wish is the purest expression of Christian friendship, of which the whole Letter is so exquisite an example. Written as it is about a common everyday matter, which could have been settled without a single religious reference, it is saturated with Christian thought and feeling. So it becomes an example how to blend Christian sentiment with ordinary affairs, and to carry a Christian atmosphere everywhere. Friendship and social intercourse will be all the nobler and happier, if pervaded by such a tone. Such words as these closing ones would be a sad contrast to much of the intercourse of professedly Christian men. But every Christian ought by his life to be, as it were, floating the grace of God to others sinking for want of it, to lay hold of; and all his speech should be of a piece with this benediction.

"A Christian's life should be 'an Epistle of Christ,' written with His own hand, wherein dim eyes might read the transcript of His own gracious love; and through all his words and deeds should shine the image of his Master, even as it does through the delicate tendernesses and gracious pleadings of this pure pearl of a letter, which the slave, become a brother, bore to the responsive hearts in quiet Colossæ."

INDEX

TO INTRODUCTION, NOTES, AND APPENDICES

*** From this Index (to subjects, and to names) are omitted for the most part such references as are obviously indicated by chapter and verse of the Text.

Abercius, 17
Aelfric of Cerne, 46
Æschylus, 126
Alexander, Bp, 92, 146, 183
Alford, Dean, 23, 77, 83, 85, 92, 96, 97, 123, 148, 169, 170
Ambrose, St, 107
angelic orders, 79, 186
angelolatry, 13, 15, 31, 32, 111
Apphia, 152, 168
Apocalypse, 13
Apocrypha, 97
Apostolic Constitutions, 105
Archippus, 144, 152, 153, 168
Aristides the Apologist, 163
Aristotle, 155, 175
Augustine, St, 107, 189, 190, 191
Augustus, 156

baptism, 105, 189
Basil, St, 77, 80
Baur, F. C., 17, 38, 148
Baxter, 72
Becker, *Gallus* and *Charicles*, 155, 157
Bengel, 150
Berlenburg Bible, 162
Beveridge, Bp, 105
Bingham, 143
Brown, Dr D., 13
Burgon, Dean, 191
Burrus, 27

Calvin, 122
Catechism, English, 103

Cecil, R., 145
Cerinthus, 33, 36
Chonæ, Chonos, 20
CHRIST, Godhead of, 66, 71, 72, 82, etc.
—— Headship of, 82, 84, etc.
—— His relation to the Universe, 77—8, 184, 185
—— His relation to the Eternal FATHER, 80, etc.
Christianity and Essenism, 183
—— —— property, 152
—— —— revolution, 158
—— —— slavery, 158, etc.
Christians, morality of early, 163
Chrysostom, St, 107, 125, 128, 147, 148, 179, 181
Church, the word and thing, 81, 188
Cibyratic Union, 11, 13, 44
Cicero, at Laodicea, 13
Clark, Professor, 8, 191
Claudius, 156
Clement, St, of Alexandria, 37, 101
—— —— Rome, 38
Clementine Homilies, 140
Coleridge, S. T., 75
COLOSSÆ, name, history, topography, etc., 18 etc., 180
COLOSSIANS, EPISTLE TO THE,
—— —— its date, 22
—— —— authenticity, 37, 52
—— —— argument, 53—61
—— —— title, 63
—— —— relations with *Ephesians*, 47—50, 50—52

193

194 / Index

Colossian heresy, 29, 30, etc.
Conybeare and Howson, *Life, etc. of St Paul*, 116, 120
Cowper, 166, 185
Cyrus Junior, 19

Dante, 187
Deity, the word, 102
development of certain doctrines, 186
Dictionary of the Bible, 138, 142
─────── *Christian Biography*, 17, 187
─────── *Classical Antiquities*, 155, 157, 176
Dion Cassius, 157
"Dionysius the Areopagite," 187
docetism, 87, 183
doctrinal proportion, need of, 185

Ellicott, Bp. 72, 75, 77, 78, 80, 82, 83, 92, 95—97, 99, 110—112, 137, 169, 170, 174
Epaphras, 21, 29, 69
Ephesians, Epistle to the, 39, 41—44, 47—52, 180, 181
Epictetus, 18, 27
epistolary past tense, 137
Erasmus, 39, 46, 150
Essenes, 33 etc.
Essenism and Christianity, 183
Euripides, 156
Eusebius, 16, 17, 24, 35, 139, 140
Euthalius, 145

Farrar, Dr F. W., 116, 142, 143, 153
Francis of Assisi, St, 116
Franke, A. H., 150
freedmen, position of, 151

Galatia, 21, 179
Gallio, 27
gnosticism, 33, 101, 182
Gregory the Great, 46
Grimm, *Lexicon to N. T.*, 70, 76, 102, 110, 125
Guyon, Mme, 71

Hamilton, *Travels in Asia Minor*, 13, 15, 19, 180
Harris, Mr J. Rendel, 164, 183
─────── Mrs J. Rendel, 164
Herodotus, 19, 126, 180
Hierapolis, topography, etc. of, 15 etc.
Hilary (Ambrosiaster), 107, 190
Holtzmann, 50, 51
HOLY SPIRIT, the, scarcely alluded to in *Colossians*, 50
Homer, 132
Hooker, 82, 88, 188
Horace, 156, 176
Hort, Professor, 22, 32, 35, 36, 50
Hymns of Consecration and Faith, 71

Ignatius, St, and Ignatian Letters, 38, 124, 147, 153

Irenæus, St, 37, 111

Jerome, St, 87, 98, 134, 147, 148, 190, 191
Josephus, 34, 116
Justin Martyr, St, 38, 111
Justinian, 160

Laodicea, topography, etc. of, 13, etc.
─────── council, of, 14, 111
─────── epistle from, 42—44
─────── "*epistle to*," 39, 44—47
Leibnitz, 128
Lewin, *Life, etc. of St Paul*, 24, 95
Lightfoot, Bp, 8, *et passim*
Lombard, Peter, 105, 189
"longanimity," 73
Lord's Supper, the, and slavery, 160
Lucan, 27
Luther, 110, 118, 130, 132, 146, 149
Lycus, valley and churches of the, 11—21, 180

Maclaren, Dr A., 192
Mahaffy, Professor, 39
Malan, Dr S. C., 12, 191
Mansel, Dean, 36, 40
Marcion, 38, 147
"mawmetis," 122
Mayerhoff, 38
Melito, 14
Meyer, 23, 39, 40
Milton, *Paradise Lost*, 187
Monod, Adolphe, 90
mysteries, pagan, 91, 93

Noel, Miss Caroline, 62

Œcumenius, 171
Onesimus, 25, 29, 153, 172, 192
Origen, 37, 147, 187, 190
Outlines of Doctrine, 65, 84
Ovid, 168

Paley, F. A., 157
───── W., *Horæ Paulinæ*, 178
Papias, 16, 17
Parsism, 35
Paschal controversy, 14
Paul, St, at Rome, 24 etc., *et aliter passim*
Pearson, Bp, 64, 66
Pedanius, 157
perseverance of the saints, 88
Peter, St, First Epistle of, 24, 180
Philo, 34, 35, 80, 116
philosophy, 32, 101
Philemon, 152, 167, etc.
PHILEMON, Epistle to,
─────── its authenticity, 147
─────── — testimonies, 148
─────── — argument, 165
Philemon and Baucis, fable of, 167
Plato, 156
Pliny the Elder, 34

Pliny the Younger, 150, 151
Polycarp, St, 66
Pomponia Græcina, 27
Ptolemy the geographer, 19
Pythagoras, 101

Quesnel, Père, *Nouveau Testament en François*, 89, 98, 101, 111, 116, 128, 130—132, 171, 175

Ramsay, Professor, 8, 12, 13, 15, 18, 19, 21, 152, 179—181
Renan, E., 16, 17, 20, 40, 130, 152
Rigg, Dr J. H., 185
Rogers, Professor H., 159

Sagaris, 14
Salmon, Dr G., 39, 139, 178, 182
Schneider, Rev. G. A., 8, 22
Schoettgen, 115
Scott, T., 173
—— Sir W., 172, 183
Scrivener, Dr, 96, 145
Seneca, 26, 136, 157
servants and masters, Christian, 162, 163
Sinker, Dr R., 8, 36
slave names, 173
slavery, ancient, 154—117, 191
—— and Christianity, 158—161, 163
Smith, Goldwin, *Does the Bible sanction American slavery?* 157, etc.
—— Bp W. S., 84
Strabo, 19, 180
Suetonius, 156
Sumner, Abp, 116

Svoboda, *Seven Churches*, 15, 16

Tacitus, 24
Taylor, Bp. Jeremy, 73
Teaching of the Twelve Apostles, 105
Tersteegen, 71
Tertullian, 37, 101, 190
Testaments of the Twelve Patriarchs, 187
Theodore of Mopsuestia, 107, 116, 191
Theodoret, 111, 191
Theophilus of Antioch, 38
Theophylact, 171
Therapeutæ, the, 35
Thoughts on Union with Christ, 76
Trench, Abp, 102, 106, 123, 127, 145

universe, relation of Christ to the, 50, 78, 184
Ussher, Abp, 42

Vedius Pollio, 156

Waller, Dr C. H., 162
Waterland, 80
Wayland, 159
Weiss, 22, 23, 44, 180, 181
Westcott, Bp, 14, 38
—— and Hort, *N.T. in Greek*, 191
Worcester, Bishop of, 108
Wordsworth, Bp. Chr., 82

Xenophon, 19, 39

Zend Avesta, 35

www.ingramcontent.com/pod-product-compliance
Lightning Source LLC
Chambersburg PA
CBHW071424160426
43195CB00013B/1797